BI SCIENCE
ENTREPRENEURSHIP
IN ASIA

Creating Value with Biology

BIOSCIENCE
ENTREPRENEURSHIP
IN ASIA

Creating Value with Biology

PAUL S TENG

National Institute of Education, Singapore

 **World Scientific**

NEW JERSEY · LONDON · SINGAPORE · BEIJING · SHANGHAI · HONG KONG · TAIPEI · CHENNAI

Published by

World Scientific Publishing Co. Pte. Ltd.

5 Toh Tuck Link, Singapore 596224

USA office: 27 Warren Street, Suite 401-402, Hackensack, NJ 07601

UK office: 57 Shelton Street, Covent Garden, London WC2H 9HE

Library of Congress Cataloging-in-Publication Data
Teng, P. S.
  Bioscience entrepreneurship in Asia : creating value with biology / by Paul S. Teng.
    p. ; cm.
  Includes bibliographical references and index.
  ISBN-13: 978-981-270-020-9
  ISBN-10: 981-270-020-X
  1. Biotechnology--Asia. 2. Biotechnology industries--Asia. I. Title.
  HD9999.B443A7825 2008
  338.4'76606095--dc22

                                                                   2008023244

British Library Cataloguing-in-Publication Data
A catalogue record for this book is available from the British Library.

Typeset by Stallion Press
Email: enquiries@stallionpress.com

Printed in Singapore by World Scientific Printers

This book is dedicated to the millions of unrecognized bioscience entrepreneurs in the Asian region, who collectively are responsible for making it so vibrant and liveable

Foreword

The Asian continent is one of the most vibrant regions of the world today, characterized by rapid economic growth and technological advances. Asia is also home to more than half the world's population. At the annual meeting of the Asian Development Bank in Manila in 1999, I warned about the dangers of complacency and the need to produce more food, feed and fiber to meet the demands of more people in this region. This need presents tremendous challenges but also offers much potential for innovation and entrepreneurship, both in the public and private sectors. When this is viewed in the context of the much-touted "Biology Century" of the new millennium, then it is in Asia that modern science, especially biology, can be harnessed to meet the needs of humankind in a practical manner.

Asia needs a vibrant and growing agricultural sector in the 21st century. With fast-improving standards of living, typical diets are shifting more and more towards those based on animal protein. Farmers are one of the key links in the supply chain for cereals and other primary commodities, which get converted into secondary products such as animal feed, and even tertiary products like bioethanol. The tradeoffs between using crops for food and animal feeds versus non-food purposes will be much debated in the years ahead. Clearly, feeding people should be the highest priority. However, modern biology can harness modern science to ensure that there is enough produce to meet all the different needs.

Professor Teng's book is a timely contribution. It illustrates how Asia is using biology to create innovative products, services and technologies to meet the goals of poverty reduction, food security, livelihood improvement and wealth creation in future years. It helps entrepreneurs to understand why investments in agriculture are important and how profitable they can be.

This century has seen a revolution in the life sciences that has resulted in a booming global industry where the products of research are put into commercial use for human benefit. This up-and-coming industry, termed by most as the "biology revolution", is very likely to play an integral role in shaping the world in the 21st century and beyond.

Professor Teng has ably drawn from his long and varied experience in Asia to bring alive the applications of biology for various enterprises which serve society's needs. I hope that readers will be inspired to explore further how they can participate in increasing bioscience entrepreneurship in Asia so that more may benefit from the practical fruits of these endeavors.

Norman E. Borlaug
Nobel Peace Laureate 1971
5 September 2007
Texas, USA

Preface

The theme for this book was stimulated by the many encounters I have had with successful entrepreneurs during some 20 years of travel in Asia. It was easy to be awed by these entrepreneurs who had used biological knowledge to create value and wealth, some of whom confessed to having no technical training in biology but had been able to see the opportunities — reflecting truly a spirit of innovation.

What impressed me most was the entrepreneurial spirit that seemed inherent in so many different cultures in Asia — from the small peasant enterprises to the home-grown conglomerates, and, in this globalized environment, the presence of multinationals. Mushroom culture, biofermentation and biopesticides have been practised before the era of modern science. Value had been created. Of course, with the advent of computers, gene technology and the knowledge economy, it was inevitable that bioscience enterprises would increase in scope, scale and sophistication.

This book is therefore my humble effort to capture some of the excitement of applied biology, especially as we move into the "Biology Century". This book aims to share with a broader audience the tremendous possibilities of using one body of knowledge to benefit humankind. Bioscience entrepreneurship is just one example of how "innovation and enterprise" can move from being a mindset to practical outcomes. An entrepreneur sees possibilities to meet some needs of society. Often, the ideas may remain just ideas. Innovations need to become reality before there is successful entrepreneurship.

Value creation is at the heart of entrepreneurship. Creating value from knowledge is the modern, successful equivalent of the age-old, fruitless quest to turn base metals into gold. Where alchemy has not succeeded, biology has, and in the process, has brought wealth to many.

This book is also an attempt to set right a negative. In my many years as an educator, too often have I heard statements like "There is no money in science", "You can't get rich being a scientist", "You become a scientist because you love science, not because you want to be rich", etc. Yet, as this book will show, there have been many scientists who have taken the extra step beyond their comfort zones and have become very successful in enterprises, gotten very rich, and at the same time, helped to meet some of the most important needs of human society like food and fiber.

Yes, science provides the knowledge to drive entrepreneurship. But creating value and wealth are not the end-points in themselves. Bioscience products meet basic human needs and are truly renewable and sustainable. Nobel Laureate Norman Borlaug has noted in his Foreword to this book the "food versus fuel" dilemma that faces many countries. This is a dilemma of success, because alternative uses have to be decided for the successful production of basic biocommodities like corn and rice.

In this new knowledge-empowered age, scientists are well-positioned to "have their cake and eat it" too. The lines between so-called ivory-towered laboratory research and product development, and ways to cross them, have become clearer. Scientist-entrepreneurs are now many, with good role models in many countries. My hope is that books such as this one can help further bridge the gap between R&D and product development, because knowledge does empower.

It has not been possible to give equal treatment to all the enterprises covered as some are more developed than others. When the research for this book first started, I had aimed at providing a simplified primer on the science and technology behind each of the bioscience enterprises so that more can appreciate the tremendous remaining potential. It has not been altogether possible. For that, I crave understanding from the reader and have suggested a reading sequence.

To guide the reader, a suggested reading sequence is to start with Chapter 1, followed by Chapter 10. Then, selectively, the chapters from two to nine provide details of ten bioscience enterprises. Where appropriate, sources of further information such as websites have been provided.

This book would not have been possible without the cooperation and support of many. Acknowledgments and thanks are due to the following:

- My faithful and dedicated research assistant, Joanne Khew, who spent many hours sourcing and checking on material;
- Dr Norman Borlaug, Nobel Peace Laureate, for finding time and energy despite his illness to write the Foreword;
- Professors Leo Tan and Lee Sing Kong, respectively past Director and Director of the National Institute of Education (NIE), for their encouragement and guidance in publishing;
- Many colleagues in NIE/NTU for insightful discussions, especially Jean Yong of the Natural Sciences and Science Education Academic Group of NIE;
- Many colleagues in government and industry for sharing their leads, information and for giving referrals — Wyn Ellis of the National Innovation Agency, Thailand; Andrew Powell of Asia Biobusiness, Singapore; Danny Manayaga of Secura International, Philippines; and Lai S.P. of Jalur Lipur Sdn. Bhd., Malaysia;
- Yasmin Ortiga and Desiree Chang for many of the illustrations; and lastly but most importantly
- My spouse, Siew-Fing, for putting up with the writer's syndrome, best described by the expression "you are here but not here".

Lastly, as a biologist, I continue to be impressed by how supposedly uneducated people have successfully mastered the intricacies of using biological knowledge to make products. This book has focused on the bioscience aspects of entrepreneurship. However, entrepreneurship is more than just knowledge and skills; it is also a mindset. Being an entrepreneur means having the ability to spot opportunities and use them to create value. I hope this book will both enlighten and inspire a mindset change in some readers.

Paul Teng
December 2007
Singapore

About the Author

Paul S. Teng is a microbiologist by training, and professionally has practised as a research scientist, research manager, educator and entrepreneur. He belongs to that group of individuals with the capacity to straddle both East and West, public sector and private sector, national versus international sectors, and in all, make contributions in both.

After graduating from Lincoln College, University of Canterbury, New Zealand, he held professorial and academic administrative positions in the USA, respectively at the University of Minnesota and the University of Hawaii. During this time, he also concurrently was Technical Assistance Specialist to a US Agency for International Development (US AID) global program on Integrated Pest

Management, and travelled extensively in Asia and Africa on projects to minimize and ensure safe use of pesticides.

This was followed by positions in the international agricultural research system as Program Leader at the International Rice Research Institute, Philippines, and Deputy Director-General, WorldFish Center, Malaysia. Professor Teng worked with industry in the early 2000s as Asia-Pacific Vice President for a major agricultural biotechnology company, the St. Louis-based Monsanto.

He has been recognized for his work through conferment of the Eriksson Prize (awarded every five years to a scientist who has made significant contributions to solve plant disease problems) by the Royal Swedish Academy of Sciences, and election to The World Academy of Sciences (TWAS), Trieste, Italy. Professor Teng is also a Fellow of the American Phytopathological Society.

Paul Teng is currently a Professor at the Nanyang Technological University, Singapore. He holds the appointment of Dean for Graduate Programs and Research, National Institute of Education, Nanyang Technological University.

He also is Vice-Chair of the Board for the international non-profit organization, International Service for the Acquisition of Agribiotech Applications (ISAAA — www.isaaa.org), Non-Executive Chair of Asia Biobusiness (www.asiabiobusiness.com) and Chief Technical Adviser to a public company, HLH Corp. (SGX — www.hlhcorp.com.sg) which is aggressively expanding its modern agriculture investments. Paul also provides advice to several ASEAN SMEs engaging in agricultural and aquacultural applications of biotechnology.

Although a naturalized American citizen, Paul considers himself a cosmopolitan Asian. He was born in the small seaside town of Muar in present-day Johor State, Malaysia, educated in the "British" educational system prevailing in post-independence Malaysia, spent his formative early adult years in Christchurch, New Zealand, started his professional career in the USA, and honed it in Asia. He frequently commutes between homes in Singapore and Manila, and visits to family in the USA and Malaysia.

Contents

Chapter 1

Exploiting Developments in Science for New Bioscience Enterprises

"We are now starting the Century of Biology.... Just as information technology undergirds today's booming economy, biology may drive tomorrow's," says J. Craig Venter, President of the Institute for Genomic Research and pioneering gene finder.

"We have a chance to achieve incredible economic benefits," says Henri A. Termeer, President and CEO of biotech company Genzyme Corp. (GENZ).

— John Carey
in http://www.businessweek.com/1998/35/b3593020.htm

The 21st century has been accompanied by great expectations of knowledge and wealth creation. In response to these rapid evolvements, many prominent scientists and public figures have dubbed the 21st century as the "Biology Century" (Woese, 2004). How has this come about? Part of the answer lies in the myriad advances in science during the last half of the 20th century, especially in molecular biology, and in the transformation of knowledge into technologies that give rise to products.

However, the use of biological knowledge to serve human needs is not new, and neither are the enterprises associated with exploiting that knowledge. Human society has tapped biological knowledge for millennia to produce food, feed, beverages and fiber, but the advent of modern technologies and new biological knowledge has vastly expanded the applications of biology. Our early ancestors domesticated

1

plants and animals, and, with the selective breeding of preferred species, they formed the biological foundation for today's plant and animal varieties, many of which are vastly different from their original parents. Indeed, few of today's crop plants are unimproved or harvested from the wild.

The extent and speed of new bioscience applications have caught the general public, and even some scientists, by surprise. The sequencing of the genomes of entire species, such the small flowering plant *Arabidopsis* (in 2000) and rice (*Oryza sativa* in 2005), means that humankind is literally unraveling the "Books of Life" of major organisms, and consequently gaining the potential to alter some very basic elements in these books. Genetically modified organisms (GMOs) have become a lightning rod for those who fear the rapid changes birthed from the acquisition of new knowledge. GMOs have also come to illustrate how basic science can be turned into a multi-billion-dollar growth industry in less than a decade. Promises and fears are the "yang" and "ying" of the new products from biotechnology. Many have warned that society is barely seeing the tip of the iceberg for bioscience products, and if this is the case, then tremendous opportunities for value creation in biology still exist, and with that, the certainty of more controversy.

In this chapter, the reader will be introduced to the basics of bioscience and the enterprises that have been created from bioscience. This chapter provides an overview of the main groups of applications from various branches of bioscience, and the context set for the markets associated with their products and their demand. In today's society, any value created from knowledge requires protection, both locally and internationally. This chapter will also discuss the important issue of value protection and its relationship to technology transfer for less developed countries, which collectively constitute the world's largest potential market.

1.1 What is "Bioscience"?

Several terms need explanation. *Biology* is the study of the life sciences, with two main branches (botany and zoology) and many disciplines (e.g., physiology, genetics, morphology). *Bioscience* includes all the sciences devoted to an understanding of life, while *biobusinesses* are enterprises based on utilization of biological knowledge.

> BIOLOGY — Study of the life sciences; science of life, with two main branches (botany and zoology) and many disciplines (physiology, genetics, morphology, etc.)
> BIOSCIENCE — All the sciences devoted to an understanding of life
> BIOBUSINESS — Business enterprises based on utilization of biological knowledge

Modern bioscience, and indeed what is generally considered modern science based on verifiable research using internationally accepted standards, is only several centuries old. Our use of nature and its products has evolved through a long history of "trial and error" and experience. Much has been written about this local, indigenous knowledge, the basis of which is still being unraveled today using current concepts and modern tools. Chinese traditional medicine, the Indian ayurvedic approach to health, Egyptian and Tibetan sacred texts all attest to how various human civilizations in different parts of the world have accumulated their knowledge base of the life sciences.

It is not possible to pinpoint accurately when modern bioscience started. Scientists generally accept that the publication of *The Origin of Species* by Charles Darwin in 1859 has been a key influence on bioscience development since the 19th century. This, in turn, laid the serious foundations of experimental science, which has become a hallmark of today's modern bioscience. This is not to undervalue the remarkable contributions that earlier, mostly unknown scientists and farmers have made in improving crops and bioprocesses in several continents. Without the efforts of the early pioneers, we would not have today's rice or wheat, from which our major staples are derived.

Modern genetics underpins many aspects of modern biology, and with that, bioscience entrepreneurship. Modern genetics is considered to have started when Mendel's laws were rediscovered in The Netherlands in 1900 by Hugo de Vries. Subsequent to this, several decades of research followed. The first known commercial hybrid seed was developed by Henry Wallace in the USA, who also founded one of today's most successful seed companies, Pioneer Hi-Bred.

The first hybrid corn seeds were sold in the USA in 1924, sparking significant corn yield increases per hectare in North America. Due to the huge agricultural success of hybrid corn, all "natural" corn grown in the USA was replaced by their hybrid counterparts by 1960. The strategic shift from natural to hybrid corn subsequently snagged the USA the title of the "world's largest exporter of corn".

Parallel research and development (R&D) work on vegetables led to the commercialization of hybrid cabbage in Japan in 1951, while conventional breeding work markedly improved the yield and performance of important food crops such as rice and wheat. The "Green Revolution" of the 1960s bore testimony to the powerful impact of hybrid crops. The Revolution has been attributed to staving off famine in large parts of developing Asia then, and won for its chief architect, Norman Borlaug, the Nobel Peace Prize in 1971.

Bioscience has been tightly linked to agriculture, especially the growing of crops. Historians have shown that agriculture gave the stability needed for our nomadic foreparents to put down roots and develop the features of human civilizations. However, traditional agriculture aimed at supplying calories has today been supplanted by the "*New Agriculture*", in which crops have become "biofactories", converting the sun's enormous energy into a myriad of useful products.

Traditional "biofarming", or the growing of crops such as rice and wheat to meet basic sustenance needs, gave way to the rubber and palm oil plantations such as those in Malaysia and Indonesia, to produce value-added hydrocarbon products to meet the needs of a changing world. The plantations were early examples of the use of mass production techniques which treated plants as biofactories to produce rubber and palm oil. Biofarming has now evolved into "Biopharming", and has branched out further into "biofuels", "bioplastics", "biofertilizers", "biopesticides" and "bioremediation". Collectively, these constitute the New Agriculture, with significant opportunities for value creation.

The last quarter of the 20th century saw the emergence of multinational seed companies and the multiplication of smaller domestic seed companies as beneficiaries of the genetics revolution in bioscience. Much has been written about the role of public sector institutions in producing improved seed for poor farmers and serving the socially responsible role of food security. Much less has been written about the role that private companies have played in developing and making available improved seed material to move poor farmers away from subsistence to farming for cash. The cash generated from the agriculture of plantation crops like rubber and palm oil moved generations of people out of the poverty trap in Southeast Asia. Today, agriculture remains an important driver of economic development, premised on entrepreneurship, in this part of the world. This last quarter also evidenced the beginning of the second revolution in genetics, expressed through the so-called biotechnology revolution (see the Annex at the end of this chapter for a brief chronology).

1.2 What are "Bioscience Enterprises"?

A bioscience enterprise is any commercial activity which involves the application of biology and the understanding of life processes and creates economic value for its owner. This generally would include many activities in the biomedical industry, agriculture, food processing and environmental areas. For the purpose of this book, only plant and microbe-based activities are being considered, namely:

- Raw biocommodities
- High-quality seed material using hybrids
- High-quality seed material using tissue culture
- Biofermentation
- Biofertilizers
- Biopesticides
- Biofuels
- Bioremediation, and
- Biotech seeds.

Each of these will be previewed in the following sections of this chapter and described in detail in subsequent chapters.

Bioscience enterprises include more than those activities dealing with the production of specific primary (e.g., rice or corn) or secondary products (e.g., rice bran oil or corn oil). Ever since international trade regimes recognized the value of intellectual property (IP) through organizations such as the World Trade Organization and World Intellectual Property Organization, value creation through the commercialization of services, and through licensing of IP, has become common. In bioscience, the landmark decision in 1980 of the US Supreme Court to grant a patent on a microbial life form that could break down oil spills (see Annex) also meant that new opportunities were created for companies to invest in R&D that led to patentable processes and products.

1.3 Creating Value from Bioscience Through Entrepreneurship

The value chain in a bioscience enterprise (Figure 1.1) therefore starts with discoveries made during the R&D stage. In modern biotechnology applications such as the development of biotech seeds, some of the early transgenic plants were made using a process called particle bombardment, which required a special piece of equipment called a "gene gun". This particle gun was initially developed by Cornell University scientists, but later patented by DuPont company. Companies selling commercial transgenic plants made from the first transgenic produced using the patented gun have to pay to DuPont a percentage of any value created.

Figure 1.1.   A comparative value chain in bioscience enterprises.

Figure 1.1 also shows the steps involved in developing bioscience-based products, many of which are regulated for safe use by government agencies. New industries have developed as governments (urged by a more enlightened and more demanding public) have put into place information requirements to support safety, to support traceability (i.e., where does a particular product in the market trace its origins from?), and to support consumer choice. Animal-testing laboratories for GM food products, detection systems for specific ingredients, and certification services for organic crops are examples of a growing industry aimed at providing more information on products. Collectively, they are valued at hundred of millions in US dollars.

Perhaps one of the biggest value additions in the value chain is further processing of raw commodity into secondary, tertiary and other products (Table 1.1). While a metric ton of rice is traded at between US$300–US$400 on the global market, a metric ton of rice bran oil (tertiary product) is worth about US$3,000–US$11,000. The extraction percent of rice bran oil is only about 0.9% of milled rice, so any R&D that gives rice varieties with higher

Table 1.1. Amplifying value through multiple secondary and tertiary processing for new products, exemplified by rice.

Plant Part	1st Stage Product	2nd Stage Product	3rd Stage Product
Panicle (Grains)	Milled rice	Human food staple Flour	Alcoholic drinks, etc.
	Brown rice	Fuel	Noodles, etc.
	Hull (husks)	Briquettes	Silica-based products
	Embryo and/or endosperm	Bran Bran oil	Tocotrienols Vitamin E Antioxidants
Leaves	Straw	Fuel	
	Phytochemicals	Paper Medium for mushroom growing Purified compounds	
Culms (Stems)	Straw	As above	
	Phytochemicals	As above	
Roots	Straw	As above	

oil content would create significant added value to the rice and the extraction process. Subsequent processing of a tertiary product like rice bran oil by extracting pharmaceuticals such as the compound, oryzanol (a known active anti-oxidant), would give even more value to rice. Organizations such as the National Innovation Agency, Thailand, have commissioned studies on how to add value to Thailand's rice crop beyond the traditional market niche of aromatic rice (NIA, 2006).

The new value chaining for a new agriculture strongly suggests that there can be different players in different countries to add to this chain. The company that owns the IP does not have to be in the same country that uses the IP to produce the bioscience product!

This is a significant, obvious fact that seems to have escaped the attention of so many national planners in countries that desire to be in the mainstream of the "Biology Century". Indeed, the new playing field argues strongly for the need to develop comparative advantages in some parts of the value chain for bioscience entrepreneurship.

Small countries with only human resources and knowledge economies can compete effectively in IP generation, provided investments are made to support R&D and effective IP protection regimes are in place. Of course, many countries have desired to do well in all parts of the value chain. This is shown by the number of science and technology parks that have mushroomed in Asia, even in countries which, analytically, do not have the comparative and competitive advantages to exploit their strengths.

1.4 Creating Value in Biotech Seed Enterprises

In the first paragraph of this chapter, reference was made to the "Biology Century", which is mainly due to the powerful discoveries and developments in genetics backed by computer power. The unraveling, literally, of the "Books of Life" (Ridley, 1999), means the ability to link specific gene(s) to specific functions and traits. The availability of technology and techniques for gene-splicing also means that novel plants or microbes with economically important traits can be created

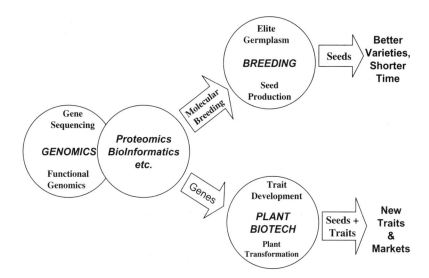

Figure 1.2. Schematic of a new biotechnology-based R&D to market chain (Courtesy: Monsanto Company, St. Louis, USA).

using genes from outside that plant's genome. Companies like Monsanto have put into practice a new biotechnology-based R&D to market chain to produce new plant varieties that meet specific grower needs for competitive farming.

Subdisciplines of modern genetics have evolved which are truly multi-disciplinary and require knowledge from traditional chemistry, biology and mathematics, to name a few. In Figure 1.2, only a few such subdisciplines are named — genomics, proteomics and bioinformatics. The net result, however, is to get competitive advantage by getting to market faster a particular new variety with the desired traits which is also protected by law.

A generic value chain for modern bioscience enterprises (Table 1.2) would show distinctions between activities aimed at value creation, value addition, value capture and value preservation. Important market development decisions to introduce a new product have been made based on the existence of value capture and value preservation mechanisms in a particular country.

Table 1.2.   A new value chain in modern bioscience enterprises.

Value Chain	Activity	{Note}
Value creation	Gene identified & cloned, expressing protein to confer a trait	IP protection for novel gene discoveries
Value addition	Incorporating desired gene into popular local crop variety	Licensing trait to small seed companies
Value capture	Hybrid seed Non-reproductive seed	Commercial seed production and distribution system
Value preservation	IP protection system for seeds	Seed Law, PVP

1.5   Value of the Biosciences Product Market

Bioscience applications in the modern era (post-World War II) have been mainly in agriculture, fisheries and forestry. These industries, with their related bioscience applications, have been a source of employment for the majority of the world's people, as well as a significant contributor to the gross domestic products (GDPs) of many developing countries.

The overall picture is fast changing, with newer applications of the biosciences, such as biotechnology, fostering new sectors especially in the industrialized world. Modern biotechnology products, services and technology solutions were estimated in 2001 to have generated about US$40 billion of value worldwide.

While it is difficult to get comparable statistics because different baskets of enterprises are included under the term biotechnology or biobusiness or bioenterprise, the global value in 2006 was estimated at around US$60 billion for modern biotechnology alone (A. Ilaga at National Biotechnology Week, Philippines, July 2006). This is but a small fraction of the global value of bioproducts shown in Table 1.3.

These figures do not fully show the substantial value addition from secondary processing of bioproducts such as rice bran, from which rice bran oil is extracted, or the use of bioproducts such as corn starch for ethanol biofuel production. Needless to say,

Table 1.3.   Relative contribution of various biobusiness sectors to economic activity (US$ billions and % GDP), 2001.

Biobusiness Sector	Global, US$ Billions (% of Global GDP)	South Asia, US$ Billions (% of Global GDP)	East Asia and Pacific Islands (Excluding Japan), US$ Billions (% of Global GDP)	USA, US$ Billions (% of Global GDP)
Agriculture, fisheries and forestry	2,611.4 (8.1%)	223.2 (28%)	362.1 (15%)	529.4 (5%)
Healthcare	2,933.8 (9.1%)	33.5 (4.2%)	108.6 (4.5%)	1,588.2 (15%)
Food sector (processing, manufacturing)	3,288.4 (10.2%)	100.5 (12.6%)	277.6 (11.5%)	1,016.4 (9.6%)
Biotechnology	40 (0.1%)	1.4 (0.18%)	4.1 (0.17%)	25 (0.24%)
Biobusiness related R&D	257.9 (0.8%)	2.4 (0.35%)	12.1 (0.5%)	105.9 (1%)
Other biobusiness	644.8 (2%)	15.9 (2%)	48.3 (2%)	211.8 (2%)
Total biobusiness	9,776.3 (30.3%)	376.9 (47.3%)	812.8 (33.7%)	3,476.7 (32.8%)
Estimated GDP	32,239.0	797.3	2,414.2	10,588.0
GDP as % of global GDP	100%	2.5%	7.5%	32.8%

Source: BioEnterprise Asia (2003); United Nations Statistics Division (2002); Food and Agriculture Organization (2002); and World Bank (2002).

the bioenterprise sector is growing in Asia at an estimated rate of > 10% p.a.

Research conducted by BioEnterprise Asia (www.bioenterpriseasia. org) showed that about 6,000 companies worldwide classified themselves as biotech companies in 2004. Within the Asia-Pacific region alone, the number of companies which classified themselves as biotech increased from 1,200 to over 2,500 from 2001 to 2004.

However, in Asia, most countries have tended to include both traditional biotechnology (e.g., tissue culture, biofermentation for food production) and modern biotechnology (e.g., drug production using genetically modified microorganisms), making it difficult to separate out the relative contributions of individual enterprises to the national economy. Countries like the Philippines and Vietnam, however, have identified specific niche areas in which to position themselves, such as in the production of natural food coloring or additives by extraction processes using plant material. Examples from the Philippines are papain extraction from papaya and a red dye from seeds of the anatto plant.

1.6 Why Excitement over Bioscience Enterprise?

Bioscience enterprises have only created a small fraction of the potential value that they are capable of generating.

Figure 1.3 is a schematic drawn from different sources to graphically show the unexploited potential of bioscience enterprises according to sector. The pharmaceutical (biomedical) industry up to today

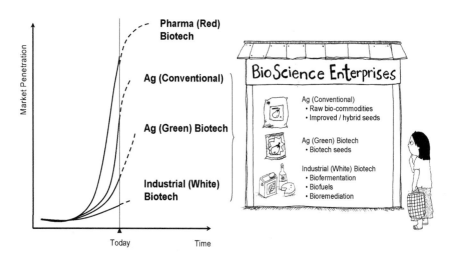

Figure 1.3.   Relative market potential for development of various bioscience products.

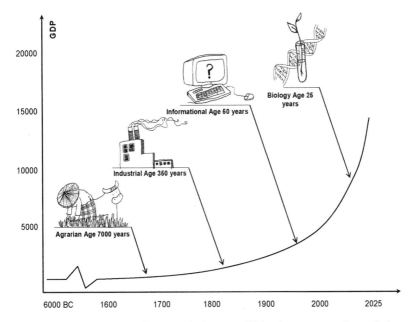

Figure 1.4. Comparison of economic impact of bioscience enterprises relative to other industries in history.

has created the most value, while agriculture (biofarming) is more matured than bioscience applications in industrial processes. Albeit a simple classification, it is meant to illustrate the growth potential and large market size of the bioscience entrepreneurship in industrial uses such as biofuel and bioremediation.

When compared with other significant global phases, modern bioscience enterprises have created much value in a relatively short time (Figure 1.4).

1.7 A Brief Description of Conventional Bioscience Enterprises

Conventional bioscience enterprises, which include agriculture, are collectively the world's largest employer! This is because much of the world today still consists mainly of rural communities, consuming what they produce, especially in Asia.

1.7.1 *Raw biocommodities*

Asia has been an important producer of some of the world's major biocommodities, such as rice, corn (maize), cashew nuts, rubber, palm oil and cacao. Asia is also the world's largest producer of natural timber and aquacultured fish.

While the commodities themselves remain important as food sources, increasing pressure is being put on their traditional role to supply calories for humans and feed for animals, especially on those commodities with potential for secondary exploitation such as conversion into higher valued biofuel or pharmaceuticals. This development is not surprising as plants have always been viewed as "primary producers" in the food chain because of their ability to capture energy from sunlight to make useful products. It is logical to expect that plants as "biofactories" will evolve in their role as human society evolves in its relative needs to use plants.

Asia is currently a net food importer despite its eminence in the production of raw biocommodities. As a region, it is self-sufficient in food commodities like rice, palm oil and fish, but is a large importer of corn, wheat, potatoes, soybean as well as various meats. Even with the food commodities for which there is sufficiency, such as rice and fish, the situation is a fragile one. Some countries are persistent net rice importers, either by design or by need (Table 1.4).

Most rice is consumed where it is grown and the global market for trade is a very "thin" market, with 5%–7% annually of milled rice being available for trade, such that any natural catastrophe has been known to dramatically disrupt availability and cause social consequences. Asia imports most of the surplus export corn (average 45%–50% of global surplus production) and because the global surplus is only 10%–15% of total production, it is projected that the market for corn will become tighter due to competing uses such as bioethanol production.

Furthermore, this region, which holds > 60% of the world's population, only has about 35% of the world's cultivable lands, with a significant area each year being degraded. The Food and Agriculture Organization, United Nations, has predicted shortages of usable land

Table 1.4.   Production and trade in four commodities important to Asia.

Crop	Item	2004/ 2005	2005/ 2006	2006/ 2007
Corn (Maize)	Global Production Million M T (million tons)	714.0	696.0	698.0
	Global Exports Million M T (% of global production)	76.0 (11%)	82.7 (12%)	84.4 (12%)
	Asian Imports[1] Million M T (% of global exports)	35.5 (47%)	36.3 (44%)	43.3 (51%)
Rice (Milled)	Global Production Million M T	401.0	418.0	417.0
	Global Exports Million M T (% of global production)	29.0 (7%)	28.5 (7%)	29.0 (7%)
	Asian Imports[2] Million M T (% of global exports)	6.3 (22%)	6.2 (22%)	7.4 (25%)
Wheat	Global Production Million M T	629.0	622.0	594.0
	Global Exports Million M T (% of global production)	112.0 (18%)	113.0 (18%)	110.0 (19%)
	Asian Imports[3] Million M T (% of global exports)	22.4 (20%)	23.2 (21%)	28.8 (26%)
Soybean (For Meal)	Global Production Million M T	216.0	220.0	234.0
	Global Exports Million M T (% of global production)	46.6 (22%)	51.3 (23%)	53.6 (23%)
	Asian Imports[4] Million M T (% of global exports)	9.9 (21%)	12.1 (24%)	12.8 (24%)

[1]Top 7 Asian countries. [2,3,4]Top 9 Asian countries.
Source: United States Department of Agriculture, Foreign Agriculture Service (www.fas.usda.gov).

and water for farming if more action is not taken to use environmentally friendly technology such as bioremediation (discussed further in Chapter 7).

The 1971 Nobel Peace Prize winner, Norman Borlaug, warned in his address to the Asian Development Bank's annual meeting in 1999 that farmers in Asia will have to produce 50%–75% more grain if a food scarcity crisis is to be averted. The International Rice Research Institute has predicted that by 2020, Asia will need about 700 million tons of milled rice just to be sufficient, and this will require a doubling of raw commodity yields in some countries from the present.

The demand for proteins in Asia, especially from poultry and hogs, has also fuelled the demand for corn as animal feed. Corn is also used to make food products such as corn bread, corn chips and cereals, and as a vegetable, it is consumed as green corn and baby corn. Corn grain is a key industrial raw material used for making starch, glucose and oil. Corn syrup is widely used as sweetener for baked goods. Corn starch is used for a variety of purposes including making pills and sweeteners and for coating paper. Recently, corn has been diverted from these uses in large amounts to make ethanol for biofuel.

What does this all mean in terms of bioscience entrepreneurship?

The increasing demand for raw commodities with a potential to be converted into products in high demand — biofuel, animal and fish feed, etc. — suggests that investments in their efficient production will likely be relatively safe ones. Although there is value creation in the first stage and value capture as raw commodity, the value addition is through further processing.

While trading of the initial dried corn is a profitable business in view of the current high prices due to shortages from biofuel conversion, value addition is high from milling into animal feed and subsequent formulation for specific purposes. As a value proposition in bioscience entrepreneurship, however, experience has shown that companies that have entered into the intellectual property (IP) ownership of the genetic material for high-quality hybrid seeds are the ones that have outperformed their contemporaries in commodity trading, in terms of value capture.

1.7.2 *High-quality seed material using hybrids*

Seed for planting includes all plant material that can be used to grow new plants, from real seeds to plant suckers to cloned plantlets produced from tissue culture. The global seed market is valued at over US$30 billion per year, dominated by about ten multinational companies. Currently, no major seed company of Asian origin has yet to dominate the global seed trade, although Asia has the potential to be the world's biggest market for certified, high-quality seed.

Value capture in the seed industry is done through IP ownership of plant varieties protected by law and the offering of value to growers who purchase the seed material. Hybridization as a bioscience technical process is well-studied, but its use as an enterprise only started in the 1920s with corn in the USA. This led to the founding of one of today's largest seed companies (Pioneer Hi-Bred).

Hybrids offer a scientific means to preserve value as such seeds commonly lose their hybrid vigor (which confers 10%–15% yield advantage over non-hybrids) if the seeds from hybrids are reused for subsequent planting. The seed market includes hybrid and non-hybrid, improved seed.

Data from the United Nations Development Program shows that worldwide, the majority of growers are already planting improved crop varieties (> 90% of wheat is improved; > 65% of rice; > 80% of corn). However, crops like cassava and sweet potato are still largely unimproved. With the hybrids, there is a continual battle to uplift the traits which add to yield, such as pest resistance, and this is an area in which science can create value through new discoveries.

Without exception, all multinational seed companies have large R&D teams which use modern molecular biology and breeding techniques in their product development process. The value creation takes place when the scientific knowledge is translated into a new, improved crop variety which is able to be registered and sold. Companies recover their R&D costs through their own marketing and sales efforts or by licensing their technology to third-party seed companies without the capacity to do their own R&D. Almost a third of the cost price in a kilogram of seed may be from the technology licensing fee, passed on to the grower-buyer by the third-party seed company. However, in the context of bioscience entrepreneurship, this is an area where countries with significant R&D capacity but without the production capacity (i.e., land) can become key players. Good seed depends on good genetics, which in turn depends on basic advances in bioscience and solid R&D.

1.7.3 *High-quality seed material using tissue culture*

Tissue culture refers to a set of techniques and scientific knowledge which enables the growth of cells into tissues and whole organisms under artificial conditions. Tissue culture was among the earliest applications of modern bioscience to develop into a multi-million-dollar business for producing genetically identical seed material with the desired characteristics such as high yield, good eating quality or resistance to pests and diseases. The technique was also one of the earliest commonly included in biotechnology to create value for investors. However, even on its own, it has led to applications just as important as those of genetic engineering, for example, the selection and subsequent mass propagation of plant varieties showing resistance to specific diseases. Indeed, most of the large plantations of rubber and palm oil in Southeast Asia have their origins in tissue-cultured clones.

The varieties of plants propagated by tissue culture in Asia and around the world are numerous and include herbaceous ornamentals, ferns, orchids, roots, tubers, tree species, tropical and subtropical crops. The benefits of propagating plants using tissue culture are manifold, apart from the uniformity in all the plants and the rapid multiplication. Plants grown in tissue culture are often disease- and virus-free. The economic value also is that tissue-cultured plants are easily exported in small lightweight containers. As plants are free of soil, disease quarantine problems are minimized.

With these advantages, export and import of tissue culture products are greatly facilitated. Tissue culture is a multi-million-dollar business in several Asian countries such as Singapore, Thailand, Australia, China and Taiwan. Taiwan alone exported over US$10 million of tissue-cultured orchids in 2003. Several tissue culture companies are now publicly listed companies and investors appear recently to have recognized the inherent value in this subsector. With the ongoing interest in biofuel, it is likely that tissue culture will be tapped to provide clonal seed material needed for the large areas planned in several countries of species like Jatropha.

1.7.4 *Biofermentation*

Biofermentation is a process whereby food and organic products are produced through large-scale fermentation in a bioreactor by organisms like yeast, fungi and algae. Some of the more familiar products produced through the process of biofermentation include natto and tempe. The process of biofermentation involves selection of a suitable microbial culture that has the metabolic potential to produce the desired end product. The medium in which the culture is fermented is carefully chosen.

The development of a suitable, economical medium is a balance between the nutritional requirements of the microorganism and the cost and availability of the medium components. The bioreactor in which the process of fermentation takes place should also be able to provide the culture with the optimal environmental conditions for growth. Producing products by biofermentation has been deemed advantageous as fermentation utilizes renewable feedstocks instead of petrochemicals. Also, the by-products of fermentation are usually environmentally benign compared to the organic chemicals and reaction by-products of chemical manufacturing. Often, the cell mass and other major by-products are highly nutritious and can be used in animal feeds.

There is now renewed interest in bioreactor technology for growing single-celled organisms such as algae which are capable of producing high yields of biodiesel. Algae are potentially the most efficient crop to grow for biodiesel as algal cells have high growth rates, and may have > 50% oil content formed when they convert carbon dioxide from the air and sunlight into energy. Studies suggest that algae are capable of yielding 30 times more oil per acre than the crops currently used in biodiesel production. Algae can create up to 32,000 liters of oil per hectare per year, far in excess of palm oil, presently considered one of the best crops for biodiesel production. The R&D to identify or selectively improve algal strains is in its early days. If the orders of magnitude in yield which have been gained from improving higher plants and microbes is any indication, then there is very high potential for significant improvement in oil yield of algal cells.

1.7.5 Biofertilizers

Fertilizers are needed to provide plants with the macronutrients for growth and development. In the modern era, high crop yields have been achieved because proper levels of fertilizer application have allowed the genetic potential of seeds to be expressed. Most of the fertilizer use today is made from petroleum-based products (i.e., synthetic fertilizers); some are organic. The high cost of synthetic fertilizers, coupled with concerns on sustainability, has led to the search for alternatives. Biofertilizers are organisms that enrich the quality of the soil through their natural processes and are commonly bacteria, fungi and cynobacteria (blue-green algae). Some of the more common types of biofertilizers include mycorrhiza, rhizobium and cyanophyceae. Natural soil already serves as a reservoir of millions of microorganisms, of which more than 85% are beneficial to plant life. Fertile soil usually consists of 93% mineral and 7% bioorganic substances.

Among the myriad of biofertilizers in use today, the use of mycorrhiza fungi to enhance plant health has been one of the most widespread. Mycorrhizal fungi are unique root-inhabiting fungi that colonize plants externally (ectomycorrhizae) or internally (endomycorrhizae). However, the mycorrhiza fungi and its host plant share a symbiotic relationship. The many benefits which the mycorrhiza fungus confers to its host are of much significance in its vast usage as a component of commercial fertilizers. According to Plant Health Care Inc., a leading manufacturer of biofertilizers, endomycorrhizae colonize the insides of plant root cells to benefit plants like fruits, grasses, most ornamental plants, hardwoods and fruit and nut trees.

The Biotech Consortium India Ltd. has been one of the main producers of BGA (Blue-Green Algae) biofertilizer in Asia. The BGA biofertilizer sold is a mix of different strains of BGA and carrier (cattle feed pulverized wheat straw). Elsewhere in Asia, fungi-based concoctions are commonly sold to augment synthetic fertilizers and have proven effective in maintaining high crop yields whilst reducing the overall cost of fertilizer per unit area. Several countries have, for environmental health reasons, launched campaigns to promote increased use of biofertilizers for food and plantation, commercial crops (e.g., palm oil in Malaysia), and to reduce dependency on synthetic, often imported fertilizers. The biofertilizer market is still a small one, but primed to grow in concert with increased demand for organic food, which is grown without synthetic chemicals including fertilizers. In Taiwan, the biofertilizer subsector was valued at US$4.2 million in 2003.

1.7.6 *Biopesticides*

Pests cause an estimated 20%–30% loss in production per crop harvest and the global pesticide market is a multi-billion-dollar one, valued at about US$39 billion in 2006. Almost every modern crop is produced using one or more pesticides and much has been invested in R&D to produce new plant varieties which can naturally resist pests and diseases. Most of the pesticides in current use are synthetic petrochemicals, hence their cost to growers has risen in response to the increase in oil prices.

Pesticides are regulated by governments, but often their misuse has had negative effects on human health and also on ecosystems. Biopesticides are considered a safe alternative and preferred in the growing of organic food. Biopesticides have received increased global attention from the late 19th and early 20th centuries and have sparked renewed attention in the 21st century due to current social issues surrounding their usage, notably, market globalization and sustainable development. Even before their commercialization, biopesticides have been prevalent in nature, with more than 2,000 plant species with insecticidal properties having been characterized.

The first generation of biopesticides essentially resulted from the use of readily available products, such as arsenic and its derivatives, animal oils and compounds from traditionally used plants. In the 19th century, a few compounds of plant origin were identified and used as repellents or toxins. This included alkaloids extracted from tobacco, nicotine and its isomer anabasine isolated from a plant growing in the Russian steppes and high plateaus of North Africa, and families of compounds represented by rotenone, rotenoids and pyrethrins. There are certain criteria for the selection of biopesticides for commercial use, namely, its activity, specificity, low mammalian toxicity, environmental acceptability and safety with regards to non-target organisms.

The value of the global insecticide market for 1998 was estimated to be approximately $15 billion, of which agriculture made up 60% and industrial uses (including consumers) 40%. Estimates of the total market commanded by botanical insecticides are difficult to come by, but it is probably fair to say that botanicals hold less than 1% of the global insecticide market (i.e., < $150 million). Among botanicals, pyrethrum enjoys a dominant place, likely constituting 75%–80% of the total. Neem insecticides are expected to challenge pyrethrum in the market. Pesticides based on plant essential oils are, in commercial terms, in their infancy. However, botanicals may well see annual sales growth of 10%–15% or greater, in contrast to the shrinking market for traditional synthetic insecticides. At present, registered products for insect control include 104 products on the market (mostly *Bacillus thuringiensis*), nematodes (44 products), fungi (12 products), viruses (8 products) and protozoa (6 products). Commercialization in developing countries is limited but growing.

The future of the biopesticide industry seems to be bright. The industry is expected to grow 5.4% annually from 2005 to 2009, led by gains in the Asia-Pacific region.

1.7.7 *Biofuels*

Biofuels are fuel sources that utilize biomass to produce bioenergy in order to provide a wide variety of energy services and to produce biomaterials as substitutes for those presently manufactured from petrochemicals. Biofuels could be an integrating response to a number of global problems including equity, development, energy supply severity, rural employment and climate change mitigation. Biomass provides fuel flexibility to match a wide range of energy demands and is a renewable energy source that can be stored, which is an advantage over several other forms of renewable energy.

Two principal biofuels are currently in use — bioethanol produced from sugar cane, corn and other starchy grains; and biodiesel produced from oil sources such as palm oil, soybean and rapeseed.

The global production of biofuel is estimated at about 45 million liters for bioethanol (or about 3% of global gasoline needs) and 4 million liters for biodiesel (insignificant proportion of global needs). In 2005, Brazil, the USA and China, in descending order, were the top three producers of bioethanol, while Germany, France and the USA were similarly so for biodiesel.

Many predictions have been made about Asia's need for increased energy and fuel as countries in the region modernize and industrialize. As such, many countries are expected to turn to biofuels as an important source of energy in lieu of the current global shortage of fossil fuels. Brazil has probably the longest experience with blending bioethanol into fuel for motor vehicles, which, by some accounts, meets almost half the country's fuel needs.

In Asia, several countries have embarked on accelerated programs to produce biofuel, notably the giant countries of China and India, and also ASEAN countries like Malaysia, Thailand, the Philippines and Singapore. China has always been one of the major players in the Asian biofuel scene. The Chinese government has consistently attached great importance to new and renewable sources of energy development and utilization. Their 21st century agenda emphasized that renewable energy would be the basis of the future energy structure, and that renewable energy development should be preferred in national energy strategies. The government of India has also given high priority to the development of renewable energy.

Energy crops are important to long-term energy strategies because they can be expanded to significantly shift the pattern of world energy supply. Volumes of other forms of waste biomass available are limited as they are by-products of other processes. Plant species that can be grown as energy crops and used for bioenergy purposes are so diverse that they can be grown in virtually every part of the world. Representative energy plant species, apart from those currently used, that have been proposed for tropical and subtropical climates include: Aleman grass (*Echinochloa polystachya*), Babassu palm (*Orbignya oleifera*), Bamboo (*Bambusa spp.*), Banana (*Musa spp.*), Black locus (*Robinia pseudoacacia*), Brown beetle grass (*Leptochloa fusca*), Castor oil plant (*Ricinus communis*), Coconut palm (*Cocos nucifera*), Jatropha (*Jatropha curcas*), Jute (*Crocorus spp.*), Leucaena (*Leucaena leucoceohala*) and the Neem tree (*Azadirachta indica*).

As is the case with algae cultivation for biofuel, many of the proposed and current plant species for biofuel extraction have not undergone as much R&D to select for higher oil yields as has been done for the selection of other agronomic traits. Scientists have estimated that conventional breeding may lead to 15%–20% increases in oil yield in the mid-term, with higher increases possible with genetic engineering. This is a very promising arena with great potential for huge value capture.

1.7.8 *Bioremediation*

Industrial and farming activities have contaminated large tracts of land with toxic chemicals such as arsenic, mercury or high levels of salts, making the land uninhabitable or unsuitable for crops. Fresh water bodies have similarly been contaminated. While mechanical and chemical cures are known for removing the toxic or unwanted chemicals, governments are increasingly searching for environmentally friendly techniques to "clean up" polluted lands and waters. One such set of techniques is collectively called "bioremediation", or the use of microbes, plants or their enzymes to remedy contaminated land and water. An appealing feature of bioremediation is that the contaminated soil or water may be acted upon by organisms *in situ* (i.e., without removing them from their original site).

Several types of bioremediation techniques are in use; in the case where plants are used to clean up the environment, the technique is called "phytoremediation" — phytoextraction, phytodegradation, phytotransformation, phytostabilization and rhizofiltration (use of plant roots to reduce contamination in wetlands and estuaries). Phytoextraction is a popular technique, and much experience has been accumulated and shared within the scientific community to use specific plants for cleaning soil contaminated with heavy metals; the plant material is subsequently removed from the locale and incinerated.

About 400 plants have been reported to hyperaccumulate metals. The families dominating these members are Asteraceae, Brassicaceae, Caryophyllaceae, Cyperaceae, Cunouniaceae, Fabaceae, Flacourtiaceae, Lamiaceae, Poaceae, Violaceae and Euphobiaceae. Brassicaceae (this family includes cabbage) has the largest number of different genera known to accumulate different metals. Nickel hyperaccumulation is reported in 7 genera and 72 species, and zinc accumulation in 3 genera and 20 species. *Thlaspi* species are known to hyperaccumulate more than one metal. Specifically, *T. caerulescence*, a species of *Thlaspi*, is known to accumulate heavy metals such as cadmium, nickel, lead and zinc. Another species of *Thlaspi*, *T. goesingense*, is known for its accumulation of nickel and zinc. *T. ochroleucum* has been known to phytoremediate nickel and zinc, while *T. rotundifolium* has been discovered to supersede the former with an additional phytoremediation ability of accumulating lead.

Several common aquatic species also have the ability to remove heavy metals from water, e.g., water hyacinth (*Eichhornia crassipes* (Mart.) Solms) and duckweed (*Lemna minor* L.). Microbes that are known to degrade pesticides and hydrocarbons generally are exemplified by species like *Pseudomonas* and *Alcaligenes*, which use the contaminant as a source of energy and carbon. Even mushroom fungi such as *Phanaerochate chrysosporium* have been shown capable of degrading environmental pollutants. Laboratory studies in Singapore have shown that common ferns (*Pteris vittata* and *Pityrogramma calomelanos*) are able to bioaccumulate arsenic at levels significantly higher than those found in the environment. One by-product of phytoextraction is the recovery of valuable metals from the metal-rich ash, which serves as a source of revenue and offsets the expense of remediation, which often requires many cropping cycles to reduce metal concentrations to acceptable levels.

As a plant-based technology, the success of phytoextraction is inherently dependent upon proper plant selection. Plants used for phytoextraction must be fast growing and have the ability to accumulate large quantities of environmentally important metal contaminants in their shoot tissue or leaf. Genetic variation in metal-accumulating ability is known within populations of the same plant. In Asia, there is much ongoing R&D in countries like China, Pakistan and India where large tracts of land are unusable due to chemical contamination.

Bioremediation is not a new phenomenon, but modern science has made it a potentially powerful ally by improving the efficiency of the organisms concerned, either using conventional selection or through genetic improvement. Much "upside" has yet to be exploited and can be done only through further investments in R&D.

1.7.9 *Novel bioscience enterprises based on genetic engineering (genetically modified plants and biotech crops)*

About a decade ago, a significant new phenomenon emerged on the agriculture scene — biotech seeds (also known as genetically modified seeds), in which new traits had been introduced using the new tools of biotechnology such as "gene-splicing". Despite controversy over the use of such "gene-splicing" techniques, the uptake of biotech

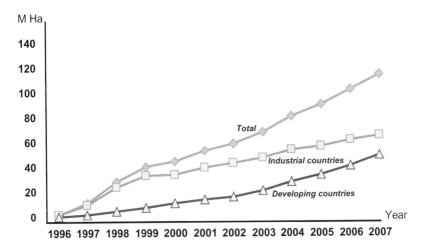

Figure 1.5. Global area of biotech crops, 1996–2007: Industrial and developing countries (million hectares).

Source: James (2007).

seeds has been remarkable and many independent academic studies have shown their value to poor farmers and commercial growers alike, as well as attesting to their biosafety and food/feed safety. The international non-profit organization based at Cornell University in the USA, called the International Service for the Acquisition of Agribiotech Applications (or ISAAA), has documented this remarkable phenomenon (Figure 1.5).

The global area with biotech seeds is now about 114 million hectares, a double digit percent increase each year since its first commercial planting in 1996. And this has been achieved with only four major crops — corn, cotton, soybean and canola — planted in 23 countries by over 10 million farmers. During that period, the share value of the leading biotech seed company, Monsanto, more than quadrupled over its IPO value. Worldwide, over 670 seed products have been approved by some 53 countries for safe use by consumers, including countries in the European Union! As a bioscience enterprise, biotech seeds have created much wealth for many companies and individuals. However, the potential has only been marginally tapped.

Many private and government-funded institutions are actively researching applications of biotech for plants, creating traits such as the following in new varieties:

- Agronomic Traits for
  - Biotic stress
    - Insect resistance
    - Disease resistance viral, bacterial, fungal, nematode
    - Weed-herbicide tolerance
  - Abiotic stress
    - Drought, cold, heat, poor soils
  - Yield
    - Nitrogen assimilation, starch biosynthesis, O2 assimilation
- Quality Traits for
  - Processing
  - Shelf-life
  - Reproduction: e.g., seedlessness
  - Nutrients (Nutraceuticals)
    - Macro: protein, carbohydrates, fats
    - Micro: vitamins, antioxidants, minerals, isoflavonoids, glucosinolates, phytoestrogens, lignins, condensed tannins
    - Anti-nutrients: phytase, allergen and toxin reduction
  - Taste
  - Architecture
  - Fiber
  - Ornamentals: color, shelf-life, morphology, fragrance
- Novel Crop Products for
  - Oils
  - Proteins: nutraceuticals, therapeutics, vaccines
  - Polymers
- Renewable Resources: biomass conversion, feedstocks, biofuels.

Various estimates put the untapped potential in US$ billions of new value creation to those who take out the IP protection. Again, in this arena, the countries and their institutions which exercise the most innovation are those most likely to reap the benefits.

1.8 Who are the Players in Bioscience Enterprises? (Private versus Public)

The range of bioscience enterprises has seen differential roles for the public and private sectors. Raw commodities such as rice, wheat, soybeans and corn initially saw much public sector investment. But this has gradually been replaced by the private sector, especially with soybean and corn. There is almost no public sector investment in corn or soybean R&D in the USA, the world's largest producer. Rice, because it is such a sensitive crop for food security in Asia, remains much in the hands of the public sector, with some companies entering into hybrid seed production only relatively recently. The other bioscience enterprises, from tissue culture to biotech seeds, are dominated by small-medium enterprises (SMEs) and MNCs. It is noteworthy that in Asia, governments have belatedly invested more into R&D than the private sector, and in crops which companies have ignored because of difficulties with capturing value. These crops have sometimes been called "orphan crops", for example cassava and sweet potato.

Biotech seeds have grown significantly in total value since their commercial introduction a decade ago. About 90% of the total number of approved biotech seed products today are owned by a handful of private entities which have been able to capitalize on their "first-entry" advantage arising from investments in R&D and market development — Monsanto, Bayer CropScience, Aventis Crop Science, Syngenta Seeds, Dow AgroSciences, Pioneer (DuPont), DeKalb and Hoechst/AgrEvo. Data from various public databases such as AGBIOS (www.agbios.com) show that the remaining 14% are owned by nine private companies (Agritope Inc.; Bejo Zaden BV; Calgene Inc.; DNA Plant Technology Corporation; Florigene Pty Ltd.; Mycogen (Dow AgroSciences); Plant Genetic Systems; Vector Tobacco Inc.;

Zeneca Seeds) and six public institutions (Beijing University; Cornell University; Chinese Academy of Agricultural Sciences; Huazhong Agricultural University; Societe National d'Exploitation des Tabacs et Allumettes; University of Saskatchewan).

These companies have been willing to share their IP through technology licensing agreements with SMEs in different parts of the world and even with government institutions. The royalty fees arising from such licensing is substantial and although the price of seed is higher than the equivalent non-biotech seed, growers have been willing to purchase on the potential of higher and more stable yields. The total value of biotech seeds has increased by some 5,000% in one decade, and the share equity of some of the pioneering companies has seen similar spectacular increases, creating much wealth for some of the early investors.

1.9 The Issue of Intellectual Property Protection for Biological Material and Processes

Consolidations in the form of acquisitions, mergers and alliances have been a noted feature of the biotechnology industry. Since 1996, more than 25 major acquisitions and alliances valued at $15 billion have taken place among agrobiotech, seed and farm chemical firms (James, 2004). While these are expected to result in increased efficiencies for the private sector, it raises fears of dominance and of marginalization of the role of public sector institutions charged with helping the "poorest of the poor". The challenge to both sectors is on identifying common ground for action to benefit resource-poor farmers, based on the common vision of ensuring food security for both the rural and urban population.

One issue that epitomizes social and ethical concern about biotechnology is intellectual property protection. Multinational companies are increasing their ownership of biological material, which will be protected by patents, relative to the public sector. Supporters of patenting point out that if the private sector is to mobilize and invest large sums of money in biotechnology R&D for agriculture, it must protect and recoup what it has put in. This is especially so when the returns to investment in agriculture do not compare as favorably as with pharmaceuticals. On the other side of the argument is fear that patenting will lead to monopolization of knowledge, restricted access to germplasm, controls over the research process, selectivity in research focus, and increasing marginalization of the majority of the world's population (Serageldin, 1999).

The new developments in biotechnology and information technology have forced a reexamination of the traditional roles of the public sector relative to the private. This has affected crops which traditionally have been only of interest to the public sector, such as rice; opportunities for the private sector started with the introduction of hybrid rice but is now extending possibly into biotech rice.

When the US Supreme Court upheld a patent in 1980 for a genetically engineered bacterium, it probably triggered what is now called by some as a new "gold rush" to own genes. An illustration of the proprietary nature of future rice varieties is given for *B.t.*-rice with resistance to stemborers — an insect-resistant rice variety could have as many as seven patents associated with it. This new situation has caused much discussion within international fora with regards to its impact on plant breeders' rights (PBR) and farmers' rights protected by conventions such as UPOV. Most Asian countries as yet do not have patent protection for biological material, although plant varietal protection laws exist. The direct effect of intellectual property protection on germplasm exchange is likely to be the requirement for companies or institutions using proprietary material to acknowledge its use in some way. It is also likely that trade issues will become intermingled with development objectives, especially in resource-poor countries.

The concerns about private sector domination of the factors of agricultural production cannot and must not be ignored. Effective regulatory mechanisms and safeguards need to be universal so that the impact of biotechnology is both productive and benign. Intellectual property protection and private sector participation in research are keys to continued technological innovations, but there is also a moral obligation to ensure that scientific research helps address the needs of poor people and safeguards the environment for future generations.

It should also be noted that a small number of public institutions have taken out IP protection on their genetic resources as well. Protection of intellectual property rights encourages private sector investment, but in developing countries, the needs of smallholder farmers and environmental conservation are unlikely to attract private funds. Public investment will be needed, and new and imaginative public-private collaboration can make the gene revolution beneficial to developing countries (Serageldin, 1999).

1.10 Outlook on Bioscience Products for the Marketplace — A New Playing Field and the New Agriculture

Bioscience enterprises reflect not only the dynamic changes occurring in science and technology throughout Asia, but also the infective spirit of entrepreneurship spreading throughout the region. In the past decade, many Asian nations, notably the so-called "Tigers", have invested heavily in building science capacity in educational institutions at all levels, and leveraged that by similar investments in technology capacity. Countries like Singapore and Korea have purposely targeted specific sectors, such as the Life Sciences, for exploitation. The goal has been to broaden the base of the current economies through future diversification beyond current strengths like manufacturing and ICT.

As the demand for basic commodities such as food, fiber and fuel continues, so too will the need for creative solutions to their supply through bioscience entrepreneurship. Innovation in products and processes will likely increase as the creative pursuits in science and technology start showing results in more countries within Asia. Asia as a region currently accounts for only a small fraction of all the patents filed worldwide. Again, there are purposeful efforts to improve on this and on related indices of research performance.

Table 1.5. Relative investment effort for major bioscience enterprises in Asia.

	Small-Medium Enterprises	Multinational Companies	Government Public Institutions
Biocommodities	+++	+++	+++
Hybrid Seeds	++	+++	+
Tissue Culture	+++	+++	+
Biofermentation	+	+++	+
Biodegradation	+++	++	+
Biofertilizers	+++	+	+
Biopesticides	+++	+	+
Biofuels	+	+++	+
Bioremediation	++	+	++
Biodetection	+++	+	+
Biotech Seeds	+	++	+++

The outlook is for a tighter link between creativity, innovation and enterprises.

Asia has great need for the products arising from bioscience enterprises. The relative investments in different biosciences suggest that there is much opportunity for growth (Table 1.5).

Education to participate in the exciting opportunities from rapid knowledge change in the biosciences is likely to be a key factor influencing success. The outstanding performance of several Asian countries in international assessments (such as the "Trends in International Mathematics and Science Study" or TIMSS), and in the regular international science olympiads, augurs well for the future. Without this sound base of science and mathematics education, it will be difficult to imagine competitive ability in the global marketplace.

"Today's students need to learn Biology..."

"We have entered a time of continuous learning, and the biotech revolution will require more of that from more of us than at any time in history."

— Richard W. Oliver in *The Biotech Age*, 2003

Annex: Brief Chronology of the Biotechnology Revolution

(Adapted from www.abc.net.au/science/features/biotech/default.htm; www.isaaa.org)

- 1973 — The discovery that created modern biotechnology. *Herb Boyer and Stanley Cohen showed it was possible to take a human gene and put it in a bacterium that could then mass produce quantities of that gene. This immediately opened up enormous industrial possibilities by presenting an easy way to mass produce hormones.*
- 1975 — *The Alsilomar conference of 1975 was where the first safety regulations for biotechnology were hammered out.*
- 1976 — World's first genetic engineering company is formed. *Herb Boyer teamed up with a venture capitalist to form Gentech, with the goal of genetically modifying bacteria to produce human insulin. Gentech was the world's first genetic engineering company and Boyer became the first molecular multi-millionaire.*
- 1978 — Scientists win Nobel Prize for discovering biological "snips" for DNA. *The 1978 Nobel Prize for Medicine went to Dr Hamilton Smith and Dr Daniel Nathans of Johns Hopkins University in America, and Prof Werner Arber of Switzerland. The prize was awarded for discovering enzymes that are like biological scissors. The enzymes cut DNA into pieces, an essential tool in genetic research and fundamental for Boyer and Cohen's 1973 breakthrough.*
- 1980 — First biotechnology patent granted. *In 1980, Cohen and Boyer were awarded a US patent for gene cloning that allowed them to make human insulin from genetically modified (GM) bacteria. Also in 1980, a landmark decision by the US Supreme Court granted a patent for a GM bacterium that could break down oil.*
- 1980 — Genetically engineered vaccine created. *In 1980, a vaccine for hepatitis B was genetically engineered. Hepatitis B was a major cause of liver disease and the genetically engineered vaccine, along*

with genetically engineered drugs, were immediately popular. People could see the advantages of the medical applications of biotechnology and accepted the new vaccines and drugs.

- 1983 — Genetically modified organism (GMO) approved for environmental release. *In 1983, Dr Stephen Lindow from Berkeley in the USA was given approval to release the first GM bacteria into the environment. Bacteria living on potato plants made the plants sensitive to frosts. Lindow wanted to release GM bacteria, which did not make the plants frost-sensitive, to compete with the non-GM bacteria on the leaves of potato plants; the potato plants were able to withstand temperatures as low as minus five degrees.*

- 1984 — Scientists stumble upon DNA fingerprinting. *Alec Jeffries from the University of Leicester in the UK created the first DNA fingerprint while researching the evolution of genes. Also in the 1980s, Nobel Prize winner Kary Mullis came up with an idea leading to the development of a technique called polymerase chain reaction (PCR). PCR is a technique that replicates a sample of DNA and enables scientists to amplify or multiply DNA from a sample as small as a single cell. The potential of PCR and DNA fingerprinting were quickly realized and used for fighting crime as well as establishing family and evolutionary relationships.*

- 1987 — GM foods start to grow. *In 1987, Dr Mike Bevan, from the Institute of Plant Research in Cambridge in the UK, grew genetically modified potatoes. Genes were added to potato plants to make them produce more protein and increase their nutritional value. Research into other foods included supplementing rice with vitamin A and removing allergy-causing proteins from peanuts.*

- The 1990s — *In the past decade, GM crops became commercialized and spread to many countries through double digit percent growth in planted area each year. Dolly the sheep was cloned and scientists finished a draft of the human genome.*

- Early 2000s — *Several genomes of public interest are mapped, e.g., human, rice.*

- 2006 — *Biotech crops exceed 100 million hectares planted by farmers in 22 countries. More than 500 plant-based biotech seed products are approved by regulatory agencies in 51 countries for public use.*

References

James, C. (2004). Global review of commercialized biotech/GM crops: 2004. ISAAA Brief No. 32. Ithaca, New York.

James, C. (2007). Global status of commercialized biotech/GM crops: 2007. ISAAA Brief No. 37. Ithaca, New York.

National Innovation Agency (NIA), Thailand (2006). *Potential World Markets for Innovative Rice Businesses in Thailand*. NIA, MOST. (www.nia.or.th)

Oliver, R.W. (2003). *The Biotech Age*. McGraw-Hill.

Ridley, M. (1999). *Genome: The Autobiography of a Species in 23 Chapters*. London: Fourth Estate.

Serageldin, I. (1999). Biotechnology and food security in the 21st century. *Science*, 285: 5426.

Woese, C.R. (2004). A new biology for a new century. *Microbiology and Molecular Biology Reviews*, 68(2): 173–186.

Chapter 2
Hybrid Plant and Seed Varieties

2.1 Introduction

One of the most recognized applications of modern bioscience is the development of improved seeds of important crops like wheat and rice. Starting in the 1960s, plant breeders catalyzed a "Green Revolution" in India and China, which later spread to other parts of the world and which has saved millions from dying of starvation. Norman Borlaug was recognized for his efforts in this when he was awarded the Nobel Peace Prize in 1971. Today, we see the continuing application of modern genetics and breeding for improving all crops on which humans depend. In the process, much value has been created, many lives have been saved, and successful entrepreneurship examples have been spawned in all continents!

Seed for planting refers to all plant material that can be used to grow new plants. The variety of planting seeds can range from real seeds and plant suckers to cloned plantlets produced from tissue culture.

Almost all seeds sold commercially are hybrid seeds produced through the process called "hybridization". Hybridization as a bioscience technical process has been well-studied, but its use as an enterprise only started in the 1920s with corn in the USA. This led to the founding of one of today's largest seed companies, Pioneer Hi-Bred.

Hybrids offer a scientific means to preserve seed value as seeds commonly lose their hybrid vigor (which confers 10%–15% yield advantage over non-hybrids) if the seeds are reused for subsequent planting. To date, the seed market includes hybrid and non-hybrid, improved seed. Data from the United Nations Development Program shows that the majority of growers are already planting improved crop varieties (> 90% of wheat is improved; > 65% of rice; > 80% of corn) worldwide. However, crops like cassava and sweet potato are still largely unimproved. With hybrid seeds, there is a continual battle to improve the traits which add to yield, such as pest resistance, and this is an area in the hybrid seed industry for which science can create value through new discoveries.

There is much value to be created in the research and subsequent improvement of hybrid seeds. It is therefore not surprising that all multinational seed companies have large R&D teams which use modern molecular biology and breeding techniques in their product development process.

The global seed market is valued at over US$30 billion per year, dominated by about ten multinational companies. Currently, two major seed companies of Asian origin on the global seed scene are in the top 11 by annual revenue, although Asia has the potential to be the world's biggest market for certified, high-quality seed. Value capture in the seed industry is done through IP ownership of plant varieties protected by law and the offering of value to growers who purchase the seed material.

Value creation takes place when the scientific knowledge is translated into a new, improved crop variety which is able to be registered and sold. Companies recover their R&D costs through their own marketing and sales efforts or by licensing their technology to third-party seed companies without the capacity to do their own R&D. Almost a third of the cost price in a kilogram of seed may be from the technology licensing fee, passed on to the grower-buyer by the third-party seed company.

However, in the context of bioscience entrepreneurship, making money from the technology of hybridizing seeds is an area where countries with significant R&D capacity but without the production capacity (i.e., land) can become key players. Good seed depends on good genetics, which in turn depends on basic advances in bioscience and solid R&D. This chapter will focus on hybrid seeds as an effective value creation, bioscience enterprise.

2.1.1 *History of hybrid plant and seed varieties*

When a plant or seed is referred to as a "hybrid", it is the progeny of a cross between two different varieties of plants. The hybrid offspring is also termed the F_1 generation (first generation) and has a heterozygous genotype. Maternal and paternal genes of differing characteristics make up the genotype of the hybrid plant or seed.

In the early 19th century, Charles Darwin first introduced the possibility of creating hybrid plants by proposing that species of plants and animals would change over time to better adapt to their environment. Such a process is commonly known as natural selection. Ever since humans knew how to farm for food, they have unknowingly aided nature's course of natural selection by picking out the best crops to plant the next year, promoting the best quality in species over each agricultural cycle.

Over time, as the global population increased, humans realized that selective breeding of the best crop strains would not be enough to sustain a growing population. Crop yields had to be improved by the creation of more vigorous crop strains with more desired traits. However, this idea only originated in the 1860s, stemming from an experiment on the study of inheritance traits in pea plants by an Augustinian abbot. The abbot, Gregor Mendel, discovered that he could cross-breed different strains of pea plants and predict the traits of the offspring. From his experiment, he concluded that there was a genetic basis for inherited traits and that selective breeding could control the expression of these traits. Unfortunately, Mendel's work languished until after the turn of the century when his work was rediscovered.

The progeny of a cross between genetically different plants are generally bigger, more vigorous and higher-yielding than their parents. The American geneticist G.H. Shull in 1914 suggested the term "heterosis" to describe this phenomenon. He understood heterosis as the increased productivity in the heterozygous F_1 compared to the mean of the two homozygous parents (Becker, 1984).

The United States was the first country to capitalize on the hybrid plant and seed industry. It pioneered the production of hybrids which had desirable traits of both the paternal and maternal plant. As early as 1909, G.H. Shull proposed to commercially utilize heterosis for the purposes of crossing inbred lines of maize. However, the first inbred strains did not provide sufficient yields for profitable seed production. It was only when the idea of producing double-cross hybrids (i.e., hybrids that are the progeny of two different parent hybrids) was put forward that the breakthrough for the method of inbreeding and crossing in American maize breeding was made. The first double-cross hybrid entered the market in 1921, and by 1944, already more than 80% of the maize-growing areas in the USA were sown in hybrid maize (Kloppenburg, 1988).

In the course of the 20th century, dramatic yield increases were achieved in maize crops: American farmers harvested an average of 1,400–1,500 kg/ha in 1910. However, yields had increased roughly sixfold to 8,500 kg/ha by 2002/2003, according to statistics available from the US Department of Agriculture. Hybrid corn is still the most important economic crop grown in the United States. Today, somewhere around 99% of United States' corn is grown from hybrid seed.

Other countries soon followed in the footsteps of the United States. China was the first country to breed hybrid rice in 1974. Hybrid rice varieties were found to yield 15%–20% more crop than even the best of the improved or high-yielding varieties of rice. Fifteen million hectares of land in China (about half of China's total rice area) are now under hybrid rice cultivation. National average rice yields have increased from 3.5 tons to 6.2 tons per hectare in the 21st century.

The hybrid plant and seed revolutions have also produced household names in the field. Iowan Henry A. Wallace was one of the first people to successfully market hybrid corn seed. Wallace worked with his father to develop the first commercial hybrid seed at Pioneer Seed in Des Moines. He later went on to become the Vice President of the United States.

Plant breeding research by Nebraskan Henry Beachell was reputed to have saved millions from starvation. When working in the US Department of Agriculture in Texas, he created nine rice varieties, which eventually accounted for more than 90% of the US long-grain rice production. Beachell received the 1996 World Food Prize for his efforts.

In China, Professor Yuan Longping is a household name as the "father" of hybrid rice. He began his research in hybrid rice development in 1964. After nine years of study, he developed the genetic materials (the A-, B- and R-line) for breeding hybrid rice varieties in 1973. The method was a success and hybrid rice was produced commercially in China from 1976 onwards. Prof Yuan's research provided an effective approach for China to increase its rice yield on a large scale — in general, the yield from hybrid rice was 20% higher than from conventional varieties. Prof Yuan was also the recipient of many awards, including the 1987 UNESCO Science Prize for outstanding contributions in the field of Science and Technology.

Practically all crop plant species today have their hybrid varieties.

2.2 The Science and Technology Behind the Hybrid Seed Business

2.2.1 *What are hybrid varieties?*

Hybrid varieties result from a targeted cross of two different pure breeding lines, with the progeny surpassing the parental lines in terms of yield. They represent the first generation originating from the cross (F_1 generation). Figure 2.1 illustrates the development of a hybrid variety in a maize plant.

A mature maize plant is monoecious (i.e., it has both male and female reproductive structures on the same plant). The male reproductive structure (tassel) is located at the top of the plant, while the female reproductive structure (ears) is located at several points along the stem (Figure 2.1a). Each ear bears silk that directs the pollen from the tassel into the embryos in the ear. There is one silk for each embryo in the ear.

Initially, the maize plants are allowed to self-pollinate (top half, Figure 2.1b). In this process, the male portion of the maize fertilizes the embryo in the same maize plant. The first generation offspring

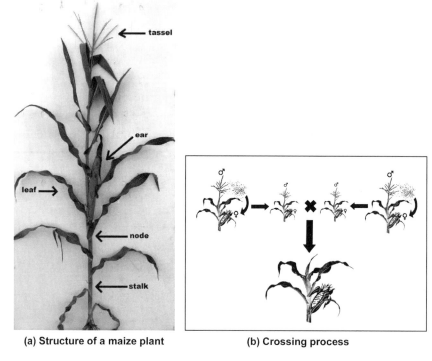

(a) Structure of a maize plant   (b) Crossing process

Figure 2.1.   Simplified diagram showing development of a maize hybrid.

would thus be genetically identical to the mother plant. Ideally, both the mother plant and the daughter plant should be allowed to prop-agate because they possess desirable characteristics which researchers hope to strengthen through inbreeding.

Among the many first generation offspring produced by self-pollination, top-performing individuals are selected and crossed. The offspring of the cross are then self-pollinated for several generations.

During early parent line development, each inbred is unique due to their different gene combinations. Researchers then select the inbred plants which display the most desirable traits for further prop-agation for about five generations.

Once the desired inbreds have been identified, scientists then identify combinations of parent lines which are able to produce the highest-yielding hybrids. To create hybrids for testing, unrelated parents are crossed to produce experimental hybrids, and their performance is tested year after year. In reality, hybrids can either be the result of a cross between two purebred varieties, a cross of two hybrid varieties or three-way hybrids (these are generated by pollinating a hybrid maternal line with an inbred line).

Hybrid plant technology also allows hybrids to be conferred unique traits like resistance to insect pests. Hybrid plants differ from pure line plants and open-pollinated varieties in that the seed they produce cannot produce viable offspring. As such, seeds of a particular hybrid plant have to be bought yearly.

2.2.2 Uniformity in hybrid varieties

A very important aspect of hybrid breeding concerns the high uniformity of the plants after the crossing of the two inbred lines. This aspect may be more important than heterosis itself; however, it only applies to self-sterile plants. In self-sterile plants, nature uses a number of biological ways to prevent the pollen of a plant from fertilizing its own inflorescence. In most such self-sterile plants, an example of such a preventive mechanism is genetic self-incompatibility. Successful fertilization requires the pollinating plant to be genetically different from the seed parent plant. This is the reason why such species always exhibit a degree of difference and diversity in their population.

Such varieties of self-sterile plants are termed "open-pollinated varieties". Open-pollinated varieties are subject to constant change and evolution, which has two effects: firstly, maintenance breeding is required to keep the desired characteristics; and secondly, every open-pollinated variety contains a certain undeveloped future potential. In the language of genetics, these are recessive genes which are not expressed. It is only when inbreeding brings two such recessive genes together in the one plant that they find expression and can, if they represent desirable traits, be bred for; or, if they are not desirable, they can be eliminated. Both actions are considered in hybrid breeding as the parental lines of hybrid varieties are bred from various original populations by means of inbreeding (forced self-pollination).

2.2.3 Hybridizing mechanism

Essential to the production of hybrid seed is the sterility of the pollen. Pollen from a hybrid plant cannot be allowed to self-pollinate the same plant. This is especially so for the maternal line of hybrid plants. If the following generations of progeny are self-pollinated, performance of the hybrid gradually drops. Inbreeding depression becomes evident until the plants are once again more or less homozygous (the genetic characteristics contained in each of the plant cells as inherited from the maternal and paternal sides respectively are similar). At that point, the mean performance level of all homozygous lines would be similar to that of the original non-hybrid parents.

The large-scale production of hybrid seed requires a hybridizing mechanism which prevents self-pollination in the maternal line. Selfing can be prevented by mechanical, chemical and genetic means.

2.2.3.1 The mechanical route

Hybridizing maize is often done through mechanical breeding of the plants because of their monoecious flower morphology, where male and female inflorescences are on the same plant but physically separate. The male inflorescences (panicles) at the terminal end of the plant can be pulled out or cut off, either manually or by machines. Seed parent and pollenizer are grown in strips adjacent to one another. Seeds formed from the plants from which the panicles were removed would thus be the offspring of the desired cross. In this way, plants are forced to cross-pollinate.

2.2.3.2 The chemical route

The chemical route of treating the seed parents with gametocides is predominantly used in self-fertile plants such as wheat. Gametocides generate complete pollen sterility, which are as independent as possible from weather conditions and the developmental stage of plants, and which at the same time do not have side effects on plants, the environment or human health. Despite intensive research in this field, there is as yet no fully satisfactory gametocide for any plant species.

2.2.3.3 *The genetic route*

The genetic route is based on the fact that in all plant species, there are occasional pollen-sterile individuals. Pollen sterility can be caused by a number of factors, but most important for hybrid breeding is a genetic system based on the combined action of nucleic and cytoplasmic genes: cytoplasmic male sterility (CMS). CMS is based on the modification of mitochondrial DNA which, in conjunction with certain nucleic genes, leads to pollen sterility, but which in conjunction with other nucleic genes results in fully fertile plants. The nucleic genes that maintain pollen sterility are called maintainers, while nucleic genes that restore pollen fertility are called restorers. The latter are dominant.

With the aid of CMS, hybrid seed can be produced economically and at a large scale. At first, the maternal line is developed through breeding before CMS is implemented. In order to maintain and propagate the maternal line, the plants in the maternal line are pollinated with a paternal maintainer line. All progeny produced should be pollen-sterile. However, for crop species where the seed is the actual crop, the hybrid variety itself must not be pollen-sterile. Therefore, the hybrid variety's paternal line must be a restorer in order to allow for normal seed development.

Functioning and established CMS systems are available for a large number of plant species. CMS mostly arises when cytoplasm and nucleic genes do not "match", i.e., if they have come together through the crossing of genetically extremely distant lines. Primitive forms or wild species of crops are often used as CMS sources, and the nucleic genes of the highly bred material are crossed into such CMS mother plants by means of repeated backcrossing. If no restorers can be found in the highly bred material, these will also have to be transferred from the primitive or wild species through backcrossing (Kloppenburg, 1988). Such a process takes many years to complete.

2.3 SWOT Analysis

2.3.1 *Strengths*

There are many outstanding advantages to hybrid plants. A testimony to this is the extensive marketing, sale and use of hybrid varieties in the international market today. Research on plant breeding has enabled scientists to develop hybrids which are superior to their non-hybrid parents. Hybrids are usually higher-yielding than their parents. The higher performance of hybrids is usually referred to as "heterosis". Heterosis is much more pronounced for the yield trait than for qualitative traits. With continued inbreeding and selection, the individual line performance of the inbred lines increases while the relative importance of heterosis slowly declines. Currently, better yields can be achieved in most crops with hybrid varieties rather than open-pollinated or pureline varieties. Hybrid varieties of major crops such as corn and rice have been shown to increase profit to the farmers who plant them.

Hybrid varieties are also known to be more uniform than open-pollinated varieties. Such uniformity cannot be achieved by population breeding. Self-sterile plants allow for quick establishment of many desirable characteristics like disease resistance in hybrid varieties. For the trait of disease resistance, which is often inherited in a dominant fashion, it is sufficient if one of the two inbred lines carries the resistance in order for the hybrid variety to have disease resistance. Thus, hybrid varieties can be said to have "inherent" product protection for the breeder.

2.3.2 *Weaknesses*

Hybrid seeds inherently have higher yield potential than non-hybrids (open- or self-pollinated) seeds by virtue of their genetics. However, much of this yield potential may not be reached unless the farmer/grower also uses "best management practices" (BMP) for the crop. This BMP includes proper soil preparation, fertilizer application, and water and pest management practices. It is common to see differences of up to 50% between actual on-farm yields and potential yields because of inconsistent management practices. This is particularly common in developing countries where the variability between farmers in management skills and in access to inputs is highest.

A major concern in the propagation of hybrid varieties is the loss of so-called intrinsic quality in the plant or seed, expressed by some groups such as those advocating biodynamic farming. However, this cannot yet be proven using purely analytical methods of mainstream science.

The uniformity of the hybrid varieties is a decisive reason for their success, especially where vegetables are concerned. However, this uniformity also makes the entire population of a hybrid variety equally vulnerable — in the case of a resistance breakdown, an epidemic can affect all plants in the field in the same manner.

2.3.3 *Opportunities*

Of the world's important food crops, several are yet to be hybridized. Commercial vegetable breeding research in Asia began only about 20 years ago. As Asia enters into the biotechnology age of the 21st century, it is inevitable that advances in biotechnology would enable Asia to produce improved strains of hybrid seeds and plants.

Biosciences involved in the production of hybrid seeds include plant pathology, plant tissue culture and molecular marker-assisted tools. Advances in plant pathology technology would enable hybrid seed companies to quickly diagnose diseases in parent plant or test hybrid plant lines. Selection of a successful parent plant breeding line would thus be much more efficient. Breeding plants in tissue culture enables the mass propagation of desired hybrid seeds. Also, growing plants in tissue culture enables researchers to control the growth of the seedlings, increasing their chances of survival. Improvement in DNA marker technology would also enable researchers to map and identify disease and quality traits in breeding lines quickly and efficiently.

Expected advances in plant pathology include the improvement and subsequent adoption of technologies like ELISA and PCR (Polymerase Chain Reaction). The application of these technologies would aim to offer quick and accurate identification of potentially important plant diseases in advance of the critical state. It is even possible to determine accurately which pathogen(s) causes a particular disease in plants and if it is similar or different from that in another species or area.

Improvements in plant tissue culture techniques would enable the more efficient mass production of haploid breeding lines through somatic embryogenesis. Tissue culture also makes possible the crossing of incompatible parents through techniques like embryo rescue, and acquisition of cytoplasmic-inherited traits through fusion of protoplasts.

Molecular marker-assisted tools have yet to be used in most plant breeding programs to date as they are initially costly and require experienced staff for data interpretation. However, the use of such DNA markers potentially offers many advantages including reducing breeding cycles of plants. Their use can also remove the need for large field selection trails and allow the early identification of quantitative traits.

2.3.4 *Threats*

Hybrid varieties and seeds face competition from open-pollinated and purebred varieties of plants and seeds. Open-pollinated varieties refer to self-sterile plants (e.g., maize). In self-fertile crop species like wheat and barley, pureline varieties are the alternative to hybrid varieties. Open-pollinated seeds or plants are a result of either natural or human selection for specific traits which are then reselected in every crop. The seed is kept true to type through selection and isolation; the flowers or seeds of open-pollinated varieties are pollinated by bees or wind. Their traits are relatively fixed within a range of variability.

Perhaps the biggest threat to hybrids is the non-realization of their yield potential because of improper crop and pest management, leading to a loss of confidence in their performance. Because hybrid seeds are relatively more costly than non-hybrids, farmers have the potential to become indebted due to this underperformance, resulting in reduced social acceptance.

2.4 "Freedom to Operate" Issues

Hybrid seeds and plants have been controversial since their creation. Some argue that hybrid seeds cause farmers to be overdependent on hybrid seed companies. Others are concerned about the commercialization of the food production process. But scientists argue that farmers do have a choice whether to use the new hybrids which have a 15%–20% yield advantage.

2.4.1 *Farmers' dependence on hybrid seeds*

Due to the heterozygous nature of hybrid crops and seeds, saving and replanting the seed of a hybrid variety results in a non-uniform crop. Various traits segregate during the formation of an offspring from its parents. It is therefore unlikely that such seed will give a similar yield and quality to the bought-in F_1 seed. Because of this, farmers are encouraged to purchase new hybrid seed on an annual basis.

When breeders and scientists first started to breed hybrid plants, there was no law on plant variety protection, which meant that a breeder had no way of living off the fruits of his labor. Only a few years after the scientific introduction of hybrid plants, commercial maize breeding companies were set up (e.g., Pioneer Hi-Bred). Breeding thus transformed hobby and research into big business. This was the beginning of today's largely complete division of labor between variety breeding and cultivation.

The expensive groundwork required by every hybrid breeding program has often been done by public institutions such as universities, i.e., the development of inbred lines, the search for pollen-sterile lines, the development of useful statistics programs for test cross-matings and much more — so the division of labor is also evident in this field: expensive and time-consuming (publicly financed) research, and practical breeding (privately financed and with private returns). The concurrent division of labor between farmer and seed producer would probably have happened eventually, but has been criticized by groups concerned about farmers' dependence on private industries.

If at some point only hybrid seed is available, it is conceivable that the seed could be used to pressurize farmers. Seed sales could, for example, be tied to supply contracts, which would allow for control over quantities and prices. Another possible scenario would be that political conditions were attached to seed purchases: only those who please politically would be allowed to grow food. All these are currently highly speculative, as farmers generally do have the right to choose what they plant.

2.4.2 Ethical issues

Some groups reject hybrid breeding for ethical reasons on account of its intervention into the plants' flowering biology and fertility. The inability to save seed and replant hybrid varieties is considered by ecologically and socially motivated movements as unethical. The protection of plant variety rights in the future is also an ethical problem. Who should "own" the crop plants? Is it right to support a breeding process which turns the breeder effectively into the owner? These questions should rightly be asked, but their answers also need to take into account the benefits from hybrid technology, and the costs of not using the technology.

For many plant species, hybrid breeding is not yet feasible today because of a lack of workable hybridizing mechanisms. It is likely that, with the aid of biotechnology, significant progress will be made in this regard in the future, especially with the application of techniques involving mutagenics, protoplast fusion and gene transfer.

Patenting and hybrid breeding turn cultural assets into private property. Many seed and breeding initiatives associated with the organic farming sector try to present alternatives to this development by maintaining threatened varieties on a voluntary basis or by searching for new ways of financing plant breeding.

2.5 Product Range

The product range of hybrid seeds in the market is very wide as seed companies view hybrid seeds as a practical way to capture and preserve the value of their R&D investments. Each crop species that has seen hybrid development is represented by a wide choice of hybrids, each promoted for its particular set of traits, apart from the yield advantage. Companies commonly add value to a hybrid variety by introducing an additional trait (such as resistance to a specific disease) over that of a competitor's variety. Table 2.1 gives examples of hybrid plant and seed varieties in some commercial crop species. The companies listed in the table exemplify hybrid biobusinesses. More complete listings are found in trade-related websites.

2.6 How Value is Created from Hybrid Seeds

Value creation in hybrid seeds is usually achieved through research and innovations in the science and technology behind the business. Much of the information on actual value multiplication is proprietary, although some public organizations such as the International Rice Research Institute and the Philippines Rice Research Institute have published figures on the costs of producing hybrid rice seeds.

Apart from financial value creation, social value creation has been proposed for vegetable hybrids, especially with regards to the number of people involved or impacted through livelihoods or food security. Figure 2.2 provides a concise summary of this value creation process in the hybrid seed industry with the East West Seed Company in Thailand as an example (East West Seed Company, 2003).

Figure 2.3 looks at the potential number of people who can be provided access to high-quality vegetables through a supply chain that starts with 50 scientists and technicians, and ramps up to 500,000 vegetable farmers who grow enough for 50 million consumers. These estimates provide strong arguments to use hybrid seeds as a social service supported by governments in the form of hybrid seeds distributed to farmers. From an enterprise perspective, the multiplication factor is significant in terms of potential value addition from the initial investment in R&D.

Table 2.1.   Examples of hybrid varieties in some commercial crop species.

Product	Company	Remarks
"Celebrity" (hybrid tomato)	Growquest; Good Earth Gardens	A great all-purpose slicing tomato with good size and uniform shape. Good in all climate zones. Indeterminate
"Early Girl" (hybrid tomato)	Ed Hume Seeds, Tomato Growers Supply Company	Classic American variety that ripens early with medium, smooth, globe fruits with excellent flavor. Indeterminate
"San Remo" (Italian hybrid tomato)	Renee's Garden	Tall, vigorous plants with sausage-shaped fruit. Great fresh or for sauce. Mid-season. Indeterminate
A&C Hybrid #500 (hybrid giant pumpkin of size 12"–14")	Not fully commercialized yet or sold under the collective umbrella of pumpkin plants. Seedquest is one company selling pumpkin seeds	Takes about 95 days to mature in North American climate and has a bright orange skin. Round medium-sized fruit with medium deep ribs. Excellent for carving. Strong handles
Mammoth Gold (hybrid giant pumpkin of weight 20–40 pounds)	Not fully commercialized yet or sold under the collective umbrella of pumpkin plants. Seedquest is one company selling pumpkin seeds	Takes about 105 days to mature in North American climate and has a deep orange coloration. A large, irregular globe fruit with excellent orange rind. Fruit is slightly ribbed and flattened where it rests on the ground
75-Day Stealth-5475 (hybrid corn)	Dairyland Seeds Co. Inc.	A true 75-day flint/dent combination hybrid that flowers very early. Vigorous plant growth and fast grain establishment. Taller statured plant with semi-erect leaves. Superior test weight. Excellent adaptation to the extreme northern corn market

(*Continued*)

Table 2.1. (*Continued*)

Product	Company	Remarks
HybriForce®-420/Wet (hybrid alfalfa)	Dairyland Seeds Co. Inc.	Strengths of HybriForce®-420/Wet include its aggressive forage yield capabilities, high forage quality, distinctive rapid regrowth after harvest, solid persistence and excellent winter survival abilities. The hybrid was designed with greater degree of the branched-root trait, which helps keep more of the root system above the water level and better anchors the plant in the ground when freezing and thawing occurs. The hybrid is also highly resistant to phytophthora root, bacterial wilt, Fusarium wilt, stem nematode and northern root knot nematode
HybriForce®400 (the world's first hybrid alfalfa)	Dairyland Seeds Co. Inc.	The hybrid shows increased vigor and stronger plants compared to non-hybrid alfalfa varieties. More aggressive growth of the hybrid alfalfa stand means yields that are 8%–15% higher over the life of the stand
DSR-0501/ RRSTS Maturity 0.5 (hybrid soybean)	Dairyland Seeds Co. Inc.	The first of its kind in this maturity that offers a versatile, dual-weed protection feature with stacked RR/STS feature. An attractive, light tawny plant, the DSR-0501/RRSTS provides strong yields that are well-protected in the presence of iron chlorosis, brown stem and phytophthora. It was bred and proven through years of research in the Red River Valley

Sources: Shepherd, R. (1999). Heirlooms versus hybrids: A common-sense approach. *Plants & Gardens News*, 14(1); The pumpkin patch. Pumpkin seeds. Pumpkin hybrids info only "rupps" (http://www.backyardgardener.com/pumpseed.html); Dairyland Seeds Co. Inc. (http://www.dairylandseed.com/), accessed 15 July 2007.

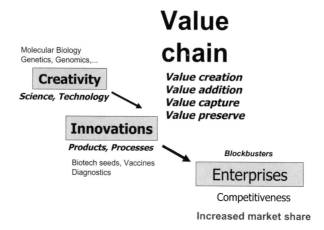

Figure 2.2.   A diagrammatic summary of the value creation process in the hybrid seed industry.

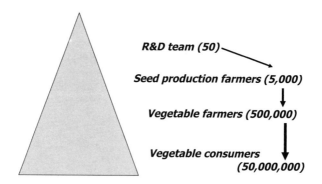

Figure 2.3.   A value chain for quality seeds.

Source: Adapted from East West Seed Company (2003).

The International Rice Research Institute (IRRI) reports that, in 1987, net return for hybrid rice cultivation in China was US$444 per hectare compared with US$322 for conventional rice cultivation. Countries with a high labor:land ratio and a high proportion of irrigated area, such as India, Indonesia, the Philippines, Sri Lanka and Vietnam, are likely to have the greatest potential demand for hybrid rice technology. Agronomic management of hybrids appears to be very important for maximizing the hybrid's yield potential.

2.7 Current Market Size

The global seed market is valued at about US$30 billion based on reported sales. This is probably an underestimate as it does not adequately account for the many SME seed companies in developing countries, private individuals and the large number of government or quasi-government entities producing and selling seed. About half of this market is generated by ten companies or merged companies — Monsanto (/Seminis), DuPont (/Pioneer), Syngenta, Groupe Limagrain, KWS AG, Land O'Lakes, Sakata, Bayer Crop Science, Taikii and DLF–Trifolium — according to industry monitors such as the International Seed Federation.

In terms of utilizing hybrid or improved seeds for farming in Asia, most farmers of the major food crops use improved seed, whether hybrid or otherwise. Even with rice, less than half of the world's rice is grown with hybrids. Hybrid seed sales are also higher in countries with strong private farming sectors and commercial agriculture. In Asia, hybrid adoption is high with vegetables. Bitter gourd hybrid seeds are now sown extensively in Thailand and Vietnam. In 1987, only open-pollinated varieties of bitter gourd were planted in Thailand. Hybrid seeds claimed just 5% of plantings in 1988, but this figure rose significantly to 15% in 1990 and 65% in 2000. In Vietnam, bitter gourd hybrids had carved a market niche worth US$15 million by 2002 (East West Seed Company, 2003). Hybrid cucumbers have also been a prominent feature in Thai and Filipino farms.

2.8 Players in the Hybrid Seed Business

All the major seed companies of the world are involved in breeding hybrid seeds. The ten largest seed companies were given above. The following paragraphs profile representative seed companies of different sizes:

- **Mahyco (India)** — Established in 1964 by Dr Badrinarayan R. Barwale, Mahyco is a pioneer and leader in the Indian seed industry. The company strives to provide quality hybrid seeds. Since its inception, it has been engaged in plant genetic research and production of quality hybrid seeds for the farming community of India. Currently, it is engaged in the research, production, processing and marketing of approximately 115 products in 30 crop species including cereals, oilseeds, fiber and vegetables. Mahyco is also developing genetically enhanced crops with the use of gene transfer technology. It has a national presence with its network across the country. Mahyco is the first private enterprise in India to produce and market hybrids of cotton, sorghum, pearl millet, sunflower and wheat. Mahyco is the first Indian company to commercially grow and market transgenic Bollgard cotton — India's first transgenic crop in 2002. An example of the hybrid plants engineered by the company are the New World cotton intra-specific hybrids (*Gossypium hirsutum*) and the inter-specific hybrids (*Gossypium hirsutum x Gossypium barbadense*). The former has good gin turnout and fiber quality as well as tolerance to sucking pests and major diseases under field conditions. The latter has fiber quality of high staple length (34.5–35 mm) and is tolerant to sucking pests. The company's New Gold wheat is also a hybrid wheat. The company also engineers other hybrids like tomatoes and radishes.
- **Pioneer Hi-Bred International (DuPont)** — The company has many hybrid plants and seeds on sale in the market, all of which are marketed under the Pioneer Hybrid name. Hybrid seeds marketed include alfalfa, canola, corn, sorghum, soybeans, sunflower and wheat. The company offers specific crops for specific regions. Pioneer Hi-Bred International, Inc., a DuPont company, is therefore a leading developer and supplier of advanced plant genetics to farmers in some 70 countries. DuPont is active in R&D.
- **Dairyland Seed Co. Inc. (Wisconsin, USA)** — Since 1907, Dairyland Seed has been the only family-owned business with

plant breeding programs in hybrid corn, soybeans and alfalfa. The company invests 15% of its revenues in plant breeding research. As a result, the industry today views Dairyland as a leading developer and provider of genetics in all three crops.

- **Indo-American Hybrid Seeds (India) Pvt. Ltd.** — Established in the year 1965, Indo-American Hybrid Seeds (India) Pvt. Ltd. has been a pioneer in the Indian hybrid vegetable seed industry. It has also been a leader in the field of commercial horticulture. It is engaged in a wide spectrum of activities — production and marketing of hybrid vegetable seeds, oil seeds, cotton seeds, flower seeds and ornamental plants; tissue culture plants; biotechnology; greenhouse construction; and landscaping. The company deals with production, marketing and export of the following seeds: Amaranthus, Beans, Beetroot, Brinjals, Cabbages, Cotton seeds, Carrots, Cantaloupes, Knol Khol, Okra, Sweet and Hot Peppers, Radish, Sunflower, Tomatoes and Watermelons. It also specializes in greenhouse construction.

- **Monsanto (International)** — Monsanto produces leading seeds for large-acre crops like corn, cotton and oilseeds as well as small-acre crops like vegetables. Hybrid seeds from Monsanto contain traits which increase yield of the plants, increase farming efficiency and decrease farming cost. Monsanto also licenses its seed products and trait technologies to other companies throughout the world to ensure a high accessibility of its products. The company uses hybrid seeds as a vehicle to capture and preserve value from its biotechnology R&D.

A valuable source of information on the seed trade and its players are the websites of industry groups such as the Asia-Pacific Seed Association and the International Seed Federation. Some countries have their own seed industry associations as well.

2.9 Growth Potential

In Chapter 1, mention was made that the majority of growers worldwide are already planting improved crop varieties (> 90% of wheat is improved; > 65% of rice; > 80% of corn). Usually, acceptance of improved varieties is a prelude to introduction of hybrid varieties, which may be considered a technological advancement in breeding. Crops like cassava and sweet potato are still largely unimproved. There is therefore a huge untapped potential for hybrid seed, which is driven by the demand to produce more on the same land area. With hybrids, there is continuing R&D to improve on the traits which add to yield, such as pest resistance. Advances in science can value-add through new discoveries. This explains the significant investments by large multinational seed companies in R&D.

Hybrid maize now has spread over all commercial maize-growing regions of the industrialized countries such as North America and Europe, and also the industrial agriculture sections of developing countries such as Argentina, Thailand, Philippines, China and Brazil. Industry estimates are that > 80% of the maize crop in Thailand is hybrid.

Biotechnology (including genetic transformation) has impacted on hybrid maize breeding everywhere, and its widespread use is certain. All the 25 million hectares of GM maize grown worldwide in 2006 was hybrid because hybrids allow R&D value capture and preservation. Although the expense of applying biotechnology is high, and biotech hybrid seeds generally cost more than their equivalent non-hybrids, millions of farmers have chosen to use these seeds due to their higher yields.

The fundamental knowledge that accrues from research in molecular biology of plants is scientifically so empowering that it is difficult to imagine a future in which biotechnology will not be beneficially applied to maize breeding (or any other biological manipulation). Add to this the continual refinements in conventional breeding technology, and it is easy to envision a future in which growth in hybrid seeds will be powered by the twin engines of breeding and biotechnology.

References

Becker, H.C. (1984). Theoretische Überlegungen und experimentelle Untersuchungen zur genetischen Basis der Heterosis. *Vorträge für Pflanzenzüchtung*, 5: 23–42.

East West Seed Company (2003). *Vegetable Breeding for Market Development.* Bangkok, Thailand: East West Seed Company Ltd.

Kloppenburg, J.R. (1988). Kapitel: Heterosis and the social division of labor. In *First the Seed: The Political Economy of Plant Biotechnology, 1492–2000*, pp. 91–129. University of Wisconsin.

Chapter 3

Tissue Culture as a Bioscience Enterprise

3.1 Introduction

Tissue culture has developed into a multi-million-dollar business for producing genetically identical planting material with the desired characteristics such as high yield, good eating quality or resistance to pests and diseases. It was among the earliest applications of modern bioscience. Tissue culture is also one of the earliest techniques commonly included in the set of biotechnology-related techniques to create value for investors, but on its own, it has also led to applications just as important as those of genetic engineering.

Tissue culture is a term which includes collectively a set of techniques and the scientific knowledge for growing unorganized cells into tissues and whole organisms under artificial sterile conditions. A notable tissue culture application is the selection and mass propagation of plant varieties showing resistance to specific diseases, such as Panama Wilt Disease in bananas, derived through selection of cell lines showing resistance in the lab to the fungus causing Panama Wilt. As such, tissue culture is a component process in modern genetic engineering (see Chapter 9).

In tissue culture, cells, tissues and organs from a selected plant are separated. These separated cells are grown in special containers with a nutrient medium under controlled conditions of temperature and light. The cultured medium contains sugars, essential salts and selected vitamins and amino acids and together, provide for the growth of the plant cells in the medium. From these cultured parts, an embryo or a shoot bud may develop, which then grows into a whole new plantlet.

3.2 The Science and Technology Behind the Tissue Culture Business

The establishment of the biological principles of tissue and organ culture has been credited to the German plant physiologist G. Haberlandt, who first enunciated them in 1902 (Haberlandt, 1902).

By 1934, P.R. White was able to grow tomato roots continuously *in vitro* by supplying them with a yeast extract containing essential ingredients like certain vitamin B types, notably B_1 (thiamine) (White, 1963).

Another major development in the history of tissue culture was the discovery of cytokinins and the hormonal control of shoot and root regeneration from tobacco callus by Skoog and his co-workers in 1948 at the University of Wisconsin. This discovery established the basis for manipulating organ initiation and provided the principles on which subsequent micropropagation depended (Skoog and Miller, 1957).

Later, George Morel, a French scientist, was attempting to obtain virus-free plants when he discovered in 1965 that he could induce a millimeter-long orchid shoot to develop into complete plantlets by growing them aseptically under certain environmental and nutrient conditions. His technique of using shoot-tip cultures to clone orchids was revisited by commercial orchid growers in the 1960s and is still being used to support the orchid industry today (Drew *et al.*, 1991).

Following the success of tissue culture in the orchid industry, many developed countries began commercial exploitation of this technology in the 1970s. During the 1980s, tissue culture was used initially to develop ornamental plants and flowers for export. However, tissue culture of woody trees remained an academic exercise until the 1990s when commercial growing of biomass and shade trees was done using species ranging from teak (*Tectona grandis*) to the Asian Fringe tree (*Chionantus retusus*). Its applications grew when large areas of tissue-cultured clones of rubber (*Hevea braziliensis*) were grown in countries like Malaysia and Indonesia.

Today, tissue culture may be even more important than before, especially in the light of rising costs for petroleum-based products. Tissue culture can be used as part of a promising solution to identify and mass produce plants with high potential for use as biofuel and bioplastic sources.

3.2.1 *What is tissue culture?*

Tissue culture refers to a set of techniques which enable unorganized cells to be cultured under artificial sterile conditions. Unorganized cells are cells which have not yet acquired a specific structure and function (i.e., cells which have yet to be differentiated). These cells are a result of undirected growth in tissue culture with no external chemical intervention to cause the cells to form definite plant structures. In commercial operations, masses of unorganized cells called calli (singular = callus) are allowed to form and grow from small plant organs, pieces of plant tissue or previously cultured cells. The process is called callus culture. There are currently three common forms — meristem culture, shoot culture and embryo culture.

The three types of plant tissue culture which are important for commercial nurseries are micropropagation, meristem culture and embryo culture.

3.2.1.1 *Micropropagation*

The aim of micropropagation is to multiply desirable plants from various tissues called explants — small plant organs or pieces of tissue from the mother plant — which commonly refer to buds, stem sections and leaves. The production of a large number of identical plants is then initiated from rapidly diving explant cells. Some of the species multiplied by micropropagation are ornamentals (orchids, indoor plants, cut flowers and woody ornamentals), fruit and vegetables (strawberry, apples) and forest trees like fir and pine.

The number of plants obtainable from a single shoot or explant ranges from a thousand to a million per year. In many cases, the rapid increase is a valuable initial boost to the establishment of large-scale populations which are then increased by conventional means. Micropropagation also provides a means of cheaply storing disease-free stock. The space required for storage is small compared to conventional stock beds. Plants are grown in a controlled environment where conditions slow the growth rate to minimize subculturing. When new stock is needed, the plants are placed in optimal growth conditions, speeding up production of new shoots and buds, which are then removed for subculturing. Labor costs are consequently reduced. Figure 3.1 is a diagrammatic representation of the process of micropropagation.

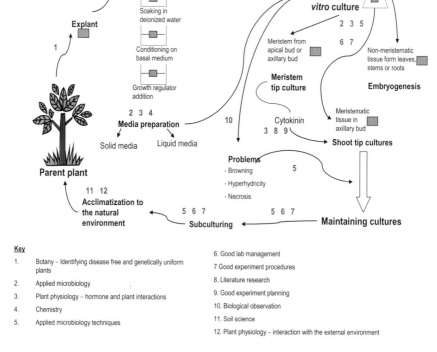

Figure 3.1.   Steps involved in micropropagation.

3.2.1.2 *Meristem culture*

Meristem cultures refer to cultures initiated from small shoot apices, each containing an apical meristematic dome with or without one or two leaf primordia (see Figure 3.2).

Meristematic cultures usually develop into a single plant shoot. Key hormones are involved in the maintenance and growth of meristematic cultures, including combinations of auxin and gibberellic acid (GA_3) growth regulators. Addition of these hormones to meristematic cultures encourages root formation and growth of meristem tips.

Meristem culture has been used most successfully to eliminate viruses from plants, and is now used routinely in quarantine stations and nurseries. It is becoming important whenever prevention or eradication of disease is essential.

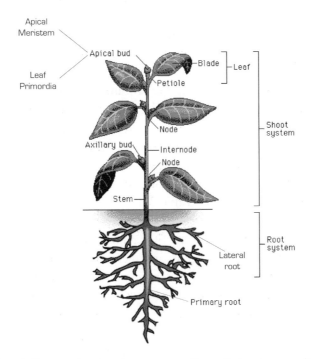

Figure 3.2.   A diagram showing the structure of a small shoot apex, which is commonly used to initiate meristem tissue culture.

3.2.1.3 *Embryo culture*

Embryo culture consists of removing the embryo from the seed and growing it in culture until it can be transferred to the soil and grown to maturity. Usually, well-developed embryos are used, but attempts have been made to culture immature embryos and even unfertilized ovules and ovaries. Late-stage embryos can usually be cultured on simple nutrient media; younger embryos have more specific hormone requirements and are more difficult to grow successfully.

Embryo culture is usually done to "rescue" embryos during attempts at crosses between distantly related plants. In many cases, genetic incompatibility results in breakdown of the endosperm that nourishes the developing embryo. By rescuing the embryo and growing it in a culture medium, the plant can be grown to maturity. Another use of embryo culture is to break dormancy in seeds (e.g., iris — embryo culture breaks dormancy and shortens the breeding cycle by months).

Shoot culture refers to cultures initiated from shoot buds having several leaf primordia and from meristem or shoot tips. However, it has become increasingly popular to use larger explants like shoot apices or stem sections carrying lateral buts to initiate shoot cultures. Shoot apices are usually cultured in such a way that each produces multiple shoots. Shoot cultures are multiplied by induction of axillary shoots. The medium used for shoot cultures is commonly the Murashige and Skoog (MS) medium, which has a relatively high concentration of salts for proper shoot culture growth. The contents of the MS media are shown in Table 3.1.

Embryo culture is initiated in either of two ways. The first method involves the dissection of fertilized or unfertilized zygotic embryos from developing seeds or fruits. These embryos are grown in tissue culture until they form seedlings. Another method of initiating embryo culture involves the induction of plant cells to produce "somatic" embryos by exposing the cells to auxin. This process, called "embryogenesis", is only initiated from cells originating from the nucellus, ovule, ovary, embryo or seeding tissue cells.

Table 3.1. Composition of MS medium, a common medium used in tissue culture.

Constituent	Amount per Liter	
	Mass	Mols
Macronutrient elements		
NH_4NO_3	1650 mg	20.6 mmol
KNO_3	1900 mg	18.8 mmol
$CaCl_2.2H_2O$	440 mg	2.99 mmol
$MgSO_4.7H_2O$	370 mg	1.50 mmol
KH_2PO_4	170 mg	1.25 mmol
Micronutrient elements		
H_3BO_3	6.2 mg	100.0 μmol
$MnSO_4.4H_2O$	22.3 mg	100.0 μmol
$ZnSO_4.7H_2O$	8.6 mg	29.9 μmol
KI	0.83 mg	3.0 μmol
$Na_2MoO_4.2H_2O$	0.25 mg	1.03 μmol
$CuSO_4.5H_2O$	0.025 mg	0.10 μmol
$CoCl_2.6H_2O$	0.025 mg	0.105 μmol
$FeSO_4.7H_2O$	27.8 mg	100.0 μmol
$Na_2EDTA.2H_2O$	37.3 mg	100.0 μmol
Sugars, auxins, cytokinins, growth factors		
Sucrose	30 g	87.6 mmol
Indole acetic acid (IAA)*	1 to 30 mg	7.71 to 171 μmol
Kinetin*	0.04 to 20 mg	0.186 to 46.5 μmol
Insoitol	100.0 mg	555.0 μmol
Nicotinic acid	0.5 mg	4.06 μmol
Pyridoxine. HCI	0.5 mg	2.431 μmol
Thiamine. HCI	0.1 mg	0.296 μmol
Glycine	2.0 mg	26.6 μmol
Casein hydrolysate	1.0 g	
Agar	10.0 g	

* These vary between species and type of cultures being grown (e.g., shoot growth usually requires kinetin or another cytokinin, while root initiation usually requires IAA or another auxin but no cytokinin).

3.2.2   Tissue culture techniques

Explants are first collected in a sterile bottle and immersed in a dilute solution of the disinfectant containing a wetting agent (e.g., alcohol). The bottle containing the disinfectant solution and the explant is then stored in a laminar flow cabinet and shaken occasionally during the sterilization period. The lid is then removed and the disinfectant solution drained out. The plant material is rinsed thoroughly in sterilized distilled water before the lid is replaced. This rinsing process is repeated two or three times over before the material is transferred to a presterilized petri dish.

The required instruments are sterilized by dipping into 100% ethanol and flamed while the plant material is being treated. The instruments are allowed to cool before using them to handle plant material. The instruments are sterilized after each time they are used to handle tissue. Suitable explants are prepared from the surface of the sterilized material using the sterilized instruments.

Explants are quickly transferred into culture vessels to minimize the time they are exposed to the environment for the maintenance of aseptic conditions. The lid of the culture vessel is quickly removed and the explant is transferred into the medium. The neck of the vessel is flamed to kill any microorganisms which may contaminate the culture and the lid is replaced. All the above are done using absolutely sterile conditions and practicing the best hygiene, commonly within a piece of equipment called a laminar hood (Figure 3.3).

3.2.2.1   Initiating tissue culture

Tissue cultures are started from explants, small plant organs or pieces of tissue. The part of the mother plant that explants are obtained from depends on the kinds of culture to be initiated, the purpose of the culture and the plant species to be used.

Plants growing *in vivo* (i.e., the normal growing situation/ environment in which a plant grows) are contaminated with microorganisms and pests which commonly reside on the outer surfaces

Figure 3.3.   A tissue culture worker preparing cultures in a laminar hood.

of the plant. However, explants have to be maintained in an aseptic environment in tissue culture, as bacteria and fungi compete adversely with plants growing *in vitro* (i.e., literarily meaning "in a glass"). This refers to the culturing of explants in a tissue culture medium. To keep explants as free from microbial contaminants as possible, stock plants are treated with disinfecting chemicals to kill superficial microbes. Tools used for dissection and the vessels and media which are used for culture are also sterilized.

Due to the heavy emphasis on a sterile environment, explants are commonly obtained from stock plants which must be typical of the variety of the species and free from any symptoms of disease. Explants are often also precultured on simple medium lacking in growth regulators to prevent them from exuding toxic substances.

3.2.2.2 *Tissue culture media*

A medium usually contains a solution of nutrients supplying the major and minor elements necessary for the growth of whole plants, together with various vitamins (optional), various amino acids (optional), a carbon and energy source (usually sucrose) and plant hormones and plant growth regulators which dictate the growth and development of plant cultures. They are compounds which are able to modify plant organogenesis at low concentrations.

The balance of components, especially plant hormones, is critical as it will determine the type of growth of the explant. Auxins encourage root initiation and callus growth. However, continual use of auxins may inhibit root development and the tissue may need to be transferred to another medium without growth substances for root development.

Cytokinins may be needed to stimulate growth of dormant buds and also to influence shoot growth. In some cases, kinetin influences single shoot growth, whereas benzyl amino pruine (BAP) causes multiple shoot growth.

Gibberellins often suppress unorganized divisions, leading to the formation of callus and stimulating the bud to produce differentiated, rapid growth. Usually, a ratio of desired hormones is applied for a desired effect. For example, an equal amount of auxin and cytokinin might encourage callus development more than root or shoot development.

A useful basic medium to start with is one devised by Murashige and Skoog (MS) in 1962. The MS medium is characterized by high concentrations of potassium, ammonium ions and meso-inositol. The composition of the MS medium is shown in Table 3.1.

Preparing media from scratch is a tedious process, requiring a large variety of chemicals, some of which have to be weighed accurately to 0.001g. An alternative is to buy ready-made media, which are sold in powdered form, and add the media powder to water.

Usually, the pH of a medium ranges from 5.5–6 pH. Agar is added to solidify the media, if needed.

3.2.2.3 *Maintaining cultures*

Plant tissue culture media not only support the growth of plants, but also the growth of microorganisms like bacteria which can affect the growth of the plants due to the toxic metabolites which they secrete. Several possible sources of contamination in the medium are the culture vessel, the medium itself, the explant, the environment of the transfer area, the instruments used to handle plant material during establishment and subculture, and the environment of the culture room.

Autoclaving media will eliminate contamination from the culture vessel or the medium. Substances like gibberellic acid, abscissic acid, urea and certain vitamins will break down upon autoclaving. These chemicals can be sterilized by filtering through filter paper with pores fine enough to exclude pathogens.

Solutions of sodium or calcium hypochlorite are usually effective in disinfecting plant tissues. Placing tissues in a 0.5%–1% solution of sodium hypochlorite for 10 to 15 minutes will disinfect most tissues. Surface sterilants are toxic to plant tissues. Therefore, tissues are exposed to them for as minimal a time as possible.

3.2.2.4 *Subculturing*

Once a particular kind of organized or unorganized growth has been started *in vitro*, it would usually continue if cultures are divided to provide new explants for culture initiation on fresh medium. Subculturing becomes necessary when density of tissue/organs becomes excessive or when there is a need to increase the volume of the culture or increase the number of organs.

Another reason for subculturing is that the growth of plant material in a closed vessel eventually leads to the accumulation of toxic metabolites and the exhaustion of the medium, or to its drying out. Shoot cultures are subcultured by segmenting individual shoot clusters.

The interval between subcultures depends on the rate at which a culture has grown: at 25°C, subculturing is required every 4 to 6 weeks. Usually, cytokinin growth hormone is added to the shoot culture to cause shoot elongation.

3.2.2.5 *Physical facilities and equipment*

The general requirements for a tissue culture enterprise include a laboratory, and grow-out facilities, required for young calli or explants to grow and develop in relatively sanitary conditions and conducive, controlled environments. When the plantlets have reached a certain size depending on plant species, they are commonly transferred to non-sterile conditions to acclimatize and grow into seedlings, either in greenhouses or shade houses; the facilities at this stage resemble those of plant nurseries (see Figures 3.4 and 3.5).

Companies and organizations which involve themselves in tissue culture often have a greenhouse facility. The greenhouse serves as a nursery for tissue-cultured plants to acclimatize to the natural surroundings. As such, when plants in tissue culture mature sufficiently, they are planted in the greenhouse to continue growing. Figure 3.5 shows the external view of a greenhouse in the National Institute of Education (NIE), Singapore, and the inside of a commercial greenhouse.

3.2.2.6 *General requirements for a tissue culture laboratory*

The size of a tissue culture lab and the quantity and type of its associated equipment depend on the nature of work and the funds available. However, a standard tissue culture lab should include space for storing lab supplies and equipment as well as for washing glassware. The lab should have a room for the sterilization and storing of cultured media and the sterile handling of plant material as well as facilities which enable the maintenance of cultures under controlled temperature and light (see Table 3.2).

At least three separate rooms are needed: one for washing used containers for storage and media preparation (i.e., dish washing

Figure 3.4.   Plant tissue cultures in a laboratory growth area with artificial lighting and temperature control. (a) Steel racks for holding glassware with tissue-cultured plant parts in grow-out room. (b) Glass dish containing calli with young developing plant parts. (c) Two types of glass containers for young plantlets to develop. (d) Young banana plantlets developing in artificial medium under sterile conditions in glass jars.

room); the second (with laminar flow or clean-air cabinets) for dissection of plant tissue and subculturing (i.e., media preparation room); and the third to incubate cultures (i.e., culture room).

Laboratory hygiene is essential in tissue culture facilities. The air supplied to the lab should be filtered through HEPA (High Efficiency Particle removal Air) filters which are capable of trapping particles greater than 0.3 um in section, particularly fungal spores and bacteria.

Entry into the clean room is commonly minimized and restricted to persons who have gone through the proper preparative procedures and have put on special lab coats and footwear.

(a)   (b)

Figure 3.5. Picture showing (a) the external view of the NIE greenhouse*, and (b) inside of a commercial greenhouse for banana tissue culture.

*Source: W.H.J. Yong and C.J. Chern.

Ideally, clean areas should be maintained at a slightly higher air pressure than other rooms and be entered through two separate sets of doors, between which there is a space. The first door is always closed before the second door is opened, thereby restricting the passage of contaminants between different environments. The final surfaces of the lab (i.e., floors or walls) should be covered to prevent dust.

The room for incubating cultures is commonly maintained at between 23°C and 27°C. Cultures are generally grown in diffuse light from cool, white, fluorescent tubes which are controlled with automatic time clocks (Figure 3.4). Generally, a 16-hour day and 8-hour night are used. Culture rooms require dust-free shelves to store cultures. Insulation between the shelf lights and the shelf above will ensure an even temperature around the cultures.

The media room is sometimes used to transfer culture from one media to another. This transfer is usually done within laminar air-low cabinets. These cabinets have a small fan which blows air through a coarse filter to remove large dust particles, then through a HEPA filter to remove microbes and their spores. The velocity of the air coming out of the fine filter is about 27m/min, which keeps airborne microorganisms out of the working area.

Table 3.2. Case study: Major equipment required in a tissue culture lab.

Area	Equipment
Preparation area	1 Bench space 2 pH meter 3 Hot plate stirrers 4 Pressure cookers or autoclave 5 Water still or de-ioniser 6 Sink 7 Balances 8 Drying oven 9 Dishwasher
Storage area	1 Refrigerator 2 Deep-freezer
Dissection room	1 Clean-air cabinet 2 Heat sterilizer 3 Binocular microscope
Growth room	1 Air (or heating/ cooling system) 2 Racks 3 Lights 4 Shakers 5 Thermograph 6 Thermostat and time clock for lights
Other apparatus	1 Beakers (100 ml, 250 ml, 1L, 2L, 5L) 2 Measuring cylinders (25 ml, 50 ml, 100 ml, 500 ml, 1L, 2L, 5L) 3 Pasteur pipettes and teats 4 Reagent bottles for storing liquid chemicals and stock solutions (glass or plastic) 5 Wire-mesh or plastic baskets 6 Filter membrane, holders and hypodermic syringes (for solutions requiring filter sterilization) 7 Large forceps (blunt and fine points) and scalpels for dissecting and subculturing plant material 8 Scalpel handles (no. 3) and blades (no. 11) 9 Chemicals and reagents for preparing culture media 10 Disposable gloves and masks

Source: Drew *et al.* (1991).

3.3 Product Range

3.3.1 *Applications of tissue culture*

3.3.1.1 *Selection of superior plants by tissue culture*

The most heavily researched area of tissue culture today is the concept of selecting disease-, insect- or stress-resistant plants through tissue culture. The selection and propagation of superior individuals can be done vegetatively via selective breeding processes, but the identification process can be sped up in *in vitro* systems. Such systems usually take advantage of the natural variability that occurs in plants. However, variability can be induced by chemical or physical agents, which are used to cause mutations.

Natural variability in the genetic makeup of plants often results in the production of bud sports and other types of chimeras (a chimera is a plant consisting of two or more genetically distinct kinds of cells). Chimeras show altered cellular expressions which are visible, but for each of these which are observed, many more differences probably exist but are masked by the overall organization of the plant as a whole.

For example, in frost-tender species, certain cells or groups of cells may be frost-hardy. However, because most of the organism is killed by frost, the tolerant cells eventually die because they are unable to support themselves without the remainder of the organized plant.

Plant tissues grown *in vitro* can be released from the organization of the whole plant through callus formation. If these groups of cells are then subjected to a selection agent such as freezing, then those tolerant ones can survive while all those which are susceptible will be killed. This concept can be applied to many types of stress as well as resistance to fungal and bacterial pathogens and various types of phytotoxic chemical agents.

The goal of selecting such resistant cell lines would be to then develop whole plants and plant populations from them. The reorganized plants would be likely to retain the selected traits. Current research in this area extends across many interests including attempts to select salt-tolerant lines of tomato, freeze-resistant tobacco plants, herbicide-resistant agronomic crops, and various species of plants with enhanced pathogen resistance.

3.3.1.2 *Selection and multiplication of pathogen-free plants*

Another purpose for which plant tissue culture is uniquely suited is in the obtaining, maintaining and mass propagating of specific pathogen-free plants. Plant tissues known to be free of the pathogen under consideration (viral, bacterial or fungal) are physically selected as the explant for tissue culture. In most cases, the apical domes of rapidly elongating shoot tips are chosen. These are allowed to enlarge and proliferate under the sterile conditions of *in vitro* culture, with the resulting plantlets tested for presence of the pathogen (a procedure called indexing).

Cultures which reveal the presence of the pathogen are destroyed, while those which are indexed free of pathogen are maintained as a stock of pathogen-free material. Procedures similar to these have been used successfully to obtain virus-free plants of a number of species and bacteria-free plants of species known to have certain leaf spot diseases. The impact of obtaining pathogen-free nursery stock can only be speculative, since little research documenting viral, bacterial or fungal diseases transmitted through propagation of woody ornamentals is available. Pathogen-tested and certified disease-free plants is a major industry in many countries such as the USA and The Netherlands.

3.3.1.3 *Somatic hybridization*

The ability to fuse plant cells from species which may be incompatible as sexual crosses and the ability of plant cells to take up and incorporate foreign genetic codes have extended the realm of plant modifications through tissue culture to the limits of the imagination. Most such manipulations are carried out using plant "protoplasts", single cells which have been stripped of their cell walls by enzymatic treatment. A single leaf treated under these conditions may yield tens of millions of single cells, each theoretically capable of eventually producing a whole plant. This concept has fueled speculation as diverse as the possibilities of obtaining nitrogen-fixing corn plants on the one extreme to discovering a yellow-flowered African violet on the other extreme.

The observation that has provided the impetus for most of this research is that when cells are stripped of their cell walls and brought into close contact, they tend to fuse with each other. This "somatic hybridization" is not subject to the same incompatibility problems that limit traditional plant breeding strategies. The potential use of somatic hybridization to bring about novel combinations of genetic material has been demonstrated in the genera *Petunia* and *Nicotiana*.

3.3.1.4 *Plant propagation*

Complete new plants can be derived from tissue culture from preexisting shoot buds or primordial buds (meristems), or following shoot morphogenesis when new shoots are induced to form in unorganized tissues or directly upon explanted tissues of the mother plant. Another method of generating complete plants from tissue culture is through the formation of somatic embryos which resemble the seed embryos of intact plants and which can grow into seedlings in the same way.

To obtain plants by the first two methods, it is necessary to treat shoots of an adequate size as miniature cuttings and induce them to produce roots. This is possible as plant cells, especially young tissues and meristems, are usually totipotent, i.e., they each retain a latent capacity to produce a whole plant.

3.3.2 *Seed material produced using tissue culture*

Tissue culture has created much commercial value by allowing the production of seed material for use by growers and farmers.

3.3.2.1 *Herbaceous ornamentals*

The multiplication of ornamental plants for the horticultural industry is, by far, the largest practical application of plant tissue culture and provides the major occupation for commercial micropropagation labs.

Table 3.3.   Examples of herbaceous ornamentals cultivated by tissue culture in the market.

Scientific Name	Common Name	Scientific Name	Common Name
Alstroemeria	Peruvian lily	*Begoniaceae begonia*	
Anthurium spp.		*Caryophyllaceae dianthus spp. and hybrids*	Carnation and pink
Caladium	Angel's wings	*Gesneriaceae saintpaulia*	African violet
Zantedeschia	Calla lily	*Gesneriaceae streptocarpus*	Cape primrose
Monstera deliciosa	Swiss cheese plant		

Ornamentals which are micropropagated are eventually sold as pot plants, plants for cut flower production or for landscaping. Most herbaceous ornamentals are propagated by shoot culture. Some examples of herbaceous ornamentals cultivated by tissue culture are given in Table 3.3.

3.3.2.2 *Plants producing bulbs and corms*

The rate of natural vegetative multiplication is slow in most species producing bulbs and corms, but can be increased by inducing the formation of shoots or new storage organs from axillary and adventitious buds. Ornamentals and plants producing bulbs and corms can be multiplied successfully by tissue culture, but although the rate of increase is improved, it is still comparatively slow and involves a lot of manual effort, thus increasing cost. Large-scale micropropagation is therefore unprofitable. Products are therefore restricted to provision of virus-free stock to growers, multiplication of material used in breeding programs and the rapid increase of foundation stock of new varieties. Some examples of bulbs and corms cultivated by tissue culture are given in Table 3.4.

Table 3.4.   Examples of bulbs and corms cultivated by tissue culture in the market.

Scientific Name (Bud)	Common Name	Scientific Name (Corm)	Common Name
Narcissus sp.	Daffodil, narcissus	*Iridaceae gladiolus*	
Hyacinthus orientalis	Hyacinth	*Iridaceae freesia*	
Lilium spp.	Lilies		
Tulipa spp.	Tulip		

3.3.2.3 *Cacti*

Cacti are frequently grown as ornamental plants. Some cacti micro-propagated are *Akersja sp.*, *Coryphantha macromeris* and *Ferocactus acanthodes*.

3.3.2.4 *Ferns and club mosses*

Spores from ferns are collected from fronds bearing mature sporangia and propagated in sterile culture. The media used usually has a low concentration of ions. Some genus of ferns are *Adiantum*, *Nephrolepis* and *Rumohra*.

3.3.2.5 *Orchids*

Orchids are micropropagated for their flowers. Raising orchid plants from seeds is not easy as the seeds are very small and need to be sown in soil infected with a symbiotic mycorrhizal fungus before they will germinate. Plants of orchid hybrids raised from seed are genetically heterogeneous and therefore, the potential to propagate orchids veg-etatively is low. Orchid seeds can grow in a plant culture medium as this provides the nutrients required for early seedling development, in the absence of a symbiotic fungus. Tissue-cultured orchids are a multi-million-dollar industry in several Asian countries (China, Singapore, Thailand and Malaysia).

3.3.2.6 *Woody ornamentals*

Where woody ornamentals can be increased cheaply from cuttings or seeds, demand may be insufficient and the cost of production too high to make propagation by tissue culture worthwhile. Tissue culture is usually done on plants which are slow or difficult to propagate by conventional means. Woody plants are frequently infected with virus diseases, which can be removed by meristem tip culture. Tissue culture techniques would obviously be useful for the maintenance and distribution of virus-free stocks. An initial culture on a dilute medium without auxins might help in the establishment of roots. Shoot cultures can be encouraged by growth in a medium with cytokinin. Some examples of woody ornamentals cultivated by tissue culture are given in Table 3.5.

3.3.2.7 *Tree species*

In vitro techniques have the potential to provide ways of propagating tree species on a large scale, especially trees cultivated for economic or aesthetic reasons, such as in forests or plantations for the production of timber and fibers, as ornamental trees planted in parks and gardens, for their edible fruits, and for the secondary products which can be obtained from them.

Table 3.5.   Examples of woody ornamentals cultivated by tissue culture in the market.

Scientific Name	Common Name	Scientific Name	Common Name
Beaucarnea recurvata	Ponytail plum	*Agavaceae yucca elephantipes*	Spineless yucca
Polianthes tuberosa	Tuber rose	*Ericaceae rhododendron*	Rhododendron
Labiatae lavandula	Lavender	*Magnoliaceae magnolia*	Magnolia
Rosa sp.	Rose	*Rosaceae amelanchier*	Service berry

Tissue culture is used to:

- Produce small clones from selected trees that can be used for evaluation in tree breeding programs;
- Reproduce genetically superior trees in large numbers so that they can be used for reforestation;
- Make available large numbers of trees that can be used in bioenergy plantations; and
- Propagate decorative trees for parks, etc.

The acceptable cost per micropropagated plantlet varies for each of these applications, being lowest in propagules intended for forest planting and highest in trees with an ornamental value. Some examples of micropropagated trees are shown in Table 3.6.

There is intense interest currently in selecting and culturing tree species capable of rapid biomass production, which in turn may be converted into biofuel.

Table 3.6.   Examples of tree species cultivated by tissue culture in the market.

Scientific Name	Common Name	Remarks
Beula spp.	Birch	Broad-leafed (angiosperm) tree. Shoot and node cultures, as well as embryogenesis are popular methods of micropropagation
Populus spp.	Poplar, cottonwood	Broad-leafed (angiosperm) tree. Shoot and node cultures, as well as embryogenesis are popular methods of micropropagation
Pinus strobus	Pine	Coniferous trees (gymnosperms). Shoots can be regenerated indirectly on callus produced on juvenile explants, direct shoot formation, formation of axillary buds or embryogenesis

3.3.2.8 *Fruit and nut crops*

Traditionally, most fruit-bearing species have been propagated vegetatively by techniques like marcotting and grafting, which not only ensure that desirable genetic characteristics are preserved, but also that fruit-bearing condition is rapidly achieved. Micropropagation is able to assist current macropropagation methods, but might not be an alternative for all crops due to the cost and nature of plants produced.

Most fruit trees are grafted onto rootstocks, which can be more suited to local soil conditions than the scion. So although macropropagation can provide a cheap source of self-rooted plant material, its use for fruit trees may be restricted to the rapid multiplication of new varieties — the mass propagation of species and cultivars where tree height and vigor are not a problem. Tissue culture initiates growth of plants, but does not sustain them to the adult stage. Some fruit and nut crops which are micropropagated are shown in Table 3.7.

3.3.2.9 *Cereals, bamboo and grasses*

Most cereals, bamboo and forage grasses are propagated efficiently and cheaply from seeds, so that vegetative multiplication is not required except for specialist purposes such as the production of clones or individual plants for evaluation and use as seed parents in breeding programs.

Table 3.7.   Examples of fruit and nut crops grown by tissue culture in the market.

Scientific Name	Common Name	Remarks
Actinidia deliciosa	Chinese gooseberry, kiwi	Propagated by shoot culture initiated from shoot apices
Ananas comosus	Pineapple	Initiated by shoot culture from axillary buds from the crown
Juglans spp.	Walnut	Shoot culture initiated with explants taken from juveniles plant material
Fragaria x ananassa	Strawberry	Meristem tip culture combined with heat treatment is used

Callus cultures of cereals and grasses can only be initiated from tissues that are young and meristematic. Explants are derived from root tips, nodes, shoot primordial, seeds and seed embryos, from young leaf tissue or from immature inflorescences. Some examples of cereals and grasses are: *Secale cereale L.* (rye), *Triticum aestivum L. em. Thell.* (wheat), *Aneurolepidium chinense* (Chinese forage grass) and *Mambusa vulgaris Achard. Ex Wendl.* (golden bamboo).

3.3.2.10 *Root and tuber crops*

Several root and tuber crops grown from tissue culture seed are available in the marketplace, namely taro (*Colocasia esculenta*), yams (*Dioscorea spp.*), and potato (*Solanum tuberosum*).

3.3.2.11 *Storage and grain legumes*

Legumes are important world crops, providing seeds which are rich in protein (grain legumes) or forage for animal feeding (forage legumes). All are nitrogen fixing and therefore require little or no nitrogen fertilizers, but leave valuable residues of nitrogen in the soil after cropping. Many legumes are self-fertile and sold as pure line varieties which breed true from seed, so that vegetative propagation is seldom used in breeding work. Vegetative propagation is, however, often used in the breeding of clovers and some other forage legumes like the *Lotus corniculatus*, and micropropagation of these species can provide a more efficient alternative to traditional methods. Apart from this limited application, interest in tissue culture of legumes is focused on its use to facilitate hybridization, gene transfer, or the induction of increased genetic variability. Meristem tip cultures have been employed to remove viruses from parental lines of some forage legumes. Some species which have been micropropagated are shown in Table 3.8.

3.3.2.12 *Tropical and subtropical crops*

Tropical and subtropical crops are grown on a very large scale to provide raw materials for industry such as rubber and food for human

Table 3.8.   Examples of storage and grain legumes grown by tissue culture in the market.

Scientific Name	Common Name
Arachis hypogaea	Peanut
Glycine max	Soybean
Trifolium spp.	Clovers

population. Examples of such crops are: *Hevea brasilinesis* (rubber), *Saccharum cvs.* (sugar cane) and *Theobroma cacao* (cocoa).

3.3.2.13 *Vegetables*

In vegetables, tissue culture techniques are mainly employed in plant breeding, and they are used in only a few species for the multiplication of plants intended for cropping. Asparagus is one of these. Some other examples of vegetables propagated in tissue culture are *Brassica spp.* (cabbage, oilseed rape, etc.) and *Apium graveolens* (celery).

3.4 Exemplifying Costs for Establishing and Operating a Biobusiness Based on Tissue Culture

Many commercial units are, understandably, reluctant to reveal the true nature of their costs to maintain a competitive advantage. An illustrative analysis of the weekly cost of operating a micropropagation laboratory capable of producing ca. 3 million plantlets per year is shown in Table 3.9.

3.5 SWOT Analysis

3.5.1 *Strengths*

Plants grown in tissue culture are often disease- and virus-free. Vegetative propagation allows viruses to be passed on to subsequent generations of plants. Meristem culture allows viruses to be removed from plants, including those which are easy to propagate by conventional means (e.g., carnations).

Table 3.9.   Illustrative costs of operating a tissue culture (micropropagation) facility.

Breakdown of Expenditure	Type of Cost	Labor Costs				Total Costs	
		Hours Worked per Week	Cost per Hour (Units)	Costs per Week		Actual Costs per Week (Units)	%
				Units	%		
Capital cost	O					1635	27.3
Depreciation & borrowing costs on buildings and equipment							
Wage costs							
Laboratory work							
Subcultures for plant production	D	1080	1.5	1620	42.4		
Culture initiation	D	120	2.0	240	6.3		
R&D transfers, etc.	O	80	2.5	200	5.2		
Media preparation and sterilization	D	80	2.0	160	4.2		
Quality assurance	D	40	2.5	100	2.6		
Washing up, cleaning	D	80	1.0	80	2.1		
Transport around laboratory	D	80	1.5	120	3.1		
Growth room work	D	80	1.5	120	3.1		

(*Continued*)

Table 3.9.   (*Continued*)

Breakdown of Expenditure	Type of Cost	Labor Costs				Total Costs	
		Hours Worked per Week	Cost per Hour (Units)	Costs per Week		Actual Costs per Week (Units)	%
				Units	%		
Greenhouse and shipment							
Planting	D	40	1.5	60	1.6		
Plant management							
Quality control	D	40	2.0	80.0	2.1		
Greenhouse controls	D	5	1.5	7.5	0.2		
Watering and feeding	D	25	1.5	37.5	1.0		
Acclimatization	D	10	1.5	15	0.4		
Dispatch	S	400	1.5	600	15.7		
Office work							
Management							
Production/planning	O	8	3.0	24	0.6		
Accountancy	O	20	3.0	60	1.6		
Other	O	12	3.0	36	0.9		
Office routine (typing, telephone)	O	40	1.5	60	1.6		
Marketing and sales	S	80	2.5	200	5.2		
Total				3820	100	3820	63.8

(*Continued*)

Table 3.9. (Continued)

Breakdown of Expenditure	Type of Cost	Labor Costs		Costs per Week		Total Costs	
		Hours Worked per Week	Cost per Hour (Units)	Units	%	Actual Costs per Week (Units)	%
Running costs							
Chemicals and consumables							
Media, sterilants, fungicides, etc.	M		71				
Minor equipment and maintenance	O		25				
Fuel and utilities							
Electricity	M		140.0				
Gas, water	M		50.0				
Packaging (assume that delivery is charged to the customer)	S		20				

(Continued)

Table 3.9. (*Continued*)

Breakdown of Expenditure	Type of Cost	Labor Costs					Total Costs	
		Hours Worked per Week	Cost per Hour (Units)	Costs per Week			Actual Costs per Week (Units)	%
				Units	%			
Maintenance of buildings	O		50					
Travel, books, journals, software	O		60					
Taxes	O		33					
Commercial fees and expenses	O		35					
Contingencies	O		50					
Total			534				534	8.9
Grand Total							5989	100

Note: It has been assumed there are 30 laminated flow hoods, each operated during a single shift of 8 hours per day, during a 5-day week. Costs are given in arbitrary currency units (one unit being equivalent to the cost of employing a technician to work at a laminar flow cabinet for 40 minutes). Costs can also be apportioned as indicated in Column 2, *viz.*: Overheads (O); Direct costs (D); Material costs (M); Sales costs (S).

Plants which are propagated in tissue culture undergo rapid multiplication. Once disease-free plants have been produced by meristem culture, they can be multiplied rapidly.

Tissue culture is also easy to initiate as it is started with very small pieces of explants. Therefore, only a small space is required to maintain the plants or to increase their number.

Plants grown in tissue culture need little attention between subcultures, and there is less labor involved compared to growing plants in the field.

Tissue culture can also be used to propagate new or difficult-to-propagate plants or plant parts. Depending on the ratio of the components in the nutrient media, especially hormones, plant tissue can be induced to produce multiple buds or embryos.

Another advantage of tissue culture is the continual production of planting material as tissue culture is not limited by seasons. The plants are propagated in an enclosed physical environment and are not affected by extreme changes in the surrounding environment.

Tissue culture is also an economic and efficient way of maintaining the parent stock culture of a number of cultivars free from disease. The parent stock of many species of plants can be maintained at very low temperatures (5°C) and subcultured once or twice a year. The parent stock material can also be stored for long periods of time.

There is great export potential in plants which are grown in tissue culture. Tissue culture plants are easily exported in small, lightweight containers. As plants are free of soil, disease quarantine problems are minimized.

There is potential to produce new types of plants through tissue culture, especially of plants which are put through a callus culture stage. This circumvents the demanding requirements of new plant types produced through genetic engineering (Chapter 9).

3.5.2 *Weaknesses*

Despite the many advantages of tissue culture, there are some areas where tissue cultures of plant materials prove troublesome. For one, it is extremely difficult to maintain a bacteria-free environment in a tissue culture lab. Once present, contamination can be difficult to contain. Bacterial contamination develops slowly and may not become visible for weeks or months. Dust mites are also known to build up their populations and destroy the cultures.

Another area where tissue culture techniques prove troublesome is the area of media formulations. One report in a scientific journal on the culture of a particular species may not guarantee a commercially feasible method of micropropagation. The documented culture of some species is difficult to repeat.

Plants in tissue culture may also suffer from certain plant physiological-related problems. Plants may suffer from phenolic oxidation. Plants, especially tropical plants, contain high concentrations of phenolic substances that are oxidized when cells are wounded or senesce.

When plants grow large enough to be transplanted to the natural environment, they may not initially be able to produce their own requirement of organic matter by photosynthesis and have to undergo a transitional period before they are capable of independent growth. Another acclimatization problem comes in the form of plants not being able to photosynthesize once they are transferred from the culture environment to the natural environment. As such, young plantlets are more susceptible to water loss in the external environment. They may need acclimatization in an environment of decreasing humidity and increasing light.

Labor issues may also be a problem. Plant tissue culture is labor-intensive and requires special skills.

It is also difficult to ensure continuity of plant supply in the tissue culture business. Although a species may be easy to micropropagate, achieving a steady supply of plants requires knowledge of multiplication rates and labor requirements. The best cultures need to be retained for further multiplication. However, continuity of supply is of limited use if the market for that certain plant product is seasonal.

3.5.3 *Opportunities*

Opportunities exist to optimize the tissue culture of specific plant species. Opportunities for micropropagation would increase if there were a possibility to provide clones at the least cost. The high cost of labor associated with tissue culture has also pushed labs to seek automation.

Another area for possible improvement is reduction of the need to subculture through liquid media. Once explants have become sufficiently large not to be submerged, plants not susceptible to vitrification (e.g., *Gerbera, Dracaena* and *Populus*) can be cultured on static liquid medium. Shoot culture is slightly less expensive in this context, for the medium is less costly and easily replaced. There is no need to remove agar if *in vitro* rooting is conducted on a liquid medium.

Spraying callus tissue with nutrient media, or maintaining it in a nutrient mist, have been found to be advantageous in the production of biomass or secondary products and has been the subject of several patent applications. There have also been instances where tissue cultures were propagated in bioreactors which are fully autoclavable and have transparent growth chambers to let in adequate light.

3.5.4 *Threats*

For countries which have only begun to create a substantive business in plant tissue culture over the past decade (e.g., Taiwan), the business of agricultural biotechnology is still far from maturity. Legal and regulatory frameworks for marketing and production of tissue culture products are still not on par with the development of the tissue culture industry.

Another threat to the tissue culture industry is the lack of connection between laboratories and factories. A good connection would enable more tissue culture products to be sold efficiently.

There is also a need for increased public awareness of tissue culture products. The lack of understanding of tissue culture products may hinder the commercialization and marketing of the products. In order for the sales of tissue culture products to increase, traditional nursery companies should also join the tissue culture business. Business in the tissue culture area would also increase if there were international cooperation in research which helps the industry formulate cost-effective means of propagating plants *in vitro*.

3.6   The Value Chain in Tissue Culture Enterprises

3.6.1   *Range of enterprises*

Tissue culture techniques are mainly used in businesses offering plants for general sale. There are several kinds of such businesses. One such includes businesses selling the immediate products of the lab only. There are no greenhouse facilities for transferring plants to soil, and cultures are sold in vessels at any stage. Such businesses have little capacity to hold plants in reserve and depend on a continuous succession of orders. Another type of business is that with a lab and associated greenhouse facilities. Products can be the same as those sold by labs without greenhouse facilities, but it is common to concentrate on the sale of rooted acclimatized plants. The larger micropropagation labs are of this kind.

Micropropagation labs have also been established by businesses which primarily use the plants produced internally. Such businesses include nursery businesses. In nursery businesses, plants are sold later at any stage of growth from plugs to mature plants. Another type of business is that which belongs to the plant breeders. These labs often use pollen and anther culture as a step towards producing homozygous parental lines; and if required, tissue culture techniques are also used to genetically transform plants.

3.6.2   *Marketing propagated plants*

Regardless of the multiplication method employed, micropropagation is at present able to offer plant material of four main saleable types:

(1)   Unrooted shoots or shoot clusters which the purchaser can use as cuttings (or occasionally as scions);
(2)   Shoots which have been rooted *in vitro*, but not yet hardened or acclimatized;
(3)   Rooted, hardened and substrate-adapted plantlets; and
(4)   Storage organs which can be directly planted into soil in greenhouses or fields.

Types 1 and 2 form specialized products which can only be sold to skilled nurserymen. Types 3 and 4 are more robust and can be sold to a wider range of customers. In some countries, the health status of tissue-cultured plants is classified into:

Class 1 — Free of all cultivatable microorganisms; free of all major diseases of the crop;
Class 2 — Free of all cultivatable microorganisms; free of all specified diseases of the crop;
Class 3 — Free of all cultivatable bacteria; and
Class 4 — Untested.

In practice, the selling price for micropropagated plants is governed by the price charged for equivalent plants which have been grown from conventional methods. Table 3.10 shows the prices of some kinds of micropropagated herbaceous and woody plants.

3.6.3 *Patents on tissue culture products*

Tissue culture science and technology has generated novelty and resulted in many patents filed for specific plant species. A short list available from public databases is shown in Table 3.11.

3.7 Market Size in Various Geographic Regions

It is hard to accurately track figures of tissue culture business worldwide as companies or laboratories often decline to give details or else present an overly optimistic picture. In the 1970s and 1980s, many new laboratories were set up in the USA and Western Europe. Later, labs propagating orchids were set up in Asia. Gradually, micropropagation labs were set up in Eastern Europe and Asia, while the number of business operations in Western Europe and USA declined. Some idea of the number of plants thought to be produced annually from tissue culture in 1988 is shown in Table 3.12.

Examples of the value of tissue culture markets with value addition through royalties is shown in Table 3.13. In some cases where the

Table 3.10.   Illustrative prices of tissue-cultured products from micropropagation.

Plant	Type	Current Average Prices per Plant ex Laboratory		
		Currency Units	UK£ (1995)	US$ (1995)
Herbaceous plants				
Nephrolepis	Types grown in pots	(0.04–0.06)	0.12–0.18*	(0.19–0.29)
	Types grown for cut flower production			
Anthurium	Types grown in pots	(0.067)	0.20*	(0.32)
	Types grown for cut flower production	(0.18)	0.55*	(0.88)
Lilium longiflorum	Plantlets of bulblets	(0.03)	0.09*	(0.14)
Lilium	Asiatic types	(0.04)	0.12*	(0.19)
Dendranthema	Virus-free chrysanthemums (large numbers)	(0.05)	0.15*	(0.24) (0.80)
grandiflorum	Virus-free plants (small numbers, i.e., 100–200)	(0.167)	0.50*	
Orchids	Small numbers of flask-grown seedlings (6–10 cm leaf span)	(0.833)	(2.50)	4.00 #
Cymbidium	Mericloned (depending on variety stage, etc.)	(0.17–0.40)	0.50–1.20*	(0.80–1.92)
				(*Continued*)

Table 3.10.   (*Continued*)

Plant	Type	Current Average Prices per Plant ex Laboratory		
		Currency Units	UK£ (1995)	US$ (1995)
Woody plants				
Rosa	Rose plantlets depending on size, variety and stage	(0.093–0.12)	0.28–0.35*	(0.45–0.56)
Rhododendron	From agar	(0.073–0.12)	0.22–0.30*	(0.35–0.48)
	Weaned in plugs (depending on variety)			
Prunus	Weaned in plugs	(0.15–0.33)	0.45–0.65*	(0.72–1.04)
Pyrus communis	Weaned in plugs	(0.24)	0.73*	(1.17)
		(0.27)	0.80*	(1.28)

*Estimates provided by Mr A.C. Brown of Plant Resources and Marketing.

#Provided by John Ewing Orchids.

Note: Values in brackets are just averages.

Table 3.11.   Illustrative patents on tissue-cultured plants.

Patent Number	Patent Description	Remarks
5–16	Regeneration via somatic embryogenesis using synthetic auxin analogs	**Assignee/Inventor:** Plant Genetics, Inc. WO Publ.: 90/01058: 2/8/90
7–16	Cotton regeneration from callus	**Assignee/Inventor:** Research Corp. US Patent: 4672035: 6/9/87
5–7	Regeneration of grape vine via embryogenesis	**Assignee/Inventor:** Champagne Moet & Chandon AU Patent: 677191: 4/17/97 EP Publ.: 641383: 3/8/95 NZ: 252209 WO Publ.: 93/23529: 11/25/93

variety being propagated is new and has been registered under the Plant Breeders' Rights (a patent organization in the UK which protects intellectual property related to plants), a royalty is payable on top of the prices shown. The price per unit plant mainly depends on the genus and the number of plantlets ordered.

The total turnover of the micropropagation industry worldwide can be estimated by multiplying the number of plants produced annually by the average price per plant. In 1990, the mean price per plant is estimated at 0.3 ECU (ca. 0.08–0.09 currency unit), making the worth of total sales of plants micropropagated in Europe to be more than 54 million ECU. Using a mean selling price of 0.08–0.09 currency units, the total turnover of micropropagation businesses worldwide can be estimated to be in the region of 40 million currency units (about equal to ca. UK £120 million or US$200 million).

In Taiwan, the tissue culture business has been growing steadily during the past decade, and recent trading has been prosperous in both local and international markets. In 2003, the total export value reached 0.272 billion NT, which is 27% more than the year 2002. About 95% of the export value came from orchids, especially *Phalaenopsis* (Liou, 2007).

In 2003, agricultural biotechnology comprised about 16% of the biotechnology industry in Taiwan (1.54 billion NT, which is about

Table 3.12.   Estimated market size for tissue-cultured products in several geographic regions.

World Region	No. of Commercial Laboratories	Annual Production (millions, US$)	Principal Crops
North America		84.7	Pot plants
	Ca. 100	Ca. 75	Foliage pot plants, woody plants
Western Europe	248	212.5	Pot plants, plants grown for cut flowers
		66.5	
		181.2	Ornamentals, Prunus, fruit trees (1990)
Eastern Europe	162*	15–23*	Foliage plants, cut flowers
Asia		55.7	
	105	76	Orchids, plants grown for cut flowers
Australia and New Zealand	20–25	Ca. 82	Ornamentals, foliage plants and plants grown for cut flowers
Latin America	15–20 #	—	Largely ornamentals #
Total	650–660	299.2–482.7	

* Information imprecise. Many small labs were previously government-supported.
\# Only imprecise information available.

US$51 million). Out of the whole agribiotechnology industry, tissue culture comprised 39.8%.

3.8 Players in the Tissue Culture Business

There are both large companies and SMEs involved in tissue culture. Several players in the tissue culture industry are profiled in this section.

- **The Consortium on Micropropagation Research and Technology Development, Department of Biotechnology, Ministry of Science**

Table 3.13.   Value addition through royalties.

Plant	Size	Seedlings in Trays			Larger Plants in Plugs		
		Currency units	UK pence	US$ cents equivalent	Currency units	UK pence	US$ cents equivalent
Begonia semperflorens F_1	Small	0.0139	4.17	6.95	0.0640–0.07095*	19.2–21.3*	32.0–35.5*
	Large	0.0355	10.65	17.75			
Impatiens F_1	Small	0.0355	10.65	17.75	0.0676–0.0748*	20.3–22.4	33.8–37.4
Petunia F_1		0.0288	8.64	14.40	0.640–0.0710*	19.2–21.3*	32.0–35.5*

* Depending on the quantity ordered.

and Technology, Government of India (India) — This is a public company formed by the government of India to bridge the gap between field research and the testing of commercial crops. The company thus has pilot scale facilities for mass cloning and testing.

The company provides services like the supply of superior quality tissue-cultured plants of species in demand, contractual research/production of plants on request by an individual or a company, inoculation of tissue-cultured plantlets with efficient mycorrhizal strains, helping in better productivity and establishment of plants, after-care of tissue-cultured plants in the field provided to harness maximum gains, help to entrepreneurs in setting up laboratories/greenhouses and transfer of technology for immediate execution, support to the tissue culture industry for virus diagnosis of tissue-cultured plants, and quality testing of tissue culture raised plants for assuring clonal fidelity.

- **Guangzhao Industrial Forest Biotechnology Group Ltd. (GIFB)** — This is a public company listed on the Singapore Stock Exchange (SGX), which started with a core business of tissue-cultured mass production of fast growing poplars. The company has since expanded into production and sale of orchids (especially *Phalaenopsis spp.*), other tree species (*Jatropha curcas* for biodiesel) and ornamentals, and also special selected poplars expressing bioremediation traits, and into several other Asian countries. The company's poplars are planted in over 18,000 hectares spread through eight provinces of China.

- **Plant Technology Ltd. (Ireland)** — Plant Technology Ltd. was established in 1989 in the Innovation Centre in University College, Dublin. It arose from biotechnological research being conducted in the Department of Horticulture by two of the company's founders. Plant Technology Ltd. moved to a new facility in Wexford in 1992 and is now the largest tissue culture company in Ireland. To date, the company has experience of culturing over 300 species of plants.

The company exports 97% of its production to locations like Europe, America, Australia, Middle East, Japan and New Zealand. The company has strong links with universities and research institutes, maintaining its reputation as a leading-edge biotechnology company. The company produces over 2.5m plants per annum in its 6,000 square foot state-of-the-art laboratory in Wexford. These include a range of tropical foliage and flowering indoor plants, such as *Calatheas*, *Streptocarpus* and gingers; plantation and food crops such as potato and date palm; and temperate outdoor ornamentals such as *Primula* and *Cordylines*, in addition to a range of material produced on an exclusive contractual basis.

- **PhytaCell Technologies, LLC (USA)** — The company, located in the mountains of Delhi, NY, subcultures plants of different species like the *Hydrangea quercifolia* "Alice", *Spigelia marilandica* and the *Asarum shuttliworhii harperi* "Callaway" for nurseries like the North Creek Nurseries Inc. or Hill Creek Nurseries. Plants are available as rooted plantlets in culture unless otherwise noted.

- **Phytocultures Ltd. (Canada)** — Phytocultures Ltd., founded in 1986 by Don Northcott, was first established to serve the needs of seed potato producers in local and international markets by assisting in the establishment and adaptation of plant tissue culture technology for seed potato production.

  Phytocultures Ltd. has been a recognized leader in the transfer and adaptation of plant tissue culture systems for micro-applications utilizing the advanced technology of *in vitro* plant tissue culture for more than 15 years. The company claims that its products are soil-free, insect-free, disease-free, and combines the advantages of the traditional ways of plant production and growing with the new advanced techniques involving micropropagation. Products include orchids, potatoes, carnivorous plants, sweet potatoes, blueberries and cranberries.

3.9 Growth Potential

Given the increasing demand for high-quality planting material, especially in the developing nations of the Asia-Pacific, it is likely that tissue culture will be the one biotechnology that can meet such demand in the short- to mid-term. As global economic forces favor shifts of labor-intensive industries to the relatively low wage rate countries, it is also foreseeable that growth in the industry will likely be fastest in the Asia-Pacific region. This is on top of the current industry in household ornamental plants (not seed material) produced using tissue culture.

References

Drew, R., Smith, M., Moisander, J. and James, J. (1991). Plant tissue culture — General principles and commercial applications. Queensland Department of Primary Industries Information Series Q189002.

Haberlandt, G. (1902). Kulturversuche nit isoliertin Pflanzenzellsn. *Sitzungsber. Akad. Der Wiss Wien, Math. — Naturwiss.*, 1(111): 69–92.

Liou, P.-C. (2007). Marching towards the market: The business potential of agricultural biotechnology in the Republic of China. In *Business Potential for Agricultural Biotechnology Products* (Ed. P.S. Teng), pp. 89–92. Tokyo: Asian Productivity Organization.

Skoog, F. and Miller, C.O. (1957). Chemical regulation of growth and organ formation in plant tissues cultured *in vitro*. *Symp. Soc. for Exp. Biol.*, 11: 118–131.

White, P.R. (1963). *The Cultivation of Animal and Plant Cells*, 2nd Ed. New York: Ronald Press.

Chapter 4

Biofermentation, Biofertilizers and Biopesticides

Microbes are organisms such as fungi, bacteria, microscopic forms of algae and viruses. Microbiology is an area within bioscience dedicated to the study of microbes. Microbes have been used by humankind since time immemorial to modify food items so that they are more digestible, and to prolong the shelf life of some kinds of food. This process is known as biofermentation. More recently, with the high price of petroleum and interest in finding alternative crop production methods, two other major applications of microbes, namely biofertilizers and biopesticides, have attracted much interest. This chapter presents information on the three applications of microbiology; biofermentation will first be discussed, followed by the production of biofertilizers and biopesticides.

4.1 Biofermentation

Humans have used fermentation from the beginning of civilization to provide products for everyday use. For many centuries, most microbial processing was to preserve or alter food products for human consumption — fermentation of grains or fruit-produced bread, beer and wine that retained much of the nutrition of the raw materials but which did not spoil easily. Lactic acid bacteria fermented milk to cheese, extending the life of milk products. Yeast that caused fermentation added vitamins to the bread or wine. The production of alcoholic beverages has been known since humans settled and produced flourishing civilizations in as diverse places as Egypt, China and modern-day

(a)   (b)

(c)   (d)

Figure 4.1.   Traditional biofermentation activities in Kampuchea. (a) Bass relief from Angkor Wat temple showing processing of local wine. (b) Sugar palm trees (*Borassus flabellifer*) growing beside rice fields in modern-day Kampuchea (Cambodia). (c) Sweet sap is harvested from the flowering fronds of the sugar palm and collected in bamboo vessels. (d) Syrup from many such bamboo vessels is concentrated for sale as substrate for biofermentation into alcoholic beverages.

Kampuchea (Cambodia). Some of these ancient civilizations have retained testimonies to their wine-making prowess, such as seen in the engravings on the walls of the Khmer temple complex called Angkor Wat in Siem Reap, Kampuchea (Figure 4.1).

No one knew that microbes were responsible for fermentation until 1857, when the French scientist, Louis Pasteur, published a paper describing the cause of failed industrial alcohol fermentations. He also quantitatively described microbial growth and metabolism for the first time and suggested heat treatment (pasteurization) to improve the storage quality of wines. This was the first step towards steriliza-tion of a fermentation medium to control fermentation conditions. In 1883, Emil Christian Hansen began using pure yeast cultures for beer production in Denmark (beer and wine were mass produced during the 18th and 19th centuries due to high demand).

In the 1920s and 1930s, the emphasis on fermentation shifted to organic acids, primarily lactic acid and citric acid. Lactic acid is used as an acidulant in foods, a biodegradable solvent in the electronics industry (ethyl lactate) and a precursor for biodegradable plastics. Citric acid is used in soft drinks, as an acidulant in foods and as a replacement for phosphates in detergents. As part of the effort to find uses for agricultural products during the Depression, the United States Department of Agriculture, Northern Regional Research Laboratory (NRRL) pioneered the use of surplus corn products such as corn steep liquor and the use of submerged fungal cultures in fer-mentation. This set the stage for the large-scale production of peni-cillin which was discovered in 1929 in Britain, developed in 1930 and commercialized in 1942 in the United States. Penicillin was initially produced as a surface culture in one-quart milk bottles. The cost, availability and handling of the bottles limited the expansion of pro-duction. Scientists at the NRRL discovered a new production culture on a moldy cantaloupe and developed submerged culture fermenta-tion, increasing the yield of penicillin through stirred tank bioreac-tors. The success of penicillin inspired many pharmaceutical companies to launch massive efforts to discover and develop many other antibiotics in the 1940s and 1950s.

Most of these fermentations were highly aerobic, requiring high aeration and agitation. As production increased, mass transfer became limiting. The field of biochemical engineering became a distinct field during this time to find solutions to the mass transfer problems and to design large-scale fermentors capable of high transfer rates.

In the 1960s, amino acid fermentors were developed in Japan. Initially, $_L$-glutamic acid (monosodium glutamate or MSG) was pro-duced as a flavor enhancer to supplement natural MSG. Using cul-tures derived from glutamic acid bacteria, production of other amino acids soon followed. Amino acids are used in foods as sweeteners and added nutrients. Commercial production of enzymes for use in industrial processes began on a large scale in the 1970s. Microbial enzymes account for 80% of all enzymes in commercial use, including grain processing, sugar production, juice and wine clarification, detergents and high fructose corn syrup. Insulin was the first product from genetically engineered fermentation and commercialized in 1977. Since then, genetically engineered products have been produced on a large scale.

4.1.1 *The product range*

Many products are manufactured by large-scale fermentation. These include amino acids, enzymes, organic acids, vitamins, antibiotics, solvents and fuels. Some of the more common products of fermentation are shown in Table 4.1.

Fermentation products can be growth associated or non-growth associated. Primary products such as ethanol and lactic acid are generally growth associated as metabolites, as are cell mass products, while secondary metabolites, energy storage compounds and polymers are non-growth associated. Other products, such as proteins, depend on the cellular or metabolic function. As such, the products mentioned in Table 4.1 can also be classified in the following manner:

- Primary metabolites: ethanol, lactic acid and acetic acid.
- Energy storage compounds: glycerol, polymers and polysaccharides.
- Proteins: extracellular and intracellular enzymes, single-cell proteins and foreign proteins.
- Intermediary metabolites: amino acids, citric acid, vitamins and malic acid.
- Secondary metabolites: antibiotics.
- Whole-cell products: single-cell protein, baker's yeast and brewer's yeast, biopesticides.

Other products of biofermentation include common food products in Asian diet like natto, tempe and yakult. Natto is a fermented

Table 4.1.   Common products of fermentation.

Category	Examples	Function
Organic acids	Lactic, citric, acetic, formic, acrylic	Food acidulants, textiles, tanning, cleaners, intermediates for plastics and organic chemicals
Organic chemicals	Ethanol, glycerol, acetone, butanediol, propylene glycol	Solvents, intermediates for plastics, rubber and chemicals, antifreeze, cosmetics, explosives
Amino acids	MSG, $_L$-Lysine, $_L$-tryphtophane, $_L$-phenylalanine	Animal feeds, flavors, sweeteners
Enzymes	Amylases, cellulases, glucose isomerase, proteases, lipases	Grain processing, cheese making, tanning, juice processing, high fructose corn syrup
Antibiotics	Penicillin, streptomycin, tetracycline, chloramphenicol	Human and animal healthcare
Biopolymers	Xanthan, dextran, poly-β-hydroxybutyrate	Stabilizers and thickeners in foods, oil well drilling, plastics
Vitamins	Vitamin B_{12}, biotin, riboflavin	Nutritional supplements, animal feed additives
Cell mass	Yeast, lactic acid bacteria	Single-cell protein, baker's and brewer's yeast, starter cultures

soybean product containing an abundance of the anti-cancer substance, isoflavone genistein. It is said to contain up to five times more genistein than that of tofu or soy milk and is a popular food in Japan. Tempe is a fermented bean product which is often eaten in Indonesian dishes, while Yakult is a Japanese yogurt-like product made by fermenting a mixture of skimmed milk with a special strain of bacterium.

4.1.2   *The science and technology behind the business*

The majority of large-scale biofermentations use bacteria, yeast and fungi, but some processes use algae, plant and animal cells.

4.1.2.1 *Process of biofermentation*

Culture selection and development

The desired products from a specific fermentation process depend on the starting population of microbe, commonly called a "culture". A culture should produce, or have the potential to produce, the desired product. Cultures are commonly selected based on substrate specificity, growth requirements, growth characteristics, range of fermentation by-products, effect of the organism on downstream processing and environmental and health effects. Successful isolation of a useful culture from the environment often requires a combination of several enrichment or selective methods. After an initial screening, there are usually many potentially useful isolates, and a second screening (semiquantitative or quantitative) is needed to narrow down the search through mass screening methods like agar plates with selective growth inhibitors or metabolic indicators. Once a few isolates have been selected, culture and process development usually begin in parallel to shorten the time to production.

Cultures often only make minute quantities of the desired product. Increasing the productivity of the initial isolates requires genetic improvement. Classical mutation and selection methods are used with most cultures selected from the environment because little is known about their genetics. Typically, a mutagen such as ultraviolet light or a chemical mutagen is applied to the culture. The survivors are isolated and tested in an iterative process; mutant strains are screened, remutagenized and reselected several times, until a culture with commercial potential is obtained. Culture improvement is an ongoing activity to improve profitability.

Process development and scale-up

Process development usually overlaps with culture development. This involves the formulation of media, optimization of culture conditions and the determination of biochemical engineering parameters used to design full-scale bioreactors. The early stages of process development are usually performed in shake flasks to determine the nutritional requirements of the culture. The next stage in process development, performed in laboratory scale fermentors, is determination of fermentation characteristics such as optimum pH, oxygen uptake rate, growth and production rates, sensitivity to nutrients and by-products, broth viscosity, heat generation and shear intensity. This information is used to determine what mode of fermentation will be used and to develop fermentation perimeters, as well as to determine the mass transfer characteristics of the fermentation used in the design of the bioreactor. Commercial bioreactors come in many sizes and shapes (Figure 4.2).

A variety of biochemical engineering methods for scale-up of bioreactors has been applied over the years. A scale-up process refers to the act of taking a process from the laboratory to full-scale production, usually though intermediate steps. It is more difficult to predict how a biological process will react at the commercial scale based on laboratory and pilot plant studies, than a chemical process. This is due to the complexity of reactions and interactions that occur in a bioreactor.

There are often unforeseen consequences of changing the scale of operation due to the effect of heat and mass transfer on the organisms. Also, as the fermentor size increases, heat generation increases

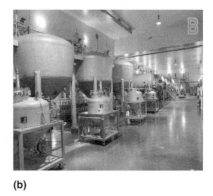

(a)   (b)

Figure 4.2. Two types of commercial bioreactors from Korea. (a) Balloon-type bubble bioreactor. (b) Drum-type bubble bioreactor.

Source: Son *et al.* (2007).

proportional to the volume, while cooling capacity increases proportional to surface area. Therefore, larger vessels require internal cooling coils to supplement the water jacket. This can, however, further aggravate mixing problems. The properties of the fermentation broth (viscosity, osmotic pressure, substrate and product and waste product concentrations) and gas/liquid interactions (gas linear velocity, surface tension, pressure gradients) are also scale-dependent. As such, fermentation scale-up is highly empirical and based on the experience of the scientists and engineers involved.

An important microbiological factor that affects the scale-up of a biological system is the increase in the number of generations required for a full-scale operation. Non-producing variant strains often arise from the parent population. Most commercially used microorganisms are mutated and selected for increased product yield and rates of production. This often decreases the growth rate and the hardiness of the culture. Therefore, a variant that either reverts to a previous condition or that short-circuits the selected pathways by additional mutations will have a competitive advantage. A stable culture is important to ensure reproducibility and profitability in a large-scale plant.

Media development and optimization

The development of a suitable, economical medium is a balance between the nutritional requirements of the microorganism and the cost and availability of the medium components. On a dry weight basis, 90%–95% of microbial biomass consists of carbon, hydrogen, nitrogen, sulfur, magnesium and potassium. The remaining 5%–10% consists of microelements (calcium, manganese, iron, copper and zinc). In most large-scale fermentations, the carbon source is carbohydrates, such as sugar or starches. The nitrogen is from a variety of organic and inorganic nitrogen sources from ammonia added to control the pH. Phosphate, sulfur and magnesium are added as salts or in complex nutrients. The micronutrients are often derived from the water or other raw materials added as mineral salts. Some commonly used fermentation substrates are shown in Table 4.2.

Table 4.2.   Commonly used fermentation substrates.

Function	Raw Material
Carbon	Glucose, sucrose, lactose, corn syrup, starch, ethanol, paraffins, vegetable oils
Carbon, vitamins, micronutrients	Beet molasses, cane molasses
Simple nitrogen	Ammonia, urea
Simple nitrogen, sulfur	Ammonium sulfate
Amino nitrogen	Cottonseed meal, casein, soy flour
Amino nitrogen, vitamins, micronutrients	Brewer's yeast, yeast extract
Carbon, amino nitrogen, vitamins, micronutrients	Whey

Large-scale operation — Inoculum production and bioreactor selection

The starting place for a large-scale fermentation is in the inoculum laboratory. Fermentation requires sterile, active inoculum. This starts with the storage of cultures under conditions which retain both genetic stability and viability. Storing cultures on agar slabs or agar slants is one of the oldest microbiology methods. Lyophilization (freeze drying) requires no refrigeration or freezing and cultures can be stored almost indefinitely at room temperature and can serve as a long-term method of safely storing culture. Once the cultures are safely stored, they have to be "activated" before they are grown in the inoculum laboratory and transferred to growth or "seed" fermentors that feed the production fermentors. Cultures are usually grown in shake flask culture in the laboratory and transferred to a suitable container for transfer to the plant.

There are a wide variety of bioreactor designs. Schugerl (1982) has good pictures of bioreactors. Selection of a reactor design for a particular process depends on a variety of factors, previously mentioned. Due to the complex nature of fermentation scale-up, a few basic reactor designs are used for most applications, the two most common being the stirred tank and the airlift reactors (Schugerl, 1982).

In addition to the mass transfer characteristics of the fermentor, other factors such as the ability to clean the vessel, sterile integrity of the vessel and maintenance costs are important in the operation of a bioreactor.

4.1.2.2 *Exemplifying costs for establishing and operating a biobusiness on biofermentation*

The main cost of operating a biofermentation lab is from the energy consumed due to sterilization, cooling, agitation and aeration.

Steam is required for sterilization of the medium, whether in the fermentor or through continuous sterilizers. During fermentation, a certain amount of steam is required to maintain the microbiological integrity of the fermentor vessel by the use of steam seals. Large amounts of steam are required for evaporation and drying in downstream processing, due to the low concentration of product in the broth. After sterilization, fermentors need to be cooled before they can be inoculated; during fermentation, cultures generate great quantities of metabolic heat. Agitators also contribute to the increase in temperature. Cooling water is used to maintain the proper incubation temperature. For downstream processing, cooling water is needed for certain types of crystallizers and for condensers on evaporators. Although cooling water is recycled, there is high-energy input for cooling towers and chillers and evaporative water loss in cooling towers. Much of the fermentor broth is water. Water is also used for some downstream processing and for cleaning and rinsing the fermentors. Agitation, compress air and water chillers require a great amount of electricity. Fermentation generates wastes with high biological oxygen demand (BOD), mainly in the form of spent cell mass. While much of it can be used for animal feed, some low solids streams are generated and must be treated as sewage. In many cases, on-site primary and secondary treatment is required to avoid paying high municipal sewage charges and fines.

4.1.3 *SWOT analysis*

4.1.3.1 *Strengths*

(1) Complex molecules that occur naturally (i.e., antibiotics, enzymes and vitamins) and optically active compounds like amino acids and organic acids (i.e., compounds with one or more chiral carbons) cannot be produced chemically, but can be produced through the fermentation process.

(2) "Natural products" can be economically derived by chemical processes, but for food purposes, are better produced by fermentation (i.e., beverage ethanol and vinegar (acetic acid)).

(3) Fermentation commonly uses renewable feedstocks instead of petrochemicals. Reaction conditions are mild, in aqueous media, and most reaction steps occur in one vessel.

(4) The by-products of fermentation are usually environmentally benign compared to the organic chemicals and reaction by-products of chemical manufacturing. Often, the cell mass and other major by-products are highly nutritious and can be used in animal feeds.

4.1.3.2 *Weaknesses*

(1) The products are made in complex solutions at low concentrations compared to chemically derived compounds.

(2) It is difficult and costly to purify the product.

(3) Microbial processes are much slower than chemical processes, increasing the fixed costs of the process.

(4) Microbial processes are subject to contamination by competing microbes, requiring the sterilization of the raw materials and the containment of the process to avoid contamination.

(5) Most microorganisms do not tolerate wide variations in pH and are also sensitive to changes in oxygen and nutrient levels. Such changes to the physical and chemical conditions in the fermentor slow the process and are also lethal to the microorganisms. Therefore, careful control of pH, nutrients, air and agitation requires close monitoring and control.

(6) Although non-toxic, waste products have a high BOD, requiring extensive sewage treatment. BOD refers to biological oxygen demand — the amount of oxygen required by microorganisms to carry out oxidative metabolism in water containing organic matter such as sewage.

4.1.3.3 *Opportunities*

Biofermentation offers significant opportunities for value creation if cheap, reliable sources of raw biomass can be found in their original form or as by-products of other bioprocessing. In the current context of high and volatile prices for petroleum-based products, biofermentation offers potential for producing bioethanol as a substitute or complement to gasoline fuel for motor vehicles. This will be discussed in detail in Chapter 6.

4.1.3.4 *Threats*

Biofermentation businesses depend on suppliers for raw materials. Therefore, any disruption in supply or price increase threaten profitability and even continued existence of the business. By integrating procurement activities into the company's global supply chain management, the risk can be reduced. Reserve inventories for supplies can also help lessen this risk.

Companies with a high vertical integration could experience production risks in the form of capacity bottlenecks, production downtimes, excessive reject rates and high amounts of working capital. This risk can be reduced by maintaining sufficient production capacity levels, using production machines and semi-automatic individual work areas along with flexitime work schedules, and by continuously monitoring the production process. A global production network helps to compensate for a product bottleneck by redirecting the product elsewhere where it is needed (Sartorius Group, 2005).

4.1.4 *Value creation and value capture*

The global market for fermentation products was estimated at US$14.1 billion in 2004, and is expected to rise at an average annual growth rate of 4.7% to US$17.8 billion in 2009. Crude antibiotics are estimated at US$5 billion in 2004. This is approximately the same value as in 1998, with volumes increased but prices eroded substantially. Amino acids are the second largest and nearly the fastest growing category, estimated at US$4.5 billion in 2004. The market in 2009 is expected to reach nearly US$5 billion. Organic acids represent the third largest category and is dominated by citric acid. The total market value is anticipated to rise to US$4 billion in 2009.

Production efficiency is key to profitability in biofermentation enterprises, and a major determinant is the biological organism itself. Hence, much R&D goes into identifying the new cultures of organisms, or in creating new strains, on which intellectual property protection is taken.

4.1.5 *Players in the biofermentation business*

Some of the notable companies in biofermentation are listed in Table 4.3.

4.1.6 *Current market size and growth potential*

Figure 4.3 graphically illustrates the market size and growth potential of some products manufactured through biofermentation processes.

4.1.7 *References*

Sartorius Group (2005). *Annual Report.*
Schugerl, K. (1982). New bioreactors for aerobic processes. *Int. Chem. Eng.*, 22: 591–610.

Table 4.3.   Players in the biofermentation business.

Company	Region	Remarks
Sartorius	Germany	The international company provides services in the areas of biotechnology and mechatronics. Out of these services, the company provides bioreactors which can be used in biofermentation plants. Some of their bioreactors include autoclavable and *in situ* sterilizable bioreactors. The company provides customized solutions to biofermentation and software required to run a biofermentation plant. The company has had a sales revenue of €467.6 million in 2004
New Brunswick Scientific Co. Ltd.	United States	This company provides bioreactors and software for the proper running of bioreactors among other products like incubators and air samplers. The bioreactors available include autoclavable, sterilizible bioreactors and cell culture bioreactors
Jiangxi Musashino Bio-Chem Co., Ltd. (JMB)	China	The company was formed in 2000 as a joint venture between China company Jiangxi Keyuan Biotech Co., Ltd., a joint-stock company held by Jiangxi Academy of Sciences and Japan's Musashino Chemical Laboratory, Ltd. (MCL), the manufacturer of high-quality lactic acid product by biofermentation. JMB now has total capacity of 5,000t high-quality L-Lactic annually

(*Continued*)

Table 4.3. (*Continued*)

Company	Region	Remarks
GDS Technology	United States	GDS provides the facility and trained staff to develop, transfer or scale up any production process within its facility. The company serves as a site to outsource projects or provide increased capacity. The company has a fermentation facility as well as a laboratory facility. The fermentation facility is designed to produce microorganisms, including recombinant organisms, from which commercially important enzymes and proteins are purified. Products include enzymes like Cholesterol Esterase, Glucose Dehydrogenase and Uricase

4.2 Biofertilizers

Biofertilizers are organisms that enrich the quality of the soil through their natural processes. The main sources of biofertilizers are bacteria, fungi and cynobacteria (blue-green algae). Some of the more common types of biofertilizers include mycorrhiza, rhizobium and cyanophyceae.

4.2.1 *The product range*

There are many varieties of biofertilizers in the market today, but only a common few are shown in Table 4.4.

4.2.2 *The science and technology behind the business*

The soil acts as a reservoir for millions of microorganisms, of which more than 85% are beneficial to plant life. Thus, the soil is a resilient

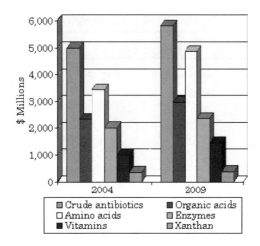

Figure 4.3.   Current market size for several biofermentation products.

Source: Marz, U. (2005). GA-103R world markets for fermentation ingredients BBC research (http://www.bccresearch.com/food/GA103R.html).

ecosystem. Good soil commonly consists of about 93% mineral and 7% bioorganic substances. The bioorganic parts are 85% humus, 10% roots and 5% edaphon. The edaphon comprises microbes, fungi, bacteria, earthworms, micro-fauna and macro-fauna.

4.2.2.1 *Mycorrhiza fungi as biofertilizers*

Mycorrhiza fungi are unique root-inhabiting fungi that colonize plants outside (ectomycorrhizae) or inside (endomycorrhizae) by the extension of internal hyphae (strands of fungal cells) called appressoria into the fine absorbing roots of the host plant to obtain important essential organic chemicals for the growth and maintenance of the fungus (Figure 4.4).

However, mycorrhiza fungi and their host plant share a symbiotic relationship. This means that both benefit from having each other. The many benefits which the mycorrhiza fungus confers to its host are of much significance in its vast usage as a component of commercial fertilizers. Endomycorrhizae and ectomycorrhizae benefit different types of plants more than others due to their colonizing nature. According to Plant Health Care Inc. (www.planthealthcare.com),

Table 4.4. Several commercial biofertilizers and their respective manufacturers.

Product	Company/Region	Remarks
BGA (blue-green algae) biofertilizer	Biotech Consortium India Ltd. (BCIL)/India	BGA biofertilizer is a mix of different strains of BGA and carrier (cattle feed pulverized wheat straw) in the ratio of 1:68.5, i.e., 1 g of wet BGA biomass is adsorbed on 68.5 g of carrier which is air dried at room temperature. The different strains of BGA on dried carrier in the specified ratio are mixed in equal proportion to prepare BGA biofertilizer. 400 g of BGA biofertilizer (mix of four strains on carrier) is packed in polythene packets
PHC BioPak™ *Plus* 3-0-20	Plant Health Care Inc./America	Rhizosphere bacteria. These provide lasting soil fertility, and help plants maintain optimal health despite adverse environmental conditions and stress
PHC Mycor™, MycorTree™	Plant Health Care Inc./America	Mycorrhizal fungus

a leading manufacturer of biofertilizers, endomycorrhizae colonize the insides of plant root cells to benefit plants like some ornamentals, hardwoods, and fruit and nut trees. Ectomycorrhizae colonize the outside of plant cells and roots of conifers and hardwoods like beech, birch, fir and oak. A summary of the differences between these two fungal types is provided in Table 4.5.

The mycorrhiza extracts water and essential elements for plant growth via vegetative strands (mycelia) that extend into the surrounding soil. Water and essential elements are then passed into the

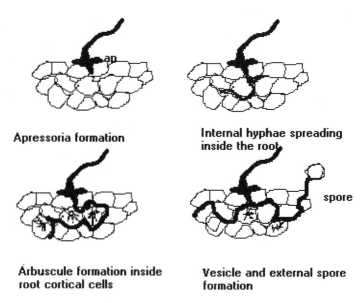

Figure 4.4.   Mechanism of establishment of endomycorrhizal symbiosis.

host plant. Studies in the biology of mycorrhizae have repeatedly demonstrated their capacity to enhance nutrient capture, especially phosphate capture. Mycorrhizal roots are able to absorb trace nutrients at a greater rate than non-mycorrhizal roots (Harley, 1969). Mycorrhizae are able to absorb, accumulate, and transfer water and all 15 major and minor elements to the host plant more rapidly than roots without mycorrhizae due to the shortening of the distance that nutrients take to diffuse from the soil to the root of the host plant.

According to scientists at Plant Health Care Inc., mycorrhizae are able to benefit more than 99% of the earth's plants and increase root absorption by 700% by an increase in root surface area to volume ratio. For a plant to produce enough absorbing roots to generate the same surface area developed by mycorrhizae, a plant would theoretically have to use 100 times more photosynthate (sugars).

Mycorrhizal infection increases the transpiration rate of their host plant. The fungus thus plays a significant part in maintaining water balance in the host plant, increasing tolerance in conditions of high

Table 4.5. Differences between endo and ecto species of mycorrhiza.

Features	Ectomycorrhizae	Endomycorrhizae (VAM)
Known number of species	2,100 species identified in North America; more than 5,000 worldwide	Most widespread; more than 150 species identified worldwide
Method of colonization	Colonizes outside of plant cells and the root	Colonizes the inside of plant root cells
Percent of plant species that benefit	Approximately 10% of plants	More than 85% of plants
Plants that benefit	Conifers and hardwoods, such as beech, birch, eucalyptus, fir, oak and willow	Turfgrasses, most ornamental plants, hardwoods, fruit and nut trees and shrubs
Visible with the naked eye?	Yes	No
Presence of large above-ground fruiting bodies	Yes	No
Spores readily dispersed by wind	Yes	No
Can be cultured in a lab	Yes	No
Spores wash into soil	Yes	No
Most effective form for inoculation	Pure hyphae with spores	Spores
Length of survival of root-mycelial fragment inocula in soil	3 to 5 weeks	10 to 12 days

Source: Plant Health Care, Inc. (www.planthealthcare.com).

soil salinity and drought. Mycorrhizal infection also increases the rate of photosynthesis in host plants, and chlorophyll content was also reported to increase in host plants infected by mycorrhiza (Allen *et al.*, 1981).

Mycorrhizae colonizing host plant roots are also known to increase the tolerance of the host plant to drought, compaction, high soil temperatures, heavy metals, soil salinity, organic and inorganic soil toxins and extremes of soil pH. These beneficial fungi also increase the lifespan, viability and productivity of the host plant's root system.

4.2.2.2 How do mycorrhiza fungi products work?

Commercial access to mycorrhizal fungi is mainly due to the research begun about 40 years ago by Dr Donald H. Marx of the United States Forest Service (he was awarded the 1991 Marcus Wallenberg Prize — considered the Nobel Prize for forestry). Now, Dr Marx is the principal scientist and chairman of Plant Health Care (PHC) Inc., a leading producer of mycorrhizal fungal products.

Mycorrhizal fungi absorb phosphorus from the soil and pass it on to the plant. Mycorrhizal plants show higher tolerance to high soil temperatures, various soil- and root-borne pathogens, and heavy metal toxicity. However, any condition that affects plant root growth influences mycorrhizal development (i.e., overfertilization and over-watering may produce rapidly growing and absorbing white roots which contain few available sugars and are much less susceptible to mycorrhizal colonization). Mycorrhizal fungi only colonize juvenile non-woody roots, not woody or white water roots.

Mycorrhizal fungi are especially effective on newly transplanted plants, as these plants need to rejuvenate their root systems as quickly as possible so they can begin to protect themselves from the normal stresses found in their new environment. Mycorrhizal fungi form a secondary root system for the plant, allowing it to become established in its new setting more quickly.

Mycorrhiza development is encouraged by high light intensity and moderate soil fertility. Once colonized, mycorrhizal fungi spread to new roots in new soil areas and continue to thrive as long as root growth is maintained and soil conditions are appropriate. Application of mycorrhizal fungi is only needed once in a plant's entire lifespan. Inoculation can occur by drenching, spraying, injection or mixing in the backfill. The fungi are applied into the soil (root zone) as vertim-ulch in the case of mature trees.

4.2.2.3 *Plant growth-promoting rhizobacteria (PGPR)*

PGPR are bacteria (such as *Rhizobium spp.*, *Azospirillum spp.*) which produce a variety of chemicals that stimulate plant growth. The bacteria grow and persist in the root surface of non-woody roots. The bacteria also live in the soil to form root nodules (i.e., outgrowth on roots) in plants such as beans, gram, groundnut and soybean. These bacteria feed on organic nutrition (sloughed root cells, exudates or organic matter) in order to grow, multiply and provide numerous plant healthcare benefits. These bacteria often fix nitrogen, an inert gas, in the soil surrounding plant roots before transferring this fixed nitrogen in the form of nitrogeneous compounds like ammonia to the plants. The ammonia is then used in processes like amino acid formation in the host plant, encouraging increase of plant dry mass. In fact, nitrogen uptake is possible only in fixed form, which is facilitated by the rhizobium bacteria present in the nodules of the root system.

PGPR benefit plants through different mechanisms of action including: (1) the production of secondary metabolites such as antibiotics, cyanide and hormone-like substances; (2) the production of siderophores (compounds produced by the microbes which capture iron from the environment); (3) antagonism to soil-bound root pathogens; (4) phosphate solubilization; and (5) denitrogen fixation. PGPR have been reported to increase the yield of crops like potato and soybean. Some examples of PGPR bacteria which are used as biofertilizers include:

(1) Free-living or non-symbiotic nitrogen-fixing bacteria — Very specialized bacteria that fix atmospheric nitrogen. This bacteria increases plant growth by supplying the plant with fixed nitrogen. The bacteria are intimately associated with the rhizosphere of roots.

(2) Phosphate-solubilizing bacteria (PSB) — Certain soil and rhizosphere bacteria that produce phosphatase enzymes which solubilize phosphorus from insoluble mineral sources.

(3) Symbiotic nitrogen-fixing bacteria — Most legumes (beans, peas, clover) in natural soils form N-fixing nodules with rhizobium bacteria. N-fixation by rhizobium nodules is greatly enhanced by vesicular-arbuscular mycorrhizae (VAM). Certain trees, e.g., alder and *Casuarina*, form VAM and N-fixing nodules with actinomycetes organisms called actinorrhizae.

Bacteria used in biofertilizers are often combined with standard NPK fertilizers. Bacteria used in biofertilizers may be dissolved in water and applied to a plant. Bacteria usually reside in the mycorrhizosphere — the zone around mycorrhizal roots, which is altered by the physical and chemical presence of the symbiotic mycorrhizal fungus. This zone supports a population of associated (helper) microbes (i.e., bacteria) that improve mycorrhizal development and their function.

4.2.2.4 *Blue-green algae*

Blue-green algae are a group of prokaryotic, photosynthetic microbes variously called myxophyceae, cyanophyceae and cyanobacteria. During the course of evolution, some of these organisms have continued to retain the primitive character of utilizing molecular nitrogen from air at the expense of solar energy. This process is known as Biological Nitrogen Fixation. Blue-green algae are thus autotrophic (i.e., capable of building up food material from inorganic materials). The nitrogen-fixing cyanobacteria generally have specialized structures known as heterocysts, which are regarded as the sites for the conversion of nitrogen to ammonia. The blue-green algae have minimum growth requirements, needing only diffused light, simple inorganic nutrients and moisture.

Algal inoculation of rice crops has both substituting as well as supplementing effects on the applied fertilizer nitrogen. Presence of algae increases the crop yield up to 20%. The effect is more pronounced at lower fertilizer levels. Superimposed inoculation for five consecutive seasons has been shown to progressively increase crop yield, suggesting the gradual build-up of the algal population in the soil.

In addition to contributing 20–25 kg N/ha of biologically fixed nitrogen, algae also add organic matter to the soil, excrete growth-promoting substances, solubilize insoluble phosphates, prevent the loss of a part of the applied fertilizer nitrogen through its metabolization which leads to the deferred availability of nitrogen, improve the fertilizer-utilizing efficiency of the crop plants, and amend the physical and chemical properties of the soil.

Blue-green algal inoculant has also been shown to increase the Fertilizer Utilization Efficiency (FUE) of the crop plants through exudation of growth-promoting substances and preventing a part of the applied fertilizer nitrogen from being lost. This is a very important contribution in view of the progressive decline in the FUE of food crops observed since 1970 in some areas (Biotech Consortium India Ltd., www.biotech.co.in).

Blue-green algae (BGA) biofertilizer is a mix of different strains of BGA and its associated carrier (cattle feed pulverized wheat straw) in the ratio of 1:68.5 (i.e., 1 g of wet BGA biomass is adsorbed on 68.5 g of carrier which is air dried at room temperature). The different strains of BGA on dried carrier in the specified ratio are mixed in equal proportion to prepare BGA biofertilizer. 400 g of BGA biofertilizer (mix of four species on carrier) is commonly packed in polythene packets. Four extremely efficient easy-to-grow *spp.* have been used. They are *Aulosira fertilisma, Tolypothrix tenuis, Anabena variabilis* and *Nostoc muscorum*. 1 kg of product (BGA on carrier) is first uniformly mixed with 10–20 kg of soil and broadcast over one hectare.

4.2.3 SWOT analysis

4.2.3.1 Strengths

Biofertilizers are organisms which enrich the quality of the soil through their natural processes. Biofertilizers share a symbiotic relationship with plants which are planted in the soil (i.e., the plants and the microorganisms used as biofertilizers derive benefits from each other) and can thus be sustained over long periods. Biofertilizers also do not pollute the soil, unlike chemical fertilizers and pesticides, which have potential to leak into the soil and waterways.

4.2.3.2 *Weaknesses*

Organisms used as biofertilizers have a typically narrow spectrum of activity compared to synthetics and often exhibit inconsistent performance in practical agriculture.

Mycorrhizal fungi are not mobile in the soil; plant roots must contact the fungi before colonization can occur. Therefore, higher numbers of mycorrhizal fungi need to be present in the soil at planting/ transplantation.

4.2.3.3 *Opportunities*

With the increasing concern about environmental pollution, with rising costs of synthetic fertilizers and with increased demand for organic produce, biofertilizers offer untapped opportunities for value creation.

4.2.3.4 *Threats*

Synthetic fertilizers are fast acting and give immediate results when applied in recommended amounts. They pose a threat to the use of biofertilizers as they are easier to use.

4.2.4 *Players in the business*

This section gives sample profiles of players in the biofertilizer business.

- **Biotech Consortium India Ltd. (BCIL), India** — BCIL was incorporated as a public limited company in 1990 under the Indian Companies Act 1956. Promoted by the Department of Biotechnology, Government of India, its core capital of Rs. 53.7 million has been contributed mainly by the All India

Financial Institutions and by the corporate sector including Ranbaxy Laboratories, Glaxo India, Cadila Laboratories, Lupin Laboratories, and Kothari Sugars and Chemicals. Its products include blue-green algae (BGA) and PGPR.

- **Plant Health Care Inc., USA** (www.planthealthcare.com) — This company is a pioneer in this enterprise area, as has been mentioned throughout this chapter, especially in the formulation of various mycorrhizal fungi as biofertilizer.

- **Advanced Green Biotechnology Inc., Taiwan** (http://agbt.en. ec21.com/company_info.jsp) — Advanced Green Biotechnology Inc. is a biofertilizer and biopesticide manufacturer. It pursues the goal of sustainable agriculture (predominantly organic), and is devoted to developing biological products for agriculture and gardening. The biofertilizer series includes: (1) Mycorrhizal Fungi (to improve root growth and broaden the nutrient absorption area of roots); (2) Phosphate-Solubilizing Bacteria Inoculant No. 1 (strong phosphate-solubilizing effects and promotes conversion of inorganic phosphate in soil into absorbable phosphate group ion); (3) Compost Inoculant No. 1 (contains bacteria to accelerate the decomposition of organic substances and putrefaction of compost); and (4) Bacillus Subtilis No. 1 (contains high concentration of live microorganisms to improve soil microenviroment of roots, and increase absorption and utility of nutrients.

- **Radar Biotech Pvt. Ltd., India** (www.radarbiotech.com) — Main product is Nature Power (biofertilizer), made up of live and latent cells of efficient strains of nitrogen-fixing, phosphate-solubilizing or cellulolyotic microorganisms.

Many countries (Philippines, Thailand, Indonesia) have home-grown SMEs producing biofertilizers and catering to the local market.

4.2.5 *Growth potential*

According to the Biotech Consortium India Ltd., out of 40 million hectares under rice, at least 15 million hectares are amenable to effective use of algal biofertilizer. In Southern India, 8 million hectares of land under rice cultivation can benefit from the use of blue-green algal biofertilizer. Assuming application of BGA biofertilizer at the rate of 250 gm per hectare, 2,000 tons per annum of BGA would be required in Southern India itself.

It has been observed that fertilizer consumption is directly correlated to the size of the holdings. Farmers owning less than 1 acre of land, amounting to more than 40% of the total arable land in the country, use only about 12% of the total fertilizer consumed in the country, in comparison to 29.9% and 11.2% used by the affluent farmers with holdings of 4 or more acres, constituting only about 15% of the cultivated land. For small and marginal farmers with limited resources, BGA biofertilizers will prove to be very useful as their supplementation effect has been shown to be more perceptible in presence of lower levels of fertilizer nitrogen.

Blue-green algae are of immense economic value as they add organic matter to the soil and increase soil fertility. Barren alkaline lands in India have been reclaimed and made productive by inducing the proper growth of certain blue-green algae. Land with similar characteristics are found in large tracts in other geographic regions as well.

4.2.6 *References*

Allen, M.F., Smith, W.K., Moore, T.S. and Christensen, M. (1981). Comparative H2O relations and photosynthesis of mycorrhizal and non-mycorrhizal *Bouteloua gracilis* H.B.K. Lag Ex Stend. *New Phytol.*, 88: 683–693.
Harley, J.L. (1969). *The Biology of Mycorrhiza*. London: Hill.

4.3 Biopesticides

The global market for crop protection chemicals is estimated to be approximately US$31 billion, most of which are synthetic, chemical pesticides such as herbicides, insecticides and fungicides.

The term "biopesticide" refers to any living microbial agent which selectively infests and kills its insect or weed host or which is a microbial antagonist of a plant pathogen. The agent is mass produced and its infective stage is applied to control the target pest. Microorganisms used for weed control are often termed "bioherbicides", while those used for insect control are often termed "bioinsecticide". The term "biopesticide" has also been used for botanical pesticides to describe natural extracts from plants used as pesticides, e.g., neem. Such plant derivatives will not be discussed in this book.

The idea of using microbial pathogens of agronomic pests as a means of biocontrol dates back to the 19th century. There are two approaches to implementing biocontrol with respect to the usage of biopesticides. These approaches are the classical approach and the inundative approach. Classical biocontrol involves the use of co-evolved, native predators or pathogens to control plants or insects which have become pests in a foreign environment. Control of the pest in the new environment is achieved through the introduction of native predators or pathogens. The goal of this method of biocontrol is to establish a sustainable host-pathogen relationship which significantly reduces the pest population. Classical biocontrol is commonly implemented in public or low value lands where there is a lack of natural pathogens and predators to control pests. The second approach to biocontrol is the inundative approach, where massive quantities of selective, aggressive microbial pathogens are used to control weeds, insects and other crop pests.

During the 1940s, chemical fertilizers were widely used to control crop diseases and insect pests. However, interest in biopesticides was sparked from the 19th century onwards due to the observation of increased pest resistance to chemical pesticides, coupled with the increasing public concern about the effects of chemical pesticides on human and animal health, as expressed through food safety and environmental pollution.

4.3.1 *The product range*

The product range of common biopesticides is shown in Table 4.6.

Table 4.6.   Product range of common biopesticides in the market.

Biopesticide	Target Pest	Method of Production
Fungi		
Beauveria bassiana	Insects	Substrate formation
Metarhizium spp.	Insects	Substrate formation
Peucilomyces fumosoroseus	Insects	Liquid culture fermentation
Fusarium spp.	Weeds, plant diseases	Liquid culture fermentation, Substrate formation
Alternaria spp.	Weeds	Substrate formation
Trichoderma spp.	Weeds	Substrate formation, Liquid culture fermentation
Bacteria		
Bacillus spp.	Insects, plant diseases	Liquid culture fermentation
Pseudomonas spp.	Weeds, plant diseases	Liquid culture fermentation
Xanthomonas spp.	Weeds	Liquid culture fermentation
Agrobacterium radiobacter	Plant diseases	Liquid culture fermentation
Virus		
Baculoviridae	Insects	In host
Bacteriophage	Plant diseases	In host

4.3.2   *The science and technology behind the business*

The use of certain types of biopesticides is based mainly on the ability of selected bacterial, fungal or viral strains to produce specific microbial, insecticidal or herbicidal compounds which are detrimental to their host — insects, weeds or other bacteria and viruses which are harmful to the target crop plant. Biopesticides act against insect pests which feed on plant tissues and act as an antagonist for the suppression of plant diseases.

4.3.2.1   *Living microbes*

During the late 19th century, European scientists including Louis Pasteur were interested in the possibility of using fungal pathogens to infect and kill insect pests. Elie Metchnikoff discovered that the fungus *Metarhizium anisopliae* (green muscardine) had the capability to infect and kill the cereal cockchafer and the sugar beet weevil, two common insect pests, via direct infection, i.e., it was a biopesticide. The use of living microbes involves initially identifying the type of organism colonizing a diseased insect (i.e., either aggressive or specific biopesticide). The pathogen is then isolated and tested to ensure that it does not harm the plant but only the pest which feeds on the plant. The pathogen is then mass produced via mass production of spores and applied to the plant in the same manner as chemical pesticides.

4.3.2.2 *Insecticidal toxins*

Insecticidal toxins refer commonly to *Bacillus* toxins produced naturally by various *Bacilli*. In 1901, a Japanese scientist, S. Ishiwata, found *Bacillus Sotto* (*thuringiensis*) to be a pathogen of the silkworm larvae. Other studies found the above-mentioned bacterium to be toxic to the Colorado Potato Beetle, the Diamond Back Moth, black flies and mosquitoes. The bacterium *Bacillus spharticus* was also found to be toxic to mosquitoes, while the bacterium *Bacillus popillae* was found to be toxic to Japanese beetle grubs. Crystalline protein toxins are formed when these bacteria differentiate to form an endospore on the host. There are four types of toxins produced by various *Bacillus* isolates:

(1) Cry I toxins, Lepidoptera (butterfly) specific
(2) Cry II toxins, Lepidoptera and Diptera (flies) specific
(3) Cry III toxins, Coleopteran (beetle) specific
(4) Cry IV toxins, Diptera specific.

The bacterium becomes active after ingestion by the insect. The alkaline digestive juices in the gut of the insect solubilize the protoxins carried by the bacteria before they are hydrolyzed by proteolytic enzymes, causing them to break into toxic fragments. The toxic fragments set into the brush border membrane lining the midgut of the insect and subsequently disrupts the permeability of the membrane. This allows excessive water and ions to flow into the intestinal cells of the insect, causing them to swell and burst. Usually, the insect host dies two to three days after ingestion of the bacteria. *Bacillus thuringiensis* ("B.t." as it is commonly called) is one of the most widespread biopesticides used to control Lepidopteran insect pests such as the Diamond Back Moth, which is very destructive on cabbages and related vegetables. B.t. is also the preferred biopesticide of most organic farmers.

Bacteria used as biopesticides are prepared using deep tank fermentations under conditions which induce bacteria sporulation for protoxin formation. Protoxins in the form of crystalline proteins are collected and used as biopesticides by direct application to plants or to the soil surrounding the plants. Another method of protoxin production is to induce bacteria sporulation through genetic engineering. Genes which encode for the synthesis of various bacteria toxins are cloned into fast growing bacteria like *Pseudomonas spp.* in order to increase the rate of protoxin synthesis. In Chapter 9, it will be shown how the B.t. gene which produces the protoxin has been genetically engineered into several crop plants like cotton and corn, and has resulted in millions of farmers in poor countries being able to grow these crops profitably with reduced use of chemicals.

4.3.2.3 *Bacteria for biocontrol of plant diseases*

Bacteria have been considered one of the most effective forms of biocontrol. Seed coatings and seedling root tips with bacterial biocontrol agents effectively suppress fungal root diseases by rapidly colonizing root tissues and producing antimicrobial compounds.

However, for bacteria to serve as effective means of biocontrol against weedy plants, the weedy plant must be compromised so that high concentrations of bacterium are able to gain entry into the plant to colonize it. For example, golf courses are often mowed to expose the vascular tissues of the *Poa Annua* (annual bluegrass), a weed which is considered a pest on golf courses. The golf course is then sprayed with *Xanthomonas campestris*, a bacterium which then colonizes the exposed cells of the weed. Wetting agents also help the bacteria to overcome host barriers to infection. Aqueous bacterial suspensions enable the bacteria to penetrate the waxy barrier on the host's epidermal cells.

An advantage of using bacteria as a form of biocontrol is the ease of production. Since bacteria are small unicellular organisms, deep tank liquid fermentation is used to produce high concentrations of spore-forming bacteria rapidly. Bacteria produced are also easily stabilized as dry preparations on seed coatings.

4.3.2.4 *Fungi for biocontrol*

Fungi are unlike bacteria in their working mechanism as biopesticides. Fungi do not require their host defenses to be compromised for infection to occur. However, free moisture must be available during the period from spore germination to germ tube penetration into the host. Once inside the host, the fungal tissue is able to spread and consume nutrients from the host. The infected host then dies, enabling the fungus to erupt to the surface to sporulate, providing effective propagules for the infection of neighboring insects and weeds. Under optimal conditions (which differ according to fungal species), epidemics may occur in a target pest population. Threats to using fungi as a means of biopesticide include the lack of free moisture in hot and dry environments.

4.3.2.5 *Viruses for biocontrol of insect pests*

Viruses are the most effective form of biocontrol against insect pests, as over 1,000 species of insects and mites are susceptible to viral infections. About 60% of the viruses used as biopesticides belong to the class of Baculoviridae (Baculoviruses). This class of virus does not infect plants and vertebrates, but are pathogenic to insects. The virus must be ingested by the insect in order to be effective. Digestive juices then disintegrate the protective structures which contain viral particles (occlusion bodies) to release the virus to infect cells throughout the insect. Usually, host death occurs four to six days after infection. Despite the effectiveness of viral biopesticides, they are not commonly used as the insect host continues to feed on the crop plant during the time before infection and death. The cost of production and the tendency of the virus to become inactivated by ultraviolet rays after spray application are additional factors on their effectiveness.

4.3.2.6 *Production methods*

Living host

The steps for producing biopesticides in a living host involve first infecting the host pest with the virus, bacteria or fungi and allowing it to grow and infest the host by providing and maintaining optimal conditions. Fungal pathogens produce spore masses and sclerotial structures when inside the body of a host. Bacteria often produce spores on the insect host cadaver, while viruses infect the insect cells with viral particles. Many pathogens (insect virus, rust fungi and some spore-forming bacteria) are obligate parasites and require a living host. This technique is generally cost-prohibitive, but technical advances in scale-up production have helped to maintain healthy aseptic host populations for the harvesting of living biopesticidal propagules without contamination.

Liquid culture fermentation

Bacteria and fungi produce spores in liquid culture. Deep tank fermentation provides a rapid and simple method of production. Liquid culture fermentation allows for the development of stable stock cultures which are stored easily after air drying, freeze drying, freezing or submersion in oil or sterile water.

Biphasic spore production

This technique is used to produce conidia for some fungal biopesticides which cannot be induced to form spores in liquid culture. The method begins with liquid culture of fungal biomass of the biopesticidal agent. The liquid medium provides the culture with appropriate nutrients for spore formation. To induce sporulation, mycelial biomass on thin mycelial mats is air dried in the presence of periodic light. As the fungal biomass dries, sporulation occurs on the surface of the mycelial mats. An example of a type of fungi sporulated by this method is the *Alternaria cassiae*, a biopesticide for the sicklepod weed. Scaling up the biphasic spore production technique is, however, problematic as scaling up requires large sterile rooms. Gas exchange and temperature control must be done to ensure optimal growth of the fungi, but this procedure is difficult in large laboratories. Furthermore, aseptic conditions must be maintained during removal of spores from the mycelial mat.

Solid substrate fermentation

This procedure is restricted to the production of fungal biopesticides. The technique involves inoculating a nutritive solid substrate (moistened grains/inert material soaked with liquid nutrients) with the fungal biomass. The fungus is provided with a conducive environment for growth. After the fungus has depleted the nutrients in the solid substrate, aerial spores are formed on the solid surface. Most fungi identified as potential biopesticides are imperfect fungi (deuteromycetes), which are amenable to aerial spore formation when grown on a solid substrate. The process is relatively simple and this technique is therefore widely practiced on a commercial scale, particularly in underdeveloped countries where inexpensive labor is readily available.

The production method of choice is dictated by the target pest, available application methodology and labor costs. For example, in underdeveloped countries of South America and some parts of Asia, the common solid substrate production method uses small bags of moistened autoclaved grains. The bags are slit open, inoculated with liquid culture of the fungal biopesticide and resealed. After nutrients in the solid substrate are consumed by the fungus, the bags are opened, allowing the contents to dry. This induces sporulation. Small bags are used as temperature and gas exchange is moderately controlled. Fungal spores are collected from the moldy grains by rinsing, vacuuming or grinding the sporulated solid substrate. The fungi

Beauveria bassiana and *Metarrhizium anisopliae* are produced by this method. More advanced methods of solid substrate fermentation have also been developed, but are more expensive to implement.

4.3.3 SWOT analysis

4.3.3.1 Strengths

Biopesticides have been marketed in developed countries as a biological product in direct competition with chemicals, which tend to be cheaper, easier to use and more reliable. However, increasingly, markets for biopesticides are becoming available as the agrochemical industry adapts to the problems of chemical insecticide resistance, reregistration of insecticides and changing public attitudes to insecticide use. Biopesticides are a sustainable and renewable resource. They can be developed in cottage industries and are cost-effective. Insect pests which are targets of biopesticides do not develop resistance to biopesticides as readily as chemical pesticides. Since house flies first developed resistance to DDT in 1946, more than 428 species of arthropods, at least 91 species of plant pathogens, five species of noxious weeds and two species of nematodes have developed strains resistant to one or more chemical pesticides (Georghiou and Saito, 1983).

Agrochemical manufacturers are only prepared to invest time and money in registering insecticides that have the potential for high-volume sales. Demands by national pesticide registration regulations for periodic reviews of active ingredients, combined with increases in development costs of pesticides, often make it unprofitable for agrochemical companies to register products for minor crop use or to maintain the larger number of formulations specific to different countries (*Agrow World Crop Protection News*, 1997). The consequence is that minor crops frequently have no chemical options available for pest control, so alternatives such as biopesticides need to be found (Tatchell, 1997).

A general decline in the use of chemical pesticides may occur in the main US and EU markets. Factors in favor of biopesticides as alternatives to chemicals include consumer preferences for pesticide-free produce and a growth in the market for organic or reduced-pesticide products; the development of more sustainable agricultural systems using integrated pest management (IPM) programs; the stabilization and harmonization of regulations governing registration of biopesticides; and the presence of many more companies in the biopesticide business (Lisansky, 1997).

Certainly, the agrochemical industry is aware that the environmental concerns of the general public are shaping the future of pesticide markets. These concerns are manifested in a demand by retailers for quality standards in pest control that are leading to traceability of produce from the farmer through the distribution and storage systems to the retailer. It will be this traceability, combined with the availability of simple and cheap residue diagnostic tests, that will influence chemical pesticide markets in the future. Market opportunities for biopesticides should increase on the basis of this.

4.3.3.2 *Weaknesses*

Microbial pesticides are living organisms and as such, their storage is limited by conditions which destroy life, such as excessively high temperatures. This weakness has been partially overcome by the production of survival modes of the microbes used, such as spores with thick cell walls and existing in a dried form. Some entrepreneurs have also developed ways to conserve the moisture of microbial cells.

4.3.3.3 *Opportunities*

The costs of developing a synthetic pesticide and taking it to market have increased significantly compared to the 1950s due to regulatory requirements. The negative view fostered by the misuse of some toxic pesticides has also made the public and governments choose to support biologically-supportive techniques to manage pests. These two factors are key drivers for future opportunities to create value.

4.3.3.4 *Threats*

The threats to the biopesticide market come from the increasing incidence of resistance to *Bacillus* bacteria biopesticides, the use of transgenic crops utilizing *Bacillus* genes and the development, manufacture and sale by the agrochemical industry of safer chemical insecticides.

Pest resistance to *Bacillus spp.* has been slow to develop, probably due to a combination of low product use and short persistence, which has limited selection pressure. However, increasing sales have led to resistance in some pests, most notably in the Diamond Back Moth (*Plutella xylostella*) in Southeast Asia (Harris, 1995) with *Bacillus* subspecies *kurstaki*. There is also concern that resistance is developing to *Bacillus* subspecies *aizawai* in Malaysia (Wright *et al.*, 1996).

Another major threat to the *Bacillus* market as a foliar spray, comes from the use of transgenic crops expressing *Bacillus* toxins. This could occur in two ways: firstly, *Bacillus* transgenic crops may replace foliar application of *Bacillus* in a number of key markets such as cotton, tomatoes and potatoes; and secondly, there is a real risk that the widespread use of such transgenic crops will accelerate the development of pest resistance to *Bacillus*; all of which would result in a decline in the market for this product.

The agrochemical industry has over the last 10 years been responding to public concerns about chemical pesticide use by reducing volume application rates and amounts of active ingredient. In addition, there has been a move towards molecules that are more selective (non-toxic to beneficials and other non-target organisms), safe (low human toxicity) and environmentally friendly (less persistent). These are the same characteristics that are associated with the benefits of biopesticides, and hence, represent another serious threat to the future of biopesticides.

4.3.4 *Value creation and value capture*

Concern for potential negative effects of pesticides have fuelled the development of alternative, more ecologically-friendly pest management tools. Biopesticides have a ready acceptance market among organic growers and among conventional farmers looking for alternatives. Value is created when technology is developed to use specific microorganisms against key pests causing significant crop losses. Potential value of a biopesticide may be estimated from the potential reduction in crop losses through pest control. The knowledge base to estimate crop losses caused by major crop pests is well-established (Savary *et al.*, 2006).

4.3.5 *Players in the business*

This section provides examples of companies involved in the biopesticide market.

- **Andermatt Biocontrol** (www.biocontrol.ch) — Andermatt Biocontrol has been the leading company in biological plant protection in Switzerland for many years. It was founded in 1988 by Dr Martin Andermatt and Dr Isabel Andermatt. The goal of the company is to replace chemical pesticides, wherever possible, with good biological alternatives such as beneficial insects and microbial control products. The first product introduced by Andermatt Biocontrol was *Madex*, a granulovirus product used to control codling moth (*Cydia pomonella*), which obtained a registration in Switzerland in 1988 and was the first granulovirus product used worldwide in food production. During the last 17 years, Andermatt Biocontrol has extended its in-house production to include more than 12 products. In addition, a wide range of around 140 commercial products allows the company to provide the producers of all the important crops in Switzerland with reliable biocontrol products. As the quality and availability of these products are of great importance in this sector, the company was certified ISO 9001 in 2004.
- **Verdera** (www.verdera.fi) — The Finnish company, Verdera Oy, Espoo, specializes in developing, manufacturing and marketing biological plant protection products for use in forestry and horticulture. Verdera is the biggest Nordic biocontrol company and

currently exports to 15 countries. Verdera's goal is to become a leading international biocontrol company with a wide range of sustainable biological solutions. R&D effort is directed not only at biological developments on crops under various cultivation systems, but also at process development including fermentation, downstream processing (especially the drying of living microorganisms), process optimization, product formulation and the scale-up of production processes.

Verdera's main product is *Rotstop*. This is a biological tree stump treatment based on *Phlebiopsis gigantea*, which provides long-term protection against annosus root rot in coniferous forests. *Mycostop*, based on *Streptomyces*, is a biological fungicide for greenhouse vegetables, ornamentals and herbs. It controls a wide range of fungal pathogens, such as *Fusarium, Alternaria* and *Phytophthora*, which cause seed and soil-borne damping-off and root diseases. *Mycostop* also strengthens the root system and enhances the growth of the host plants. It can be easily applied via drip irrigation, growing media spray, drench, incorporation, as a seed treatment or transplant and cutting dip. *Prestop* is used in control of damping-off, wilts and root diseases caused by *Pythium* and *Rhizoctonia* in greenhouse vegetables, ornamentals and herbs. It also controls certain foliar diseases such as *Didymella* gummy stem blight and *Botrytis. Gliocladium catenulatum* strain J-1446, the active ingredient of *Prestop*, has already been approved for inclusion in Annex I of Directive 91/414/EEC.

As with other bioscience enterprises, many SMEs exist in Asian countries which cater for localized markets.

4.3.6   *Market size and growth potential*

According to biocontrol specialists David Dent and Jeff Waage of the United Kingdom, the majority of the global biopesticide sales are of *Bacillus* bacteria (totalling US$119 million), a small proportion of the global insecticides market. Despite this, a biopesticide market of

$71 million in 1991 grew by 68% to reach $119 million in 1995. With the introduction of new technologies, the growth of the biopesticide market is expected to continue.

At present, biopesticides have a competitive advantage in small markets where demand for biopesticides is present and competition from conventional chemicals is limited (Georgis, 1997). Most currently registered products for insect control are produced in developing countries, and include 104 products on the market (mostly B.t.), nematodes (44 products), fungi (12 products), viruses (8 products) and protozoa (6 products) (Lisansky, 1993). Commercialization in developing countries is limited but growing.

In India, biotechnology is considered to have the potential of generating revenues to the tune of US$5 billion. It is estimated that the agricultural and industrial biotechnology which includes biopesticides is expected to have a market value of US$500 million (Department of Biotechnology, Ministry of Science and Technology, Government of India, http://dbtindia.nic.in/biotechstrategy/Biotech%20strategy.doc).

In 1992, the value of the Canadian market for pesticides and other agricultural chemicals was $557 million. By 2001, market value had risen to just over $1 billion, which amounts to an average increase of slightly more than the rate of inflation. Most of this growth came in the early 1990s, with little or no growth since 1995. Domestic manufacturing shipments of pesticides and other agricultural chemicals amounted to about $264 million in 1992 and had only risen to $376 million by 2001, indicating little or no real growth over the last decade.

In 1999, Statistics Canada reported a total of 49 active and inactive pesticide production locations in Canada. At that time, these locations were distributed as follows: 45% on the prairies, 35% in Ontario, and the remaining 20% elsewhere in Canada. None of the major pesticide companies operating in Canada are Canadian-owned. Although dozens of companies supply pesticides and related products to the Canadian market, the major companies currently supplying the vast majority are all foreign-owned (Agriculture and Agri-Food Canada, http://www.agr.gc.ca/misb/spec/index_e.php?s1=bio&page=pest2).

A report titled "World Biocides to 2009", published on 1 July 2005 (http://freedonia.ecnext.com/coms2/summary_0285-289462_ITM), has estimated that global biocide demand will grow 5.4% annually through 2009, led by gains in the Asia-Pacific region. In more mature markets, modest advances will be prompted by a mandated shift toward higher value formulations. Food and beverage processing will remain the largest and fastest growing outlet for preservatives.

The study analyzed the $5.3 billion world biocide industry. It presents historical demand data for 1994, 1999 and 2004, and forecasts to 2009 and 2014 by product (e.g., halogen compounds, organosulfurs, nitrogen compounds, metallic compounds and organic acids); by market (e.g., preservatives, water treatment, disinfectants and industrial processing); and by world region, for 22 countries.

The study also considered market environment indicators, evaluated company market share and profiled major producers including Arch Chemicals, Rohm and Haas, Dow Chemical, Lonza, Ciba Specialty Chemicals and Occidental Chemical.

Despite some of the weaknesses inherent in biopesticides because of their biological nature, the market is expected to grow mainly from the increased demand by organic growers, and the substitution by conventional farmers due to increasingly higher costs of synthetic pesticides and the development of pest resistance. The greatest threat to the biopesticide market, and also to the synthetic pesticide market, is the advent of improved resistance conferred to popular crop varieties through genetic engineering. It is possible to foresee a future genetically engineered plant with perfect pest resistance and possessing biofertilization properties.

4.3.7 *References*

Agriculture and Agri-Food Canada. Biopesticides. http://www.agr.gc.ca/misb/spec/index_e.php?s1=bio&page=pest2 (Accessed 11 July 2007).

Agrow World Crop Protection News (1997). US EPA official warns of OP losses. 298: 12.

Department of Biotechnology, Ministry of Science and Technology, Government of India. National biotechnology development strategy. http://dbtindia.nic.in/biotechstrategy/Biotech%20strategy.doc (Accessed 11 July 2007).

Georghiou, G.P. and Saito, T. (1983). *Pest Resistance to Pesticides*. New York: Plenum Press.

Georgis, R. (1997). Commercial prospects of microbial insecticides in agriculture. In *Microbial Insecticides: Novelty or Necessity?*, BCPC Symposium Proceedings No. 68, pp. 243–254.

Harris, J.G. (1995). The efficacy of different strains of Bacillus thuringiensis for diamondback moth control in South East Asia, and their strategic usage to combat resistance to chemical insecticides, especially acyl urea compounds. In *Bacillus Thuringiensis Biotechnology and Environmental Benefits* (Ed. T.-Y. Feng *et al.*), pp. 259–268. Taipei, Taiwan: Hua Shiang Yuan Publishing Co.

Lisansky, S. (1993). Crop protection without chemicals: The present and future of biopesticides. In *World Agriculture* (Ed. A. Cartwright). Sterling Publications.

Lisansky, S. (1997). Microbial biopesticides. In *Microbial Insecticides: Novelty or Necessity?*, BCPC Symposium Proceedings No. 68, pp. 3–10.

Savary, S., Teng, P.S., Wilocquet, L. and Nutter, F.W. (2006). Quantification and modeling of yield losses. *Annual Review of Phytopathology*, 44: 89–112.

Son, S.H., Yun, S.R., Kim, J.-A., Koh, S.-T. and Shin, H. (2007). Commercial-scale production of valuable plant biomass and secondary metabolites using bioreactor system. In *Business Potential for Agricultural Biotechnology Products* (Ed. P.S. Teng), pp. 67–70. Tokyo: Asian Productivity Organization.

Tatchell, M. (1997). Microbial insecticides and IPM: Current and future opportunities for the use of biopesticides. In *Microbial Insecticides: Novelty or Necessity?*, BCPC Symposium Proceedings No. 68, pp. 191–200.

Wright, D.J., Iqbal, M., Granero, F. and Ferre, J. (1996). Resistance mechanisms to Bacillus thuringiensis (Bt) subsp. kurstaki and Bt subsp. aizawai in a multi-resistant field population of diamondback moth from Serdang, Malaysia. Proceedings of the Third International Workshop on the Management of Diamondback Moth and Other Crucifer Pests.

Chapter 5
Mushroom Culture as a Bioscience Enterprise

5.1 Introduction

Human societies have cultivated mushrooms for many millennia. The collection of mushrooms from the wild for various purposes dates even further back in time. Ancient civilizations from all continents (Aztecs, Greek, Roman, early Chinese, Aryan) have all found uses for mushrooms. Mushrooms are most recognized by the unique umbrella-like shape of their fruiting bodies. Bearing testimony to the universality of the mushroom, the term "mushroom" has been widely used to describe any shape which resembles the structure of the mushroom fruiting body.

Mushrooms are a diverse group of fungi which includes both edible and poisonous varieties. Organisms that are classified in the Fungi Kingdom are unique as they possess both animal and plant qualities. Although the cell walls of fungi are rigid, similar to those of plant cells, they are made out of chitin which is a chemical compound found in the exoskeleton of insects. Some mushrooms store glycogen, an animal polysaccharide, while others form amoeboid cells and flagellated zoospores which are characteristic of animals. Mushrooms are heterotrophic (lack chlorophyll) and are unable to produce food for themselves.

Nutrients are obtained through external digestion and absorption by the mycelium. Mushrooms are prized for their unique flavor and nutritional value. Mushrooms have less protein than animals, but more than most plants. They have all the essential amino acids, and are low in fat and calories. Some of the nutritional benefits of mushrooms are as follows:

- The protein content of mushrooms is almost equal to corn, milk and legumes.
- Mushrooms are low in cholesterol and sodium.
- Although mushrooms lack vitamin A, they are high in vitamins B, C and D.
- Mushrooms contain high levels of riboflavin, thiamin and nicotinic acid.
- The amount of antipellagra vitamin, which contains the key compound niacin, is almost equal to the levels found in beef or pork.
- Mushrooms are a good source of iron, potassium, phosphorous and folic acid.
- Mushrooms largely contain water and carbohydrates, making it an essential energy- and moisture-providing food.

The market for mushrooms continues to grow due to interest in their culinary, nutritional and health benefits. They also show potential for use in waste management. Mushroom cultivation offers benefits to market gardens when it is integrated into the existing production system. Potential investors have been cautioned to conduct a careful analysis of markets before deciding whether to cultivate mushrooms (Beetz and Kustudia, 2004). Data on the worldwide production of the mushrooms are available from internet sources and the publications by Chang and Miles (1991) and Chang (1999). Many textbooks and guides have been written on mushroom cultivation for profit. Some useful information sources are given in the References section of this chapter, especially one for growing mushrooms in developing countries (Oei, 2003).

5.1.1 *Mushroom anatomy*

The term "mushroom" usually refers to the umbrella-like fruiting body which consists of a massive mesh of mycelium that arises from an extensive fungal network of underground mycelia. Usually, mushroom mycelium propagates in damp soil or in decaying organic matter, forming a fruiting body during the reproductive cycle. For the purpose of this book, the fruiting body will be referred to as the "mushroom".

Initially, the mushroom emerges as a button which may be covered by a membrane known as the universal veil. This membrane tears as the mushroom grows, leaving fragments of membrane on the cap called patches or warts. Some mushrooms have a cup-shaped remnant of the universal veil at the base of the stalk called a volva.

A mature mushroom possesses a cap and a stalk. The stalk can be attached to the cap in its center, off-center or at the side. Blade-like gills which function as spore storage spaces are formed on the underside of the cap. Not all mushrooms store spores in gills though. Alternative reproductive structures are teeth/spines or tubes. A pore is found at the end of the tubes which are packed together to form a pore surface. Figure 5.1 shows the general anatomy of a mature spore-bearing fruiting body.

5.1.2 *Lifecycle*

Mushrooms grow on raw or composted organic material (technical name is "substrate") and not directly on the surface of soil. An economic benefit of mushrooms is that the compost produced from the mushroom can be recycled as animal feed and fertilizers.

Mushroom spores germinate under specific conditions of temperature and moisture to form a mass of mycelium. Initially, the haploid and unicellular primary mycelium is formed before individual mycelia arising from different spores fuse to form a septate secondary mycelium. Fragments of this mycelium are complete and are capable of independent growth. The mycelium produces and excretes enzymes that digest carbohydrates, lipids and protein, which can be absorbed by the hyphae.

This stage of extracellular digestion and nutrient storage is known as the spawn stage, where energy is stored until the fruiting bodies emerge during the reproductive stages. The reproduction

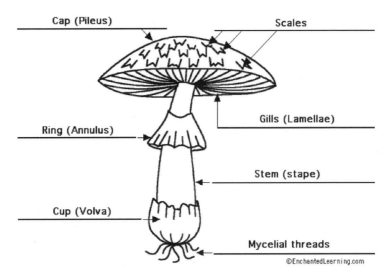

Figure 5.1.   Diagram of a typical mushroom fruiting body.

stage starts with the formation of the visible fruiting bodies which initially emerge from underground as pinheads or primordial before growing into a button-like structure. The mushroom then develops a cap and forms gills underneath. Basidia cells are formed at the edges of the gills, which later produce basidiospores that are released to start the cycle again.

5.2 The Product Range

There are many types and species of cultivated mushrooms in production today. However, this chapter only focuses on mushrooms with entrepreneurial value in the Asian biobusiness industry, as shown in Figure 5.2.

5.2.1 *Shiitake*

The shiitake mushroom (*Lentinula edodes*) grows on logs and has been prized in the Orient for centuries. The color of the shiitake fruiting body varies from very light tan to dark brown. The fruiting body also has a characteristic umbrella-shaped cap with an open veil and tan gills.

Figure 5.2. (a) Button mushrooms of different sizes. (b) Enoki mushrooms. (c) Padistraw mushroom. (d) Oyster mushroom. (e) Wood ear (*Auricularia spp.*). (f) Shiitake mushroom. (g) Reishi (ling chi).

Shiitake mushrooms are commonly incorporated into the diet of many Asians, either fresh or rehydrated from the dried form. However, the stems, which are very tough, are generally not consumed. The caps, with their firm texture and wonderful woody aroma, are cooked in soups, pastas and a wide variety of other dishes. The mushroom is described as having a dense, chewy and meaty flavor that tastes best when fried or grilled. Shiitake mushrooms provide many health benefits to consumers. It reportedly functions as an antioxidant, prevents viral infection and protects the consumers against high cholesterol.

Until recently, shiitake mushrooms were hard to cultivate, but recent scientific advances in plant breeding technology have made this mushroom one of the easiest mushrooms to grow today. Commercial production of these mushrooms often requires them to be grown on compressed sawdust logs, on the outside or inside of damp logs, or in bottles and bags. Singapore may have the only shiitake mushroom farm in Southeast Asia where the production is under controlled indoor environments (http://www.everbloom-mushroom.com.sg/).

The shiitake mushroom has earned considerable consumer demand. Shiitake mushrooms are well-suited as a low-input alternative enterprise as they can be grown on a small scale with moderate initial investment.

5.2.2 Oyster mushroom

The oyster mushroom (*Pleurotus spp.*) is one of the easiest mushrooms to grow as it is able to grow on many substrates. These mushrooms are commonly grown on sterile straw from wheat or rice, but will also grow on a wide variety of cellulose waste materials. Oyster mushrooms are popular candidates for mushroom culture as a high percentage of substrate converts to fruiting bodies, increasing profit. Oyster mushrooms come in different colors and sizes, depending on the species. Colors vary from pink, creamy yellow, white to gray, while sizes range from one to three inches.

An example of an oyster mushroom grown commercially today is the pearl oyster mushroom (*Pleurotus ostreatus* and other subspecies). This mushroom grows on woody substrates and can even be successfully grown on old espresso coffee grounds!

The consumer market for oyster mushrooms is being developed by the larger mushroom companies as they diversify their operations. However, because of the short shelf life of many oyster mushroom varieties, this species may offer a special advantage to the local grower, who markets directly and can consistently deliver a fresh, high-quality product (Beetz and Kustudia, 2004).

5.2.3 *Enoki*

The enoki (*Flammulina velutipes*), which grows on logs in the wild or on sawdust under cultivation, is perhaps one of the most interesting-looking mushrooms. The clumps of pencil-thin, long whitish caps look almost like tiny flowers. They have a mild flavor and are common in Japanese noodle dishes.

5.2.4 *Reishi or ling chi*

The reishi mushroom (*Ganoderma lucidum*) has been used by the Chinese and Japanese for hundreds of years. It was believed then that the mushroom could confer longevity and various other health-stimulating effects to the consumer. It has also been reported to induce a non-narcotic feeling of well-being. This mushroom is traditionally consumed fresh or dried in teas and soups. The dried "conks" have an attractive varnish-like appearance and can be used in dried flower and seedpod arrangements.

5.2.5 *Padistraw mushroom*

The padistraw (*Volvariella spp.*) derives its name from the substrate on which it originally grew on. Cultivation of *Volvariella* was believed to have begun in China as early as 1822. In the 1930s, straw mushroom cultivation began in the Philippines, Malaysia and other Southeast Asian countries. Production of the straw mushroom increased from 178,000 tons in 1986 to about 253,000 tons in 1991 — a 42% increase. *Volvariella* accounts for approximately 6% of the total worldwide production of edible mushrooms, and is popular as it does not require temperature control in the hot, humid tropics and can be grown by small farmers as well.

5.2.6 *Wood ear*

The wood ear (*Auricularia spp.*) is another mushroom which does not require any special temperature control for its growth in the hot, humid tropics. In the wild, many *Auricularia* species may be found growing on decaying logs such as those of rubber trees and in tropical forests. Wood ears come in black and white forms and are prized in Chinese cuisine. It is reputed to be the first cultivated mushroom. In Figure 5.2(e), a particularly large specimen is shown from a backyard cotton grower in Hebei province in China, visited by the author.

5.3 The Science and Technology Behind a Mushroom Enterprise

Mushroom culture techniques share many common features irrespective of the type or species of mushroom propagated. Hygiene and good starting stock cultures (spawn) are key for the healthy growth of mushrooms. The main features of mushroom tissue culture are illustrated diagrammatically in Figure 5.3.

5.3.1 *Growing containers*

Mushrooms are usually cultivated in trays, shelves or bags. Trays are the most commonly used, although yields per ton of compost are comparable for all systems. Plastic bags are disposable and cheap, but require extra handling as the compost must be peak heated in other

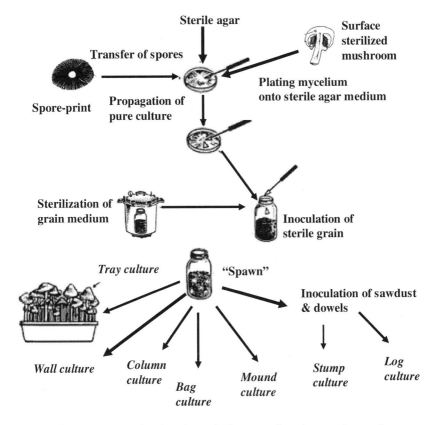

Figure 5.3.   Diagram showing the main features of mushroom tissue culture.
Source: http://attra.ncat.org/attra-pub/mushroom.html#marketing (after Paul Stamets, 1995).

containers (such as trays). In the tropics, it is common to use special heat-resistant plastic bags.

Trays can be constructed out of timber (ensure any preservative used is not detrimental to mushroom growth), concrete or rust-protected metal. Preservatives are applied to the trays to prevent the material from decomposing. However, the preservatives used are carefully selected such that they do not contain chemicals that would be detrimental to proper mushroom growth. Tray construction should also be sturdy enough to withstand rough handling. Trays are more expensive to build and maintain than shelves, but allow ease of maintenance and hygiene, and more continuous production.

The standard growing media is partially-decomposed organic compost. This compost will have a range of microorganisms contributing to the decomposition process, some of which will be detrimental to mushroom production. The growing media is therefore pasteurized (referred to as "peak heating") before the spawn is added. It should be noted that pasteurization (a process commonly used on milk) is not the same as sterilization. Unlike sterilization, pasteurization does not kill all the microorganisms in the media, but reduces them so they are unlikely to harm the growing mushroom. After peak heating, the compost should be used for growing as soon as possible to minimize possible recontamination by bacteria in the environment.

Care must be taken when preparing the compost as this is an important production stage and contamination could result in heavy losses. Ideally, the compost production area should be quarantined with limited staff access and hygienic measures implemented.

5.3.2 *Growth medium*

A diversity of medium is used to grow mushrooms, from uncomposted straw to sawdust supplemented with nutrients (Table 5.1). Special compost is usually made using industry wastes such as oil palm fruit fiber and animal manure mixed with other material. Composting transforms these products into a suitable nutritional substrate for mushrooms. Ready-mixed compost can also be produced commercially to minimize the time and manpower used in compost manufacturing from scratch.

All essential nutrients for optimal mushroom growth must be supplied in the compost as mushrooms lack chlorophyll for photosynthesis. The compost should have a pH of 6.5 to 7 for ideal mushroom growth. As the mycelium grows, the compost will become increasingly alkaline.

When compost is used as the medium, a layer of specially prepared soil is commonly spread over the compost to protect it from drying out and to allow for formation of the fruiting bodies.

Table 5.1. Cultivation media for several mushroom types.

Mushroom Cultivation Media	
Mushroom Species	Growing Medium
1. Rice Straw Mushroom (*Volvoriella*)	1 Rice Straw 2 Wheat Straw 3 Cotton Waste from Textile Industry 4 Water Hyacinth/Water Lily 5 Oil Palm Pericarp 6 Banana Leaves
2. Oyster Mushroom (*Pleurotus*)	1 Rice Straw 2 Wheat Straw 3 Coffee Pulp 4 Sawdust 5 Sawdust — Straw 6 Cotton Waste from Textile Industry 7 Corncobs 8 Paper 9 Crushed Bagasse and Molasses Wastes from Sugar Industry 10 Water Hyacinth/Water Lily 11 Bean Straw 12 Cotton Straw 13 Cocoa Shell Waste 14 Coir
3. Shiitake (*Lentinula*)	1 Coffee Pulp 2 Sawdust 3 Cottonseed Hulls 4 Logs 5 Sawdust — Rice Bran 6 Corncobs
4. Reishi (*Ganoderma*)	1 Sawdust
5. Wood Ear (*Auricularia*)	1 Sawdust 2 Sawdust — Rice Bran
6. Enoki	1 Sawdust

Chemicals to assist in pest and disease control are also often added to the casing mix.

Many types of wood are suitable as material for mushroom compost, although commercially, there needs to be a fit between mushroom species and preferred wood. A common recipe for supplemented sawdust is: 76% sawdust, 12% millet and 12% bran. The standard industry container for growing specialty mushrooms in sawdust is a heat-resistant plastic bag fitted with a filter patch, which allows gas exchange but excludes contaminating microorganisms.

5.3.3 *Spawn*

Spawn refers to the material used for propagating mushrooms. This material also contains mushroom spores with a mixture of other materials which promote growth. Spawn is commercially available from specialist spawn producers. Once purchased, it should be mixed with the compost as soon as possible; however, if required, spawn can be stored at 15–20°C for several days or at 2°C for several weeks. Spawn performance can be adversely affected by excessive temperatures or by rapid temperature changes. Spawn can also be produced using an original starter culture, and has been done even under small village conditions in developing countries. Many small entrepreneurs in Southeast Asia multiply spawn of the padi straw and oyster mushrooms for local producers (Figure 5.4).

5.3.4 *Harvesting*

Harvesting usually commences at the first sign of buttons or mature fruiting bodies, depending on the type of mushroom. Harvesting cycles vary, from 7–10 day cycles and may last for 1.5–2 months. Mushrooms may be picked at the button, cup or flat stage depending on market requirements. Timing is important as mushrooms grow quickly, doubling their size within 24 hours. Buttons are small unopened mushrooms, cups are older buttons where the cap has begun to open, and flats are cups that have fully expanded to expose all of the gills (Figure 5.1).

Figure 5.4. Various aspects of village-level oyster mushroom cultivation in a Cambodian village, 2006. (a) Plastic bags of unsterilized sawdust stored in a village house. (b) A sterilization chamber for preparing the plastic bags containing sawdust as the growth medium. (c) "Seeding" the growth medium of sterilized sawdust contained in plastic bags. (d) Close-up of a bottle of spawn produced by seeding a bottle of sterilized rice seeds with a starting culture of the fungus. (e) Bags of seeded medium with oyster mushroom fruiting bodies emerging from the openings.

The fruiting bodies are harvested by hand with a twisting motion. The stems are trimmed and the mushrooms are usually graded straight into boxes for transport and sale. Mushroom deterioration (brownish discoloration, stalk elongation, etc.) can be reduced by cooling. Mushrooms are highly perishable and need to be marketed as soon as possible after harvest. Buttons are volume-packed, whereas cups and flats are packed with the gills facing up to prevent spores from dropping onto lower layers.

Mushroom yields are influenced by compost depth and quality, length of cropping and grade of mushrooms picked, spawn productivity, moisture and climatic conditions and disease factors. The majority of mushrooms will be picked over the first three flushes (about four weeks).

Marketing costs are usually incurred from packaging, transport, commissions and levies. In modern commercial enterprises, mushrooms are grown indoors under controlled environment conditions and can be available all year round, although there are usually peaks and troughs in the market as well. Mushroom cultivation requires high capital input and labor costs and a strict adherence to hygiene procedures. Furthermore, operation efficiency is essential to maintain viability. Spent compost can be marketed as a potting mix or garden soil additive.

5.3.5 *Physical facilities and equipment*

In the tropics, mushrooms are grown in facilities ranging from modern, environment-controlled buildings, to corners of houses in small villages. There is no standard size or design of buildings for mushroom culture. Factors to include when planning include construction costs, machinery space requirements, tray or bed size, stacking design, etc.

Doors must be designed to suit all machinery and equipment that is used. Windows are not required. Although mushrooms do not require complete darkness to grow, direct sunlight is commonly avoided. Any electrical equipment installed must be able to withstand high humidity.

Cement floors with adequate drainage are required to allow for ease of cleaning and hygiene operations. Flat roofs should have sufficient slope to prevent condensation from dripping onto the beds. Insulation (commonly polystyrene panels) prevents temperature fluctuations and increases the energy efficiency of the air conditioning.

Good ventilation to supply a constant flow of fresh air and prevent carbon dioxide build-up is essential. Ventilation units should be fully adjustable in terms of circulation volumes and include a filter which will prevent entry of insects and airborne spores. The filters should be cleaned regularly. Unfiltered air between different growing rooms should not be recycled. Trays or shelving should be arranged to allow ease of air circulation.

Controlled environment rooms (temperature and humidity) are required for efficient production of high-quality mushrooms. Computer monitoring equipment to maintain the temperature and humidity at the required levels during the production cycle is expensive, but streamlines production considerably.

5.3.6 Case study: The production processes of several commercially important Asian mushrooms

5.3.6.1 Oyster mushrooms

The Golden Oyster is an attractive, fast-growing mushroom that fruits easily on a wide range of ligneous substrates. The mushrooms grow in clusters of small, thin-fleshed, funnel-shaped bright yellow caps.

The Golden Oyster is not as productive as other oyster mushrooms in terms of cultivation yield. The temperature must be at least 65°F to initiate fruiting. These mushrooms also need plenty of fresh air to develop normally. High carbon dioxide levels from mushroom metabolism will accumulate in sealed growing environments and may reduce cap size severely. Figure 5.4 shows various aspects of village-level oyster mushroom cultivation in a Cambodian village, as part of a livelihood project started by non-government organizations.

5.3.6.2 *Enoki*

Production of most enoki mushrooms in Japan is based on synthetic substrate contained in polypropylene bottles. Substrates (primarily sawdust and rice bran mixed in a 4:1 ratio) are mechanically mixed and filled into heat-resistant bottles with a capacity of 800–1,000 ml. Sawdust consisting primarily of *Cryptomeria japonica*, *Chamaecyparis obtusa* or aged (9–12 months) *Pinus spp.* appear to offer the best yields.

In the United States, a bran-supplemented medium, consisting primarily of corn cobs, serves as the primary medium. After filling into bottles, the substrate is sterilized (4 hours at 95°C and 1 hour at 120°C), mechanically inoculated and incubated at 18–20°C for 20 to 25 days. When the substrate is fully colonized, the original inoculum is removed mechanically from the surface of the substrate and the bottles may be placed upside down for a few days. At the time of original inoculum removal, the air temperature is lowered to 10–12°C for 10 to 14 days.

To further improve quality during fruiting, temperatures are lowered to 3–8°C until harvest. As the mushrooms begin to elongate above the lip of the bottle, a plastic collar is placed around the neck and secured. This collar serves to hold the mushrooms in place so that they are long and straight. When the mushrooms are 13–14 cm long, the collars are removed and the mushrooms are pulled as a bunch from the substrate. The mushrooms are then vacuum-packed and placed into boxes for shipment to market.

5.3.6.3 *Padistraw mushroom*

Many agricultural by-products and waste materials have been used to produce the straw mushroom. These include padistraw, water hyacinth, oil palm bunch, oil palm pericarp waste, banana leaves and sawdust, cotton waste and sugar cane waste. *Volvariella* is well-suited for cultivation in the tropics because of its requirement for higher production temperatures. In addition, the mushroom can be grown on non-pasteurized substrate and is therefore more desirable for low-input agricultural practices. Many lowland rice farmers in Southeast Asia cultivate this mushroom for additional income.

In recent years, cotton wastes (discarded after sorting in textile mills) have become popular as substrates for straw mushroom production. Cotton wastes give higher and more stable biological efficiencies (30% to 45%), and earlier fructification (four days after spawning) and harvesting (first nine days after spawning) than that obtained using straw as a substratum. Semi-industrialization of padistraw mushroom cultivation on cotton wastes has occurred in Hong Kong, Taiwan and Indonesia as a result of the introduction of this method.

5.3.6.4 *Wood ear*

The wood ear is commonly produced on a synthetic medium consisting of sawdust, cottonseed hulls, bran and other cereal grains, or on natural logs of broad-leaf trees. Many tropical species of both hard and softwoods have been used.

For synthetic medium production of *Auricularias*, the substrate may be composted for up to five days or used directly after mixing. In either case, the mixed substrate (about 2.5 kg wet wt) is filled into heat-resistant polypropylene bags and sterilized (substrate temperature 121°C) for 60 minutes. Composted substrate is prepared by mixing and watering ingredients [sawdust (78%) : bran (20%) : $CaCO_3$ (1%) : sucrose (1%)] in a large pile. The pile is then covered with plastic and turned (remixed) twice at two-day intervals. For direct use of substrate, a mixture of cottonseed hulls (93%), wheat bran (5%), sucrose (1%) and $CaCO_3$ (1%) is moistened to about 60% moisture and then filled into polypropylene bags.

After the substrate has cooled, it is inoculated with either grain or sawdust spawn. The spawn then is mixed into the substrate either mechanically or by hand, and the mycelium is allowed to colonize the substrate (spawn run). Temperatures for spawn run are maintained at about 25°C±2°C for about 28–30 days. Temperature, light intensity and relative humidity all interact to influence the nature and quality of the fruiting bodies.

In Fujian, China, a system has been worked out to intercrop *Auricularia spp.* with sugar cane. Bags containing colonized substrate are suspended in mid-air on a rope stretched between rows of sugar cane. The bags then are covered with a thin layer of plastic to help regulate relative humidity. Carbon dioxide generated from the growing mycelium apparently stimulates the growth of the sugar cane. In Hebei, China, cotton farmers supplement their incomes by growing wood ear using composted sawdust in plastic bags (Figure 5.2e).

5.4 Enterprise Issues in Mushroom Businesses

5.4.1 *The value chain*

Mushroom cultivation is big business in North America. Between 2002 to 2003, 260 mushroom growers in the USA produced more than 383 million kilograms of mushrooms, which had a combined farm gate value of US$889 million. Certified organic mushrooms accounted for only 1% of all sales, although 12% of growers were certified organic. The vast bulk of sales were of the *Agaricus* species, which includes white button mushrooms, portobellas and criminis (current statistics are found at http://usda.mannlib.cornell.edu/reports/nassr/other/zmu-bb/mush0803.txt).

Total production of *Auricularia spp.* in 1991 exceeded 465,000 tons in fresh weight (see Table 5.2). This value is an increase of 346,000 tons or 290% over the net weight of mushrooms produced in 1986 (Chang, 1993). *Auricularia spp.* production now represents about 11% of the total cultivated mushroom supply worldwide.

Worldwide production of *F. velutipes* (enoki) has increased from about 100,000 tons in 1986 to about 187,000 tons in 1991 (an 87% increase). Japan is the main producer of enoki. In 1986, Japan produced 74,387 tons; by 1991, production had risen to 95,123 tons. In 1993, Japan produced 103,357 tons — an increase of about 8%. From these data, it is evident that a faster growth rate, in terms of total production, is being enjoyed by other countries. In the United States, for example, enoki production has increased at an estimated rate of 25% or more per year for the last four years.

Table 5.2.   World production of cultivated edible mushrooms in 1986 and 1991.

| Species | Common Name | Fresh Wt (× 1,000 tons) | | Increase (%) |
		1986	1991	
Agaricus bisporus		1,215 (55.8%)	1,590 (37.2%)	30.9
Pleurotus spp.	Abalone mushroom, Golden mushroom, etc.	169 (7.8%)	917 (21.5%)	442.6
Lentinula edodes	Black forest, Black, Oak	320 (14.7%)	526 (12.3%)	64.4
Auricularia spp.	Black ear, Wood ear	119 (5.5%)	465 (10.9%)	290.8
Volvariella volvacea	Straw, Padistraw	178 (8.2%)	253 (5.9%)	42.1
Flammulina velutipes	Winter, Velvet stem, Golden, Snow puff	100 (4.6%)	187 (4.4%)	87.0
Tremella fuciformis	Snow fungus, Silver ear, White jelly	40 (1.8%)	140 (3.3%)	250.0
Hericium erinaceus	Monkeyhead, Bear's head	—	66 (1.5%)	—
Pholiota nameko	Viscid, Nameko	25 (1.1%)	40 (0.9%)	60.0
Hypsizygus marmoreus	Shimeji	—	32 (0.7%)	—
Grifola frondosa	Hen of the woods	—	8 (0.2%)	—
Others		—	49 (1.2%)	—
Total		2,176 (100.0%)	2,176 (100.0%)	96.4

Source: Chang (1993).

Production of the straw mushroom increased from 178,000 tons in 1986 to about 253,000 tons in 1991 — a 42% increase. *Volvariella* accounts for approximately 6% of the total worldwide production of edible mushrooms

Usually, the market prices for shiitake mushrooms fluctuate throughout the season. Prices in temperate countries are highest in the winter when supply is low, and lowest in summer when production peaks. Except in very mild climates, the only logs that fruit in winter are those maintained indoors. Using strains selected to fruit at cooler temperatures can lengthen the harvest season and allow producers to capture the higher prices.

Adding value to fresh mushrooms usually means either developing a processed product, such as a sauce, or drying surplus mushrooms for sale in the off-season, when prices are higher. Drying shiitakes and other mushrooms is an effective way to add value and avoid the low prices of the peak season. After drying, mushrooms commonly need to be stored at 0°F for four days to kill any surviving pest eggs (http://attra.ncat.org/).

The value of various mushrooms, compiled for different years, is shown in Tables 5.3 and 5.4.

5.5 Exemplifying Costs for Establishing a Biobusiness in Mushroom Culture

Tables 5.5 and 5.6 show a summary of the costs involved in establishing a bioenterprise in mushroom culture. The examples are from the USA, as it is difficult to get reliable estimates from tropical developing countries for mushrooms grown there.

5.6 Players in the Mushroom Business

Some 260 US growers produced more than 844 million pounds of mushrooms in 2002–2003, with a farm gate value of $889 million (certified organic mushrooms accounted for only 1% of all sales, although 12% of growers were certified organic). The vast bulk of sales were of the *Agaricus* species, which includes white button mushrooms,

Table 5.3.   World production of cultivated edible and medicinal mushrooms for the period 1981–1997.

Species	1981 Fresh Wt × 10²		1986 Fresh Wt × 10²		1990 Fresh Wt × 10²		1994 Fresh Wt × 10²		1997 Fresh Wt × 10²	
	M. Tons	%	M. Tons	%	M. Tons	%	M. Tons	%	M. Tons	%
Agaricus bisporus/bitorquis	900.0	71.6	1,227.0	56.2	1,420.0	37.8	1,846.0	37.6	1,955.9	31.8
Lentinula edodes	180.0	14.3	314.0	14.4	393.0	10.4	826.2	16.8	1,564.4	25.4
Pleurotus spp.	35.0	2.8	169.0	7.7	900.0	23.9	797.4	16.3	875.6	14.2
Auricularia spp.	10.0	0.8	119.0	5.5	400.0	10.6	420.1	8.5	485.3	7.9
Volvariella volvacea	54.0	4.3	178.0	8.2	207.0	5.5	298.8	6.1	180.8	3.0
Flammulina velutipes	60.0	4.8	100.0	4.6	143.0	3.8	229.8	4.7	284.7	4.6
Tremella spp.	—	—	40.0	1.8	105.0	2.8	156.2	3.2	130.5	2.1
Hypsizygus spp.	—	—	—	—	22.6	0.6	54.8	1.1	74.2	1.2
Pholiota spp.	17.0	1.3	25.0	1.1	22.0	0.6	27.0	0.6	55.5	0.9
Grifola frondosa	—	—	—	—	7.0	0.2	14.2	0.3	33.1	0.5
Others	1.2	0.1	10.0	0.5	139.4	3.7	238.8	4.8	518.4	8.4
Total	1,357.2	100.0	2,182.0	100.0	3,763.0	100.0	4,909.0	100.0	6,158.4	100.0
Increasing %			73.6		72.5		30.5		25.4	

Source: Chang (1999).

Table 5.4.   World production of cultivated edible mushrooms by major producing country and region in 1997 (thousand metric tons).

	Agaricus bisporus	*Lentinula edodes*	*Pleurotus spp.*	*Auricularia spp.*	*Volvariella volvacea*	Total
China	384.4	1,397.0	760.0	480.0	120.0	
Japan	—	115.3	13.3	—	—	
Rest of Asia	68.4	47.4	884.0	5.3	60.8	
North America	425.3	3.8	1.5	—	—	
Latin America	51.8	0.3	0.2	—	—	
EU	875.0	0.5	6.2	—	—	
Rest of Europe	115.2	0.3	5.8	—	—	
Africa	38.0	—	0.2	—	—	
Total	1,955.0	1,584.4	875.6	485.3	180.8	6,160.8
%	31.8	25.4	14.2	7.9	3.0	

Source: Chang (1999).

portobellas and criminis. The latter two are a brown strain of *Agaricus bisporus*, whose cultivation is managed for extra large (portobella) and very small (crimini) fruiting bodies. Current statistics are found at http://usda.mannlib.cornell.edu/reports/nassr/other/zmu-bb/mush0803.txt.

Large, well-established companies produce virtually all *Agaricus* mushrooms; most are located in Pennsylvania and California. Their production houses are full of mushrooms in every stage of development. Mushrooms raised in these systems can be sold profitably on the wholesale market. As a side note, shiitakes grown on logs are generally of higher quality and have a longer shelf life than shiitakes grown on sawdust substrates (the most common mass production method). Log-grown shiitakes earn prices from three to eight times higher than those grown on sawdust substrates. Locally-grown oyster mushrooms have an advantage because oysters have a very limited shelf life and are too fragile to ship easily. The grower with direct, local sales can supply a fresher product that arrives in better condition.

In almost every Asian country, there are mushroom SMEs. China, the world's largest mushroom producer, has innumerable companies to supply the local market and for export. In Southeast Asia, Ganofarm

Table 5.5.   An example of the costs required to cultivate shiitake mushrooms.

Shiitake Mushrooms — Establishment Cost (1,000 logs)			
Item	Quantity	Price (US$)/ Unit	Total
Cash Expenses			
5" × 48" green oak logs	1,000 logs	$0.75/log	$750.00
Mushroom spawn	25 gal	$16.00/gal	$400.00
Polyethylene backer rods	3 boxes	$12.00/box	$36.00
8,000 rpm drill	1 drill	$280.00/drill	$280.00
Drill bits	10 bits	$6.00/bit	$60.00
* Water tank	1 tank	$100.00/tank	$100.00
* Used refrigerators	2 frig.	$100.00/frig.	$200.00
Misc. (Sprinklers, water hoses, utilities, etc.)			
Total Non-Labor Cost			$1,926.00
Labor			
Drill, paint, cut plugs, plug and rack	70 hours	$7.00/hour	$490.00
Inspect and water	15 hours	$7.00/hour	$105.00
Total Labor Cost			$595.00
Total Establishment Cost			$2,521.00

* These items are not essential until the second year of production.
Note: Actual cost may vary considerably, depending on location, source or inputs, labor supply, weather, etc.
Source: Andy Hankins, Extension specialist. Virginia Cooperative Extension, Box 540, Virginia State University, Petersburg, VA 23803, USA.

Sdn. Bhd. in Malaysia is one of the few modern growers of reishi (ling chi) for various medicinal and food supplements. Another Malaysian company, C&C Mushroom Cultivation Farm Sdn. Bhd., produces over 140 metric tons of oyster mushroom per month for supply to local supermarkets. The Everbloom company in Singapore started operation in 1980 and produced > 1 ton of fresh shiitakes a day. Countries like Indonesia, Thailand and the Philippines have active homegrown mushroom industries supplying the fresh produce market.

Table 5.6.   Production cost of shiitake mushrooms per 1,000 logs.

Shiitake Mushrooms — Production Costs (1,000 logs)					
	Years				Total
	1	2	3	4	
Income					
No. of logs	1,000	1,000	1,000	800	
Lbs. produced	100	2,200	1,500	600	4,400
Lbs. sold (fresh)	80	1,760	1,200	1,000	4,040
20% culling rate					
Revenue $3.50/lb	$280	$6,160	$4,200	$3,500	$14,140
Expenses					
* Pro-rated estab. cost	$822	$822	$822	$822	$3,529
(Interest rate #####)					
Transportation	$40	$600	$600	$600	$1,840
Year 1 200 miles (2–100 mile trips)					
Year 2–5 3,000 miles (30–100 mile trips)					
Cost/mile: $0.20					
Boxes (3 lbs/box @ $0.50 per box)	$13	$293	$200	$167	$673
Utilities ($0.07 kWh)	$25	$200	$200	$200	$625
Total Non-Labor Cost	$961	$1,976	$1,882	$1,849	$6,668
Labor: $7.00/ hour					
Soak & repack	$117	$467	$467	$373	$1,423
(Year 1: 1time × 1 min/log)					
(Year 2–5: 4 times × 1 min/log)					
Harvest 17.5 lbs/ hour	$40	$880	$600	$240	$1,760
Delivery	$35	$525	$525	$525	$1,610

(*Continued*)

Table 5.6. (*Continued*)

Shiitake Mushrooms — Production Costs (1,000 logs)

	Years				Total
	1	2	3	4	
Wage * Distance/ speed; with speed			40mph		$40
Total Labor Cost	$192	$1,872	$1,592	$1,138	$4,793
Total Costs	$1,152	$3,847	$3,474	$2,987	$11,461
Net Revenue	($872)	$2,131	$726	$513	$2,679
Present value of net revenue flow:		#Value!	Annual Equiv.:		
Breakeven price: $2.60/Lb		Total labor cost:	$4,793.33		
		Total labor hours:	959		
Breakeven yield: 3275 Lbs		Labor as % of total cost: 42%			

Source: Andy Hankins, Extension specialist. Virginia Cooperative Extension, Box 540, Virginia State University, Petersburg, VA 23803, USA.

5.7 Growth Potential

There are excellent prospects for mushroom cultivation as a bioscience enterprise in Asia, especially in the developing Asian countries. Some reasons are as follows:

(1) Mushrooms can convert waste materials into human food — by growing on all types of wastes and degrading them by secreting extensive enzyme complexes.
(2) Mushrooms are relatively fast-growing organisms — some tropical mushrooms can be harvested and consumed 10 days after spawning. By using different varieties, mushrooms can be produced all year round.
(3) Mushroom cultivation is labor-intensive and can provide jobs for many in tropical countries.

(4) It requires minimum land unlike other crops, and is again suitable in places where land is scarce and expensive.

(5) Mushrooms have been accepted as human food from time immemorial, and can immediately supply additional protein to the human diet.

(6) Mushrooms should be used as a type of vegetable — this would be beneficial to the public once it is grown as widely and cheaply as other common vegetables.

(7) It represents one of the world's greatest relatively untapped source of nutritious and palatable food for the future.

Stella K. Naegely writes in the *American Vegetable Grower* that the key to the mushroom business is to have established buyers and be capable of consistent production. New growers might encounter an uphill educational experience for two or three years. Launching a commercial mushroom operation in the USA can cost between US$50,000 and US$250,000, depending on whether a grower starts with an appropriate building. For that reason, it is prudent to start small.

Overall, the growth potential for mushrooms is in the warmer developing countries as there is greater diversity of species and lower costs of production, as well as much greater demand. As human populations in the developing regions increase their awareness of this nutritious food item, and as more innovative ways are found to utilize agricultural and industrial wastes as substrates, supply will increase to stimulate consumption. Another upside is the technological innovations made possible through biotechnology. As yet, mushroom cultivation has benefited little from modern biotechnology, and another "green revolution" may be in the horizon.

References

Beetz, A. and Kustudia, M. (2004). Mushroom cultivation and marketing: Horticulture production guide. National Sustainable Agriculture Information Service. ATTRA publication #IP087. http://attra.ncat.org/attra-pub/mushroom.html.

Chang, S.T. (1993). Mushroom biology: The impact on mushroom production and mushroom products. In *Mushroom Biology and Mushroom Products* (Ed. S.T. Chang *et al.*). The Chinese University of Hong Kong.

Chang, S.T. (1999). World production of cultivated edible and medicinal mushrooms in 1997 with emphasis on *Lentinus edodes* (Berk.) Sing in China. *Int. J. Med. Mush.*, 1: 291–300.

Chang, S.T. and Miles, P.G. (1991). Recent trends in world production of cultivated mushrooms. *Mushroom J.*, 503: 15–18.

Hankins, A. Extension specialist. Virginia Cooperative Extension, Box 540, Virginia State University, Petersburg, VA 23803, USA.

Oei, P. (2003). *Manual on Mushroom Cultivation: Techniques, Species and Opportunities for Commercial Application in Developing Countries.* Amsterdam, The Netherlands: TOOL Publications.

Websites

- http://biotype.biology.dal.ca/museum/wildMush/wildNoFrame.htm#nutrition
- http://www.hinduonnet.com/thehindu/mp/mpcl14.htm
- http://www.shroomery.com
- http://www.mushworld.com/home/re-default.asp
- http://attra.ncat.org/attra-pub/mushroom.html#marketing
- http://www.michaelweishan.com/gardenarchives.html
- http://www.fungi.com

Chapter 6
Biofuels

6.1 Introduction

Many predictions have been made about Asia's need for increased energy and fuel as countries in the region modernize and industrialize. As such, many countries are expected to turn to biofuels as an important source of energy in lieu of the current global shortage and high price of fossil fuels.

The global production of biofuel is estimated at about 45 million liters for bioethanol (or about 3% of global gasoline needs) and 4 million liters for biodiesel (insignificant proportion of global needs). According to 2005 biofuel and biodiesel global production statistics, Brazil, the USA and China (in descending order) were the top producers of bioethanol, while Germany lead France and the USA in the production of biodiesel. To date, Brazil has probably the longest experience with blending bioethanol into fuel for motor vehicles, which, by some accounts, meets almost half the country's fuel needs.

Biofuels are fuels derived from plant biomass. Biomass is a term which collectively refers to living organisms or their metabolic by-products, such as vegetable oil. Biofuels are known to be a renewable energy source, unlike the other natural fuel sources of petroleum and coal. Two principal biofuels are currently in use — bioethanol produced from sugar cane, corn and other starchy grains; and biodiesel produced from oil sources such as palm oil, soybean and rapeseed.

Biofuels can be manufactured from a huge variety of biomass. Agricultural products specifically grown for use as biofuels in the United States include corn and soybeans. Flaxseed and rapeseed are grown primarily in Europe for use as biofuels. Waste from industry, agriculture, forestry and households can also be used to produce bioenergy; examples include straw, lumber, manure, sewage, garbage and food leftovers. Most biofuel is still burned to release its stored chemical energy. The production of biofuels to replace oil and natural gas is seeing very intensive R&D, focusing on the use of cheap organic matter (usually cellulose, agricultural and sewage waste) in the efficient production of liquid and gas biofuels which yield high net energy gain. Simple plants such as algae are touted as a rich potential source of bioenergy, but as yet have not seen large-scale commercial exploitation comparable to the production of bioethanol or biodiesel from plant oil.

The use of biomass provides fuel flexibility to match a wide range of energy demands. Some forms of biomass used to make biofuels are shown in Table 6.1.

According to the World Energy Assessment's 2002 statistics (http://www.undp.org/energy/), biomass contributes significantly to the world's primary energy supply, probably accounting for 45 ± 10 EJ (1 EJ = 10^{18}J or Joules) a year or up to 14% (traditional forms included). Its largest contribution is in developing countries, meeting on average between one-third and one-fifth of their national primary energy demand compared with 3% on average in industrialized countries.

In developing countries, traditional biomass remains the main source of energy. Several countries, particularly in Africa (e.g., Kenya) and Asia (e.g., Nepal), derive over 90% of their primary energy supply for cooking and heating from firewood and dung. In India and China, biomass provides 45% and 30% respectively (Sims and El-Bassam, 2003).

Table 6.2 shows the global energy content of potentially harvestable biomass for the use of conversion to biofuels across different regions.

The concept of "biofuels" is not a new one. As long ago as 1853, the transesterification of a vegetable oil was conducted by scientists E. Duffy and J. Patrick, many years before the first diesel engine became functional.

One of the first applications of biofuel was in Germany, where Rudolf Diesel demonstrated an engine which ran on peanut oil in

Table 6.1. Materials that are classified as "biomass".

Source	Raw Materials
Woody Biomass	1 Forest arisings (e.g., arisings remaining after log extraction or wood process residues at the sawmill or pulp plant) 2 Wood process residues (e.g., from agro-forestry and farm woodland silviculture after log extraction and used mainly for heating) 3 Recovered woodfuels from activities such as land clearance and municipal green waste
Agricultural Biomass	1 Energy crops, short rotation and annuals (e.g., vegetable oil crops to produce biodiesel; or sugar cane, beet, maize and sweet sorghum for bioethanol; or miscanthus and short rotation coppice for heat and electricity generation) 2 Aquatic vegetation (algae, water hyacinths, seaweeds, salicornia) 3 Agricultural by-products (field crop residues) and agro-industrial by-products (e.g., cereal straw, rice husks and bagasse for cogeneration) 4 Animal by-products (cattle, pigs, horses and poultry as well as humans) (e.g., anaerobic digestion of sewage sludge to produce biogas or interesterification of tallow to give biodiesel)
Municipal By-Products	1 Municipal solid and liquid residues and landfill gas (either combusted in waste-to-energy plants or placed in landfills with the methane gas collected)

Source: Sims and El-Bassam (2003, p. 27).

1893. In 1912, Rudolf Diesel predicted that "the use of vegetable oils for engine fuels may seem insignificant today, but such oils may become, in the course of time, as important as petroleum and the coal-tar products of the present time." In the 1920s, biofuels were shadowed by the petroleum industry (diesel engine manufacturers) as diesel engines were altered to utilize lower viscosity fossil fuel instead of biomass fuel (vegetable oil). This alteration was the first step in the scaling down of the production infrastructure for biomass fuels. It is interesting how matters seem to have come full cycle, with many

Table 6.2.   Global energy content of potentially harvestable crop, forest residue and animal wastes residues $(10^6 \text{ GJ})^d$.

Region	Crop Residues[a]	Forest Residues[b]	Animal Manure[c]	Total
Developing countries	21,510	16,671	13,328	51,509
Industrial countries and economies in transition	16,528	18,802	6,295	41,626
World	38,038	35,473	19,623	93,135

[a] Only the world's main crops (wheat, rice, maize, barley and sugar cane) are included and a residue recovery of 25% was assumed.
[b] Forest residues assume 40% of the total stemwood harvested for industrial roundwood.
[c] Recoverable animal manure was assumed to be 25% of that potentially harvestable or 12.5% of the production dry weight.
[d] 1 GJ = 10^9 J or Joules.
Source: Woods, J. and Hall, D. (1994). Bioenergy for development: Technical and environmental dimensions. FAO Environment and Energy Paper 13, Food and Agricultural Organization of the United Nations, Rome.

countries now expressing interest to ramp up production of biofuels as additives to the petroleum fuels mainly used in motorcars.

Biodiesel is commercially available in most oilseed-producing states in the USA. At present, biodiesel is considerably more expensive than fossil diesel.

Many farmers who farm oilseeds to manufacture biodiesel use a biodiesel blend in tractors and equipment, and it is sometimes easier to find biodiesel in rural areas than in cities. Similarly, various businesses (especially agribusinesses) with ties to oilseed farming use biodiesel.

In 2003, some tax credits were available in the US for using biodiesel. In 2002, almost 3.5 million gallons (13,000 m³) of commercially produced biodiesel were sold in the USA, up from less than 0.1 million gallons (380 m³) in 1998. Due to increasing pollution control requirements and tax relief, the US market is expected to grow to 1 or 2 billion gallons (4–8 billion liters) by 2010. The price of biodiesel has decreased from an average $3.50/gallon ($0.92/liter) in 1997 to $1.85/gallon ($0.49/liter) in 2002. However, this is still higher than petrodiesel (the industry term for diesel produced from petroleum), which averaged about \$0.85/gallon (\$0.22/liter) in 2002.

Biodiesel is available in the UK, at prices comparable with petroleum-based diesel — high fuel taxation making the cost of production a small fraction of the retail cost — but is so far not widely available or in very great demand.

In Brazil, bioethanol is produced from sugar cane, under the National Alcohol Program implemented in 1975. Since then, bioethanol production in Brazil has increased to an astonishing 14.7 billion liters per year in 2004.

Presently, all automotive gasoline in Brazil contains 25% anhydrous bioethanol, while hydrous ethanol is provided to a fleet of about 2.4 million cars. Starting from 2005, the Brazilian government has aimed to encourage the production and use of a greater amount of bioethanol through a comprehensive national policy.

In this chapter, the focus will be on biofuels derived from biomass, and not on the use of biomass on its own to generate energy.

6.2 What is the Product Range?

6.2.1 *Plant species for producing biofuels*

Plant species that can be grown as energy crops and used for bioenergy purposes are so diverse that they can be grown in virtually every part of the world (Lwin, 2003). Samples of representative C_3 and C_4 crops grown in different climatic zones are summarized in Table 6.3. Coppiced wood species, such as willow, poplar and eucalyptus are widely used energy crops. Other high-yielding crops such as perennial grasses (miscanthus, canary reed grass) are also being developed as sources of biofuels. Energy crops are important to long-term energy strategies because they can be expanded sufficiently to significantly shift the pattern of world energy supply. Volumes of other forms of waste biomass available are limited as they are by-products of other processes (Lwin, 2003).

Table 6.3.   Representative energy plant species selected for different climatic regions.

Arid and Semi-arid Climate

Argan tree (*Argania spinosa*)
Broom (Ginestra) (*Spratium junceum*)
Cardoon (*Cynara cadunculus*)
Date palm (*Phoenix dactylifera*)
Eucalyptus (*Eucalyptus spp.*)
Giant reed (*Arundo donax*)
Groundnut (*Arachis hypogaea*)
Jojoba (*Simmondsia chinensis*)

Olive (*Olea europaea*)
Poplar (*Populus spp.*)
Rape (*Brassica napus*)
Safflower (*Carthamus tinctorius*)
Salicornia (*Salicornia bigelovii*)
Sesbania (*Sesbania spp.*)
Soybean (*Glycine max*)
Sweet sorghum (*Sorghum bicolour*)

Tropical and Subtropical Climate

Aleman grass (*Echinochloa polystachya*)
Babassu palm (*Orbignya oleifera*)
Bamboo (*Bambusa spp.*)
Banana (*Musa spp.*)
Black locus (*Robinia pseudoacacia*)
Brown beetle grass (*Leptochloa fusca*)
Cassava (*Manihot esculenta*)
Castor oil plant (*Ricinus communis*)
Coconut palm (*Cocos nucifera*)
Eucalyptus (*Eucalyptus spp.*)

Jatropha (*Jatropha curcas*)
Jute (*Crocorus spp.*)
Leucaena (*Lecuaena leucoceohala*)
Neem tree (*Azadirachta indica*)
Oil palm (*Elaeis guineensis*)
Papaya (*Carica papaya*)
Rubber tree (*Acacia senegal*)
Sisal (*Agave sisalana*)
Sorghum (*Sorghum bicolour*)
Soybean (*Glycine max*)
Sugar cane (*Saccharum officinarum*)

Source: El-Bassam, N. (1998). *Energy Plant Species, Their Use and Impact on Environment and Development.* London, UK: James & James.

6.2.2 Bioalcohols currently used for transport

Liquid biofuels, primarily biodiesel and bioethanol, are processed from agricultural crops and other renewable feedstocks. Ethanol produced from sugar cane is currently being used as transport fuel in Brazil and, to a very small extent, in India (Pachauri, 2006). On the other hand, states in the USA are using ethanol produced from corn. The use of cellulosic biomass from plants for ethanol production still requires substantial development and scaling up.

Biomethanol can also be produced from ligno-cellulosic material, and may be a viable option to hydrogen fuel.

Butanol is another fuel formed by fermentation using the bacteria *Clostridiun acetobytylicum*. It can be burned directly in existing gasoline engines without any modification; can produce larger quantities of energy (higher octane fuel value); and is less corrosive and less water-soluble than ethanol. Also, it dramatically reduces vehicular emissions and can be distributed through existing infrastructures (Pachauri, 2006).

At present, much biodiesel is processed from oilseed rape and sunflower oil, whereas bioethanol is processed mainly from wheat maize, sugar beet, sweet sorghum or sugar cane. European countries often use canola oil to meet their biofuel needs.

Other raw materials used are palm oil in Malaysia, sunflower oil in Austria, France and Italy, and soybean oil in the USA. Some newer plant species such as Jatropha (Figure 6.1) are receiving intense attention in Asia as future sources of biofuel.

6.3 The Science and Technology Behind the Business

Plants are known to manufacture simple and complex sugars from sunlight through the primary process of photosynthesis. Other complex chemicals are also manufactured using different physiological processes. In this chapter, only one such set of chemicals manufactured by plants, commonly and collectively called "biofuels", is described, together with their extraction from plants or conversion from other products made by plants.

There are many ways to convert a myriad of feedstocks into biofuels. The end biofuel product is also not uniform and may be solid, liquid or gaseous biofuels. Table 6.4 gives a summary of the raw materials used to manufacture biofuels, the processes used to treat the respective feedstocks and the resultant biofuels produced.

6.3.1 *Case study: Fermentation and hydrolysis to bioethanol and biomethanol*

Fermentation is where natural hexose (6-carbon atoms) sugars are converted by yeasts into alcohol. Sugar cane has easily fermentable

(a)   **(b)**

Figure 6.1.   Picture of a Jatropha plant, a potential biofuel source in tropical and subtropical climates. (a) Jatropha plant showing leaves and fruit. (b) One-year-old Jatropha plantation in Southeast Asia. (Courtesy: Dr J. Yong, NIE, Singapore.)

free sugars present, but crops such as beet or cereals need extra processing to release yeast digestible sugars. For ligno-cellulosic feedstocks, the process requires acid or enzyme hydrolysis to break down the cellulose into glucose sugar. During this process, the lignocellulose biomass feedstock undergoes hydrolysis to release xylose from the hemicellulose. The contents are separated to obtain a solid cellulose/lignin cake. The cake undergoes further hydrolysis to release glucose.

Ethanol can be used as a straight fuel, as an oxygenate, or blended with petrol at up to 26% by volume as in Brazil. In the USA, anhydrous bioethanol is used as a 10% blend (Lim and Sims, 2003).

6.3.2 Case study: Vegetable oil extraction — Solvent extraction technique

Technology for extracting oils from vegetable seeds has undergone increasing sophistication in modern times. Historically, vegetable oils were extracted by wrapping seeds in cloth before using devices operated by stones and levers to exert pressure on them. Later, various presses were developed which extracted oil, leaving a pressed cake of seed residue (meal) as a by-product. The meal contains protein which,

Table 6.4. The major routes for the production of solid and liquid fuels from selected sources of biomass.

Production of liquid and gaseous biofuels for transport from a range of biomass feedstocks

Biomass source	Oil crops (Oil palm, rape, sunflower)		Sugar and starch crops (Sugar cane, cassava, Sugar beet, sweet sorghum, potato)	Organic wastes (Landfill gas, solid and liquid municipal wastes)
Technologies	Extraction		Fermentation and distillation	Anaerobic digestion
Biofuels	Vegetable oil	Esters by esterification	Ethanol, oxygenates	Methane (Biogas)

Production of solid, liquid and gaseous energy carriers for heat and power generation from solid biomass resources

Biomass source	Forest trees and residues → Lignocellulosic crops (Straw, energy cereals, miscanthus, poplar, willow)				
Technologies	Compaction	Pyrolysis	Gasification	Pulverization	Hydrolysis
Fuels	Solid fuels, briquettes, pallets, bales	Bio-oil, char	Syn. gas, hydrogen, methanol	Pulverized fuel	Ethanol

Sources: Department of Biotechnology, Ministry of Science and Technology, Government of India, National biotechnology development strategy, http://dbtindia.nic.in/biotechstrategy/Biotech%20strategy.doc; Shahi, G.S. (2004), *BioBusiness in Asia*, Pearson Education South Asia, p. 4.
Note: This table is modified from the above sources.

if undamaged, may be used for either human food (soy flour, for example) or animal feed such as soybean meal.

Because most press processes overheat the meal and leave too much of the high-value oil in the seed cakes, methods of extracting the oil with solvents have been developed. Seeds (like soybeans) with low oil content are processed by solvent methods alone. In other cases, presses are used first to extract part of the oil; then, solvents extract the oil that remains in the seeds.

Because of their efficiency, processes employing solvents to extract vegetable oil in large quantities are in wide use, and solvent extraction equipment is readily available commercially. Economically viable factories process from 200 tons/day to 4,000 tons/day.

6.3.3 Case study: Production of biodiesel

Biodiesel is a renewable energy fuel that can be produced from a number of sources including animal fats, algae-sourced oil and vegetable oils by lipid transesterification. It has very similar properties to petroleum-based diesel, and can be used as a complete replacement or as a mixture of petroleum and biodiesel. Because biodiesel is a renewable fuel, it is one of the most realistic candidates to replace fossil fuel as the world's primary transportation energy source. Chemically, it is a fuel comprised of monoalkyl esters of long chain fatty acids. The transesterification production process removes glycerol from the oil.

6.3.3.1 Biodiesel: Fuel quality, standards and properties

Biodiesel is a clear amber-yellow liquid with a viscosity similar to petrodiesel. Much of the world uses a system known as the "BD factor" to state the amount of biodiesel in any fuel mix. For example, 20% biodiesel is labeled BD20.

The international standard for biodiesel is ISO 14214, while the standard in Germany is referred to as DIN. There are three different sorts of biodiesel, each of which is made from different oils:

- RME (rapeseed methyl ester, from rape products, according to DIN E 51606);
- PME (vegetable methylester, purely vegetable products, according to DIN E 51606); and
- FME (fat methyl ester, vegetable and animal products, according to DIN V 51606).

Biodiesel can be mixed with petrodiesel at any concentration in most modern engines.

6.3.3.2 *Production of biodiesel*

Biodiesel can be produced from a variety of biolipids (biological oils and fats). These include:

- Virgin oil feedstock from such crops as mustard, rapeseed and soybeans, as well as other crops and algae;
- Waste vegetable oil (WVO);
- Animal fats including tallow, lard and yellow grease.

While waste vegetable oil is touted by many as the best source of oil to produce biodiesel, it is limited in supply at an amount drastically less than the amount of petroleum diesel or gasoline that is burned for transportation and home heating in the world. Although it is economically profitable to use WVO to produce biodiesel, it is even more profitable to convert WVO into other products such as soap, and hence, most WVO is used for these other purposes.

For a truly renewable source of oil, crops or other similar cultivatable source would have to be considered. Plants utilize photosynthesis to convert solar energy into chemical energy. It is this chemical energy that biodiesel stores and is released when it is burned. Therefore, plants can offer a sustainable oil source for biodiesel production.

The production of algae to harvest its oil for biodiesel has not been undertaken on a commercial scale yet, but there are many feasibility and pilot studies. Soybeans are not a very efficient crop solely for the production of biodiesel, but their common use in the USA for food has led to soybean biodiesel becoming the primary source for biodiesel in that country. Specially-bred mustard varieties can produce very high oil yields with the added benefit that the meal leftover after the oil has been pressed out can act as an effective and biodegradable pesticide.

There are three basic routes to biodiesel production from biolipids:

- Base catalyzed transesterification of the biolipid;
- Direct acid catalyzed transesterification of the biolipid; and
- Conversion of the biolipid to its fatty acids and then to biodiesel.

Almost all biodiesel is produced using base catalyzed transesterification as it is the most economical process, requiring only low temperatures and pressures and producing a 98% conversion yield. Transesterification is crucial for producing biodiesel from biolipids. The transesterification process is the reaction of a triglyceride (fat/oil) with a bioalcohol to form esters and glycerol (a biodiesel).

During the esterification process, the triglyceride is reacted with alcohol in the presence of a catalyst, usually a strong alkali (NaOH, KOH or sodium silicate). The alcohol reacts with the fatty acids to form the monoalkyl ester (or biodiesel) and crude glycerol.

6.4 Value Creation in Biofuels

The direct source of the energy content in biodiesel is solar energy captured by plants during photosynthesis. Value creation is therefore highly dependent on how much biofuel can be produced per biomass of the plant over a comparable period and area grown with the plant. Table 6.5 shows the estimated biofuel yield of several common plant species used or proposed as biofuel sources.

Different plants yield different amounts of usable oil. Some studies show the following rates of production in liters per hectare per year:

- Soybean: 374–477 liters per ha per year
- Mustard, rapeseed: 1,029–1,356 liters per ha per year
- Algae: 46,000–187,000 liters per ha per year.

A major challenge from R&D is to increase both the inherent biofuel yield as well as the efficiency of the extraction or conversion

Table 6.5. Estimated biofuel yields (in liters) for common plant species used or proposed as biomass sources.

Crop	Liters of Biofuel Produced per Hectare	Estimated Price of Biofuel (in dollars per liter)
Corn	172	6.25
Sugar cane	75.7 (liters per ton)	3.41–3.78
Soybean	446	11.73–13.56
Jatropha	1,892	—
Palm oil	5,950	—

Sources: Mitchell, D. (15 June 2007), Perspectives on biofuels and impacts on world commodity markets, Global Agri-Food Forum, 2007, Mexico City, World Bank, https://www.foroglobalagroalimentario.org.mx/ponencias/2007/magistrales/Donald_Mitchell.eng.pdf; Oil yields and characteristics: Journey to forever, http://journeytoforever.org/biodiesel_yield.html.

process. To this end, biotechnology, especially genetic engineering, has much potential to offer. For example, the relative yield of oil per biomass of some common plant materials is:

- Algae — 50%
- Jatropha — 30%
- Palm kernel — 30% from pericarp; 33% from kernel
- Soybean — 20%.

It is known that there is natural, genetic variability in the percentage oil yield. Selective breeding could increase this yield percent by several percentage points, but genetic engineering (Chapter 9) is the technology that offers the most promise for double digit increases in oil yield.

As of 2005, bioenergy covers approximately 15% of the world's energy consumption. Most bioenergy is consumed in developing countries and is used for direct heating, as opposed to electricity production. However, Sweden and Finland supply 17% and 19% respectively of their energy needs with bioenergy — a high figure for industrialized countries.

In assessing the viability of biofuel production, factors that need to be taken into consideration include the fuel equivalent of the energy required for processing, the yield of fuel from raw oil, the return on cultivating food, and the relative cost of biodiesel versus petrodiesel.

Some nations and regions have pondered the transition fully to biofuels, but have found that doing so would require immense tracts of land. Using older data on the amount of biodiesel that can be produced per acre of cultivated land, some have concluded that it is likely that the United States, which uses more energy per capita than any other country, does not have enough arable land to fuel all of the nation's vehicles. Other developed and developing nations may be in better situations, although many regions cannot afford to divert land away from food production. For Third World countries, biodiesel sources that use marginal land could make more sense.

More recent studies using a species of algae that has oil content of as high as 50% have concluded that as little as 28,000 km² or 0.3% of the land area of the US could be utilized to produce enough biodiesel to replace all transportation fuel the country currently utilizes. Further encouragement comes from the fact that the land that could be most effective in growing the algae is desert land with high solar irradiation, but lower economic value for other uses, and that the algae could utilize farm waste and excess CO_2 from factories to help speed the growth of the algae. This technology is attracting current strong interest due to the promising returns.

6.5 Current Market Size

In 2000, approximately 18 million tons of liquid biofuel were produced worldwide, with the European Union producing 0.7 million tons of biodiesel from oilseed rape and 0.3 million tons of bioethanol from cereals and sugar beet. The USA, on the other hand, produced 6 million tons of bioethanol from maize, while Brazil produced 10.7 million tons of bioethanol from sugar cane. World biofuel production is anticipated to rise by 2020 to over 20 million tons per year.

Bioethanol from Brazil has contributed a large share in the global biofuel market. Under the PROALCOOL program, Brazil has made bioethanol fully competitive with respect to gasoline in the automotive fuel market with an annual production of 14.8 billion liters (Lucon, 2005).

The European Union, on the other hand, has taken a lead in the production of biodiesel, with a current production of over 500,000 tons.

A country to note with regards to biofuel production in Asia is China. The Chinese ethanol industry comprises over 200 production facilities in 11 provinces, capable of producing more than 3 million tons of bioethanol per annum, of which more than 80% is grain-based. The market price for bioethanol in China is about 360 euros per ton (Dhavala, 2006).

Interest in biodiesel in the United States began in the late 1970s and early 1980s. The general conclusion at that time was that biodiesel was a technically acceptable substitute or blending stock for petroleum diesel, but production costs were prohibitive compared to petroleum-based diesel fuel. Subsequently, the Clean Air Act Amendments of 1990 and the Energy Policy Act of 1992 spurred activities to commercialize biodiesel in the USA.

The Clean Air Act Amendments of 1990 were enacted to address environmental concerns such as the emissions output of urban buses, new marine engines and off-road vehicle engines. An increase in demand for cleaner burning fuels has occurred. The Energy Policy Act of 1992 (EPACT) was enacted by the US Congress to strengthen the USA's energy security by displacing imported petroleum through the promotion of alternative fuels.

US biodiesel promoters chose to focus on the urban transit industry because it was the first major diesel market segment regulated as a result of the Clean Air Act Amendments. Also, it was believed that it would be easier to distribute biodiesel to industries in which vehicles are centrally fuelled.

Currently, the transit industry is the major consumer segment for biodiesel in the USA. Other markets targeted in the USA include regulated fleets, the marine market and underground mines. The US biodiesel industry is still in its infancy.

The principal US manufacturer of biodiesel is Procter & Gamble. It sells the biodiesel to other distribution companies that market the biodiesel directly to the end user. In 1994, Procter & Gamble sold 11,300 liters of biodiesel for fuel use. The major factor hindering biodiesel marketing efforts in the US is the high cost of production.

Different approaches have been tried to increase the market share of biofuels. Italy has one of the highest levels of mineral oil tax in Europe, both on diesel fuel and heating oil. Given full detaxation, it was therefore a logical step to penetrate the easier accessible market for heating oil. France has chosen another strategy by delivering biodiesel to refineries, where it is blended with 5% to fossil diesel and distributed through the existing system, mainly by Elf, Shell and Total. However, the customer is not in a position to identify the difference in the fuel. This strategy is avoiding building of a separate and costly infrastructure and big volumes of biodiesel can enter the market immediately.

Another blending strategy is tried in the USA, where 20% soya oil-methyl-ester is mixed with fossil diesel, mainly because of price reasons.

6.6 Players in the Asian Biofuel Business

Some industry players in biofuels are shown in Table 6.6. A few selected countries are profiled in the following sections.

6.6.1 *China*

China has always been one of the major players in the Asian biofuel scene. China has given high priority to rural energy planning, where biomass fuels are the main energy source. It has been very successful in popularizing the use of renewable energy planning and technologies, mainly in areas of biomass conversion, through an integrated approach. China has integrated the development and utilization of various forms of energy sources for complementary and practical purposes, taking into account local conditions. China developed an integrated rural energy development program to implement biogas,

Table 6.6.   Players in the biofuel business.

Company	Region	Remarks
Akzo Nobel Chemicals	Netherlands	Akzo Nobel is a Global Fortune 500 company and is listed on both the Euronext Amsterdam and NASDAQ stock exchange. The company manufactures crude glycerine which is sold to other companies for refinement. Other products include healthcare and coatings
Biofuels Cooperation Plc.	Europe, England	The company is producing a plant which produces biodiesel. It aims to be Europe's leader in biodiesel manufacturing. This production, equivalent to some 284 million liters of biodiesel, will use renewable vegetable oil crops as the feedstock
Phillips Biofuels	USA	The company is Vermont's largest distributor of the highest-quality American Society of Testing and Materials (ASTM) spec biofuel available within the state

energy-saving cooking stoves, biomass briquetting and other biomass conversion technologies. A unique feature of the program is the manner in which it blends the centralized and decentralized functions necessary for ensuring that local efforts are successfully implemented and managed, while maintaining coherent national planning and oversight (Lwin, 2003).

The Chinese government has consistently attached great importance to new and renewable sources of energy development and utilization. Their 21st century agenda emphasized that renewable energy would be the basis of the future energy structure, and that renewable energy development should be preferred in national energy strategies. At the national level, resources from various government departments were pooled to support R&D in renewable energy projects, with special emphasis placed on supporting market development using facilitating regulations. At the provincial level, local manufacture was promoted by developing pilot renewable energy industries, with stations established to provide after-sales service. Local industries also enjoyed preferential treatment regarding taxation and provision of raw materials, low-interest loans and subsidies. For example, several government units were mobilized to use rice husks for electricity generation and fiscal incentives were provided (Lwin, 2003).

Research and development of biodiesel in China started in the late 1980s. Research activities included selection, genetic modification, distribution and cultivation of oil-yielding plants, and processing technologies. Feedstocks used for biodiesel production included waste cooking oil, low-grade vegetable oil, and oil extracted from seeds. Major oil-bearing plants found in China are *Jatropha curcas*, *Pistacia chinensis*, *Cornus wilosoniana* and *Xanthoceras sorbifolia* (Dhavala, 2006). Data on the total land area that can be brought under biofuel plantation in China are presented in Table 6.7.

6.6.2 *India*

The government of India has also given high priority to the development of renewable energy. The Commission for Additional Sources of Energy (CASE) formulated programs for the development of new and renewable sources of energy. It has coordinated and intensified R&D activities and implemented government policies in this regard. The Ministry of Non-Conventional Energy Sources (MNES), along with the Indian Renewable Energy Development Agency (IREDA), acts as nodal points within the institutional framework for promoting renewable energy technologies. The IREDA is a unique model globally operating a revolving fund to develop and promote commercially viable renewable energy technologies throughout India. IREDA is the main financial institution which promotes, develops and finances these technologies through R&D projects, private sector projects and programs supported by government subsidies (Lwin, 2003).

The Planning Commission, India in July 2003 highlighted the increased acceptance and usage of biodiesel worldwide as a solution to the problem of environmental pollution and energy security. The MoRD (Ministry of Rural Development) has been designated as the nodal ministry for implementation of the recommendations of the

Table 6.7.   Land resources for plantation production of biodiesel in China.

	Potential Woodlands	Grain-to-Green Land	Barren and Uncultivated Land Suitable for Forestland
Proportion (Mha)	57.0	14.70	53.93
Potential utilization ratio for energy-orientated forestry (%)	60	80	40
Potential utilization area (Mha)	34.20	11.76	21.57
Total (Mha)		67,530,000	

Commission, especially for launching the NMB (National Mission on Biodiesel) to look into Jatropha plantings throughout the country. The MoRD has prepared a detailed project report on the NMB, with the help of TERI (The Energy and Resources Institute), which is presently being examined by various ministries. As part of the demonstration project under the NMB, Jatropha plantations are planned for 0.4 million hectares of land in various states across the country with funding from the government of India, against a target of 11.19 million hectares of land required for achieving 20% biodiesel blending with diesel.

6.6.3 *Philippines*

The Department of Energy of the Philippines has been mandated under the Republic Act 7638 to coordinate, supervise, control and prepare an integrated plan for all efforts, programs, projects and activities of the government relating to energy exploration, development and utilization. The Philippines' New and Renewable Energy Program aims to accelerate the promotion and commercialization of new and renewable energy systems by pursuing large-scale use of new and renewable energy sources, enhancing energy self-sufficiency through continuous exploration, development and exploitation of indigenous sources, and encouraging greater private sector investment and participation in all energy activities (Lwin, 2003).

6.6.4 *Thailand*

Another key player in Asia's biofuel industry is Thailand. Being essentially an agricultural economy, Thailand has a fairly large biomass resource base that has been partly utilized for energy purposes. The total annual supply of biomass, including fuelwood, rice husks and bagasse, amounts to 30.2% of the total energy supply or 51.9% of the indigenous supply (Tanticharoen, 1995). Energy research and development projects have been decided and budget allocations for these projects made on an annual basis (Lwin, 2003).

6.7 SWOT Analysis

6.7.1 *Strengths*

Biofuels are a renewable energy source, unlike other natural fuels like coal and oil. Biofuels can be stored for an indefinite period of time without posing any danger to the environment. The carbon in biofuels is recently extracted from atmospheric carbon dioxide by growing plants, so burning it does not result in a net increase of carbon dioxide in the earth's atmosphere. As a result, biofuels are seen by many as a way to reduce the amount of carbon dioxide released into the atmosphere by using them to replace non-renewable sources of energy.

Advocates of using biodiesel as a fuel over conventional petrochemical fuels provide these advantages:

- Biodiesel reduces emissions carbon monoxide (CO) by approximately 50% and carbon dioxide by 78.45%.
- Biodiesel contains less aromatic hydrocarbons: benzofluoranthene (56%); benzopyrenes (71%).
- It also eliminates sulfur emissions (SO_2), because biodiesel does not include sulfur.

- It reduces by as much as 65% the emission of particulates (small particles).
- Biodiesel does produce more NOx emissions than petrodiesel, but these emissions can be reduced through the use of catalytic converters. Petrodiesel vehicles have generally not included catalytic converters because the sulfur content in that fuel destroys the devices, but biodiesel does not contain sulfur.
- It has a higher cetane rating (less knocking) than petrodiesel.
- Pure biodiesel (BD100 or B100) can be used in any petroleum diesel engine, though it is more commonly used in lower concentrations. Some areas have mandated ultra-low sulfur diesel (ULSD) petroleum, which changes the natural viscosity of the fuel because certain materials have been removed. Additives are required to make it flow properly in engines, and biodiesel is one popular alternative. Ranges as low as 2% (BD2 or B2) have been shown to restore lubricity. Also, many municipalities have started using 5% biodiesel (BD5 or B5) in snow removal equipment and other systems.
- Biodiesel is non-flammable and non-explosive (flash point 150°C for biodiesel as compared to 64°C for petrodiesel). It is also biodegradable, non-toxic, and significantly reduces toxic and other emissions when burned as a fuel.
- Biodiesel is a better solvent than petrodiesel and has been known to break down deposits of residue in fuel lines of vehicles that usually run on petroleum. Fuel filters may become clogged with particulates if a quick transition to pure biodiesel is made, but the biodiesel cleans the engine in the process.

Wastes arising from agricultural production or farm woodlots often have a dispersal cost. Therefore, their conversion from waste-to-energy has good economic and market potential, particularly in rural community applications.

The economic benefits of biofuels are not always evident when competing with sources of coal, natural gas and oil. Calculating economic benefits of either of these resources pose a barrier due to factors such as exploration costs and greenhouse emissions that are currently excluded when calculating the economic "costs" of traditional fuel sources of coal, oil and natural gases. Therefore, the environmental and social issues surrounding these fuel sources have to be fully accessed (Sims and El-Bassam, 2003). The environmental benefits of biofuels would be the fact that utilization of biomass would mitigate for greenhouse gases and substitute for industrial petrochemical and plastics. These benefits have been well-understood by the community at large. Where biomass resource is in the form of agricultural waste product or crop residue, any adverse environmental impacts from the conventional methods of treatment and disposal (such as dumping animal manures in waterways or burning stray in the field) can be avoided, at least in part, by using one of the many possible waste-to-energy conversion routes (Sims and El-Bassam, 2003).

The social benefits from modern biomass use relate to improved quality of life, lower emissions of human health-harming substances compared with fossil fuel use, and local employment opportunities (Sims and El-Bassam, 2003).

In general, renewable energy systems are more labor-intensive than fossil fuel systems, and a higher proportion of the jobs require relatively highly skilled labor. To operate and maintain bioenergy plants and provide the fuel, employment opportunities are often created, particularly in rural communities.

6.7.2 Weaknesses

Energy yields from oilseed crops grown under temperate climatic conditions tend to produce only around 1,500–2,000 liters of oil per hectare, so production costs per liter are relatively high. Such crop energy yields of 60–80 GJ/ha/yr are low compared with growing short rotation forests or starch/sugar crops on the same land which can produce 300–400 GJ/ha/yr. This, together with the poor energy ratios of some systems, led the US National Research Council to advise against any further investment (NRC, 1999).

With regards to biofuel from agricultural waste products, the supply of agricultural waste is finite. Supply of such resources could also be under threat from improved waste minimization processes. However, energy crops can be grown to supplement this limited resource.

In many biofuel industries, the equipment used is extremely expensive to replace or maintain. Therefore, it is difficult for a company to risk trying a new fuel unless the manufacturer of the engine will cover any damage that may be incurred. Manufacturer approval is thus needed and is important because it means that the engine manufacturer has tested the fuel thoroughly and has determined parameters for safe use in engines. These factors ensure that the risk associated with trying a new fuel is minimal.

The lack of ability to provide flexible distribution on demand is a current weakness. Because many company sites are located in remote areas and require fuel delivery on an "as needed" basis, many companies are concerned that a biodiesel producer would be unable to meet the necessary distribution requirements.

6.7.3 *Opportunities*

Increasing the oil yield per hectare would help to bring down the production costs per liter, which tend to be two to three times the ex-refinery diesel and petrol price. This measure would be a solution to the point raised in Section 6.7.2 about cost.

A major challenge when using biomass is for it to be produced and used in a sustainable manner in order to provide an acceptable future supply of bioenergy and biomaterials with minimal inputs of water, agrichemicals, fertilizers or fossil fuel energy. With careful design of the overall system, this might be achieved by recycling nutrients through the ash, optimizing (rather than maximizing) crop yields per hectare, linking effluent treatment with energy crop production, growing mixed species tree crops, and returning to traditional crop rotations including the use of leguminous species (Sims and El-Bassam, 2003).

Genetically modified energy crops are under investigation and may well become an acceptable means of capturing and storing solar energy for future decades. Their impact on the environment and "sustainable" production is complex and requires careful evaluation before widespread energy crop production begins. Of particular significance is the "fuel versus food" debate.

6.7.4 *Threats*

Threats facing the biofuel business come mainly from three sources and include problems in the marketplace, considerations for the environment, and social impact of biofuels on society and the environment.

With regards to marketplace problems, results to date from commercialization programs worldwide indicate that there are market opportunities for most renewable technologies. However, like any new product entering a market, these technologies must be developed to customers' requirements, proven in the commercial environment and marketed effectively.

The markets in which bioenergy technologies are trying to establish themselves are dominated by well-established technologies and influenced by the convenience of an existing supply network. There is also persistent skepticism introduced by the prospect of using any new form of energy supply. Existing public policies generally work against renewable sources of energy by heavily subsidizing conventional sources, especially in rural areas. This creates the critical problem of how the market potential of renewable energies can be realized in terms of a self-sustaining business sector.

Although biomass conversion processes are effective in the disposal of organic wastes, especially in rural areas, they also generate quantities of pollutants, turning one pollution problem to another. The environmental impact of new and renewable sources of energy will depend on the technology being used and on whether dispersed or centralized systems are adopted.

The main social constraints of biomass use are directly related to user attitudes and limitations. The social constraints include lack of information, motivation and skills; social and cultural unacceptability of the technology; low literacy levels; and labor scarcity. These factors, plus the resistance to change of many villagers, makes biofuel unpopular.

The main economic constraints on the use of biomass are associated with the relatively high capital cost of acquisition, inadequate financial incentives and lack of purchasing power on the part of potential users. The lack of after-sales service is also a serious issue in rural areas where innovative technologies for new and renewable sources of energy have been diffused. This predicament has caused many installed units to become non-operational after relatively short periods, resulting in a dwindling number of operational units in particular (Lwin, 2003).

6.8 "Freedom to Operate" Issues

Many countries of the Asia-Pacific region have no national policies to specifically promote the use of biomass energy systems, and this has inhibited its development. Even in China, India, Sri Lanka, Thailand and the Philippines where such policies have become part of the national energy policy, the implementation has not always been successful because of insufficient high-level political will, until recently.

There are many areas where further action is needed for successful biofuel market entry to be achieved. In many countries, the biggest problem is the lack of a solid political framework for the exploitation of biomass resources. Such a framework should consist of a clear vision of the role of biomass in future energy supply of a country, accompanied by commitment at high levels to the achievement of the role envisaged. In addition, there must be well-established constitutional, legal, institutional and administrative systems which will translate political will into defined targets.

In rural communities, the level of technical competence and skills required for proper use of biomass systems is usually minimal, if not absent. Training programs are needed to ensure efficient operation and maintenance of the devices without which no renewable energy diffusion program will ever succeed.

Biomass training courses to "train the trainers" have been successfully organized in China, Vietnam, Laos, Cambodia and Thailand (Lwin, 2003). However, training alone may not be adequate and has to be accompanied by the strengthening of institutional frameworks, including after-sales service and product stewardship (Chapter 9).

More accurate biofuel pricing is also needed for the optimal growth of the biofuel industry. Because most companies would base their decision to purchase biodiesel on its price, cost is a necessary factor in determining if biodiesel would be used by a company.

6.9 Growth Potential

It is commonly acknowledged that Asia is experiencing increased energy and fuel consumption as countries in the region modernize and industrialize. Since the 1990s, biofuels have gained renewed interest worldwide as a sustainable source of energy whose production may make a contribution to rural development, and consequently, to national development. As such, many countries in Asia are expected to turn to biofuels as a major substitute for petroleum-based energy in lieu of the current global shortage of fossil fuels. As this book goes to press, the price of crude oil has approached US$100 per barrel and car petroleum prices all over the world have seen double digit price increases. The economics of producing affordable sources of energy look increasingly favorable for biofuel.

Ultimately, the potential market size for biofuels may be equal to the market currently occupied by petroleum-based fuel, although experts believe this is still a long way off.

References

Dhavala, P. (2006). International experiences in biofuels. In *Biofuels: Towards a Greener and Secure Energy Future* (Ed. P.P. Bhojvaid). The Energy and Resources Institute.

Lim, K.O. and Sims, R.E.H. (2003). Liquid and gaseous biomass fuels. In *Bioenergy Options for a Cleaner Environment* (Ed. R.E.H. Sims). Elsevier Ltd.

Lucon, O. (2005). Bioethanol: Lessons from the Brazilian experience. Paper presented at the International Conference and Expo on Biofuels, New Delhi, 17–18 October 2005, organized by The Energy and Resources Institute.

Lwin, K. (2003). Policy options and strategies for market development of biomass: An Asian-Pacific perspective. In *Bioenergy Options for a Cleaner Environment* (Ed. R.E.H. Sims). Elsevier Ltd.

NRC (1999). *Automotive Fuel Economy.* Washington, DC: National Research Council Committee on Fuel Economy of Automobiles and Light Trucks, Energy Engineering Board, National Academy Press.

Pachauri, R.K. (2006). Introduction. In *Biofuels: Towards a Greener and Secure Energy Future* (Ed. P.P. Bhojvaid). The Energy and Resources Institute.

Sims, R.E.H. and El-Bassam, N. (2003). Biomass and resources. In *Bioenergy Options for a Cleaner Environment* (Ed. R.E.H. Sims). Elsevier Ltd.

Tanticharoen, M. (1995). Biomass as energy source: ASEAN perspective. Paper presented at the Asia-Pacific Renewable Energy Symposium (APRES'95), Sydney, Melbourne and Perth, Australia.

Chapter 7

Bioremediation

Large tracts of land have been contaminated with toxic chemicals such as arsenic, mercury or high levels of salts because of industrial and farming activities, making these lands uninhabitable or unsuitable for crops. Fresh water bodies have similarly been contaminated. While mechanical and chemical cures are known for removing the toxic or unwanted chemicals, governments are increasingly searching for environmentally friendly techniques to "clean up" polluted lands and waters. One such set of techniques is called "bioremediation", or the use of microbes, plants or their enzymes to remedy contaminated land and water.

Bioremediation is not a new phenomenon, but modern science has made it a potentially powerful ally by improving the efficiency of the organisms concerned, either using conventional selection or through genetic improvement. Much "upside" has yet to be exploited and can be done only through further investments in R&D. An appealing feature of bioremediation is that the contaminated soil or water may be acted upon by organisms *in situ* (i.e., without removing the soil or water from their original site).

Several types of bioremediation techniques are in use; where plants are used to clean up the environment, the technique is called "phytoremediation", comprising phytoextraction, phytodegradation, phytotransformation, phytostabilization and rhizofiltration (use of plant roots to reduce contamination in wetlands and estuaries). Phytoextraction is a popular technique and much experience has been accumulated and shared within the scientific community to use specific plants for cleaning soil contaminated with heavy metals.

The plant material is subsequently removed from the locale and incinerated.

Besides using plants for bioremediation, microorganisms can be used to accumulate pollutants in the environment. Bioremediation is not a new concept in the field of applied microbiology. Microorganisms have been used to remove organic matter and toxic chemicals from domestic and manufacturing waste effluents for many years. What is new, however, is the emergence and expansion of bioremediation as an industry. Today, bioremediation by microorganisms has become accepted as an effective, economically viable alternative for cleaning soils, surface water and groundwater contaminated with a wide range of toxic chemicals like petroleum hydrocarbons.

7.1 Product Range

The process of bioremediation dates back to the ancient times. A range of organisms, from microbes to lichens, mushrooms and higher aquatic and terrestrial plants have been used by different societies.

Microbes have always been present on the surface of the earth. What we term as simple, everyday experiences like turning rotting vegetable matter into fertilizer and fermenting wine are able to occur due to the biological action of microorganisms. The early Spaniards used microorganisms in the water to degrade the sulphate on copper sulphates to obtain copper.

About 400 plants have been reported to hyperaccumulate metals. The families dominating these members are Asteraceae, Brassicaceae, Caryophyllaceae, Cyperaceae, Cunouniaceae, Fabaceae, Flacourtiaceae, Lamiaceae, Poaceae, Violaceae and Euphobiaceae. Brassicaceae (this family includes cabbage) has the largest number of different genera known to accumulate different metals. Nickel hyperaccumulation is reported in seven genera and 72 species, and zinc accumulation in three genera and 20 species. *Thlaspi* species are known to hyperaccumulate more than one metal. Specifically, *T. caerulescence*, a species of *Thlaspi*, is known to accumulate heavy metals such as cadmium, nickel, lead and zinc. Another species of *Thlaspi*, *T. goesingense*, is known for its accumulation of nickel and zinc. *T. ochroleucum* has been known to phytoremediate nickel and zinc, while *T. rotundifolium* has been discovered to supersede the former with an additional phytoremediation ability of accumulating lead.

Several common aquatic species also have the ability to remove heavy metals from water, e.g., water hyacinth (*Eichhornia crassipes* (Mart.) Solms) and duckweed (*Lemna minor* L.). Microbes that are known to degrade pesticides and hydrocarbons generally are exemplified by species like *Pseudomonas sp.* and *Alcaligenes sp.*, which use the contaminant as a source of energy and carbon. Even mushroom fungi such as *Phanaerochate chrysosporium* have been shown capable of degrading environmental pollutants. Laboratory studies in Singapore have shown that common ferns (*Pteris vittata* and *Pityrogramma calomelanos*) are able to bioaccumulate arsenic at levels significantly higher than those found in the environment. One by-product of phytoextraction is the recovery of valuable metals from the metal-rich ash, which serves as a source of revenue, and offsets the expense of remediation, which often requires many cropping cycles to reduce metal concentrations to acceptable levels.

As a plant-based technology, the success of phytoextraction depends on proper plant selection. Plants used for phytoextraction must be fast-growing and have the ability to accumulate large quantities of environmentally important metal contaminants in their shoot or leaf tissue. Genetic variation in metal-accumulating ability is known within populations of the same plant. In Asia, there is much ongoing R&D in countries like China, Pakistan and India where large tracts of land are unusable due to chemical contamination.

There are many different types of microorganisms in the bioremediation industry today. These microorganisms have helped solve many pollution problems like oil spills and water contamination. Some examples of bioremediation are described below:

- On 24 March 1989, the Exxon Valdez spilled 11 million gallons of crude oil off the Alaskan coast. Seventy miles of polluted coast were treated with a nitrogen phosphorus fertilizer, the Inipol EAP22. The fertilizer contained a bacteria native to local land, which was able to react with the pollutants in the oil spill, leaving behind messy but harmless alphast hydrocarbons.

- In 1984, Traverse City, Michigan residents had started to complain that their well water was brownish and foamed in the glass. The city was home to a military base which utilized large amounts of aviation fuel. The pollution in the groundwater was due to aviation fuel leaks. John Wilson, a researcher from the Environmental Protection Agency (EPA) laboratory in Oklahoma, used microbes to combat the contamination. In 18 months, the water quality was restored. The aviation fuel under the military station itself was cleared up using a process called "bioventing". The science of bioventing is elaborated further in Section 7.2.4 of this chapter.

- The soil surrounding the Inger oil refinery in Louisiana was once contaminated with 200 toxic compounds. It would have cost US$25 million to move the contaminated soil to a landfill site in Texas. However, Ralph Pertier of Louisiana State University encouraged the usage of a pollutant-eating bacterium already present in the soil on a test site as an answer to the pollution problem. Upon usage of this bacterium, the site was cleaned in nine months. Bioremediation of the site cost US$10 million, considerably less than the originally planned landfill solution.

- The Clean Air Act in Europe had placed a caution on bakeries, printers, car spray painters, industrial plasma sprayers and related jobs to properly dispose of any industrial gaseous by-products or else be charged. A conventional volatile organic compound filter could cost a few million dollars, enough to put many non-compliers out of business. Therefore, it was not surprising that an alternative was invented. This involved passing industrial gas through 100-feet-long hoses filled with manure, peat moss or sawdust. The microorganisms in these substances would aid in the breaking down of any toxic gas into relatively harmless compounds.

- Microorganisms are used extensively today to clean up garbage sites where pollutants are buried under the ground. The toxic cases in these sites are vented to a separate site for clean-up before microbes are injected into the dump site to bioremediate the contaminated soils.

- Bioremediation has been used extensively in the mining industry. For example, the Homestake Mine site in South Dakota, Whitewood Creek produces mercury, arsenic and sewage as by-products of gold ore processing. Usually, cyanide effluent is used for separating gold from its ore. Bioremediation specialists had a cyanide-tolerant microbe to feed on the carbon and nitrogen in the poisonous by-products.

Radiation is commonly used to keep market produce fresh. The radiation may destroy enzymes that constitute the crop's value to health. Microbes have been engineered to keep these produce fresh by attacking and degrading rot-causing bacteria.

7.2 The Science and Technology Behind the Business

The selection of microbiological processes for treating soils and groundwater contaminated with organic pollutants requires characterization of the waste, selection of an appropriate microorganism or group of microorganisms, and information about degradation pathways and rates (Admassu and Korus, 1996). This process will be elaborated further in the following sections.

7.2.1 *Site characterization*

The main objective of site characterization is to identify the contaminants, their concentration and the extent of contamination. Before process options can be selected, site characterization must determine the key chemical, physical and microbiological properties of the site. The distribution of contaminants between the soil and groundwater will largely determine the applicability of soil excavation and treatment.

In soil bioremediation, the rate limiting step is often the desorption of contaminants, since sorption to soil particles and organic matter in soils can determine the bioavailability of organic pollutants. Determining the feasibility of *in situ* bioremediation requires extensive characterization of hydrological soil properties as well. Rates of *in situ* soil bioremediation are governed by mass transfer of contaminants (desorption and diffusion), the flux of oxygen and nutrients, and the microbiological content of the soil.

7.2.2 *Microbiological characterization*

The measurement of biodegradation rates by indigenous microorganisms is the first step in microbiological characterization. These measurements may be complicated by low microbial populations or by the absence of species capable of degrading contaminants. Also, optimum conditions of temperature, oxygen nutrient supply, and contaminant availability due to low solubility and sorption can limit degradation rates, especially in early tests where these limiting factors are not well-defined.

The main objective of microbial degradation tests is to determine whether the indigenous microorganisms are capable of bioremediation when conditions are optimized, or if inoculation by non-indigenous microorganisms will be required.

7.2.3 *Environmental factors*

Along with biodegradation tests, some attention must be given to environmental factors affecting biodegradation rate measurements. Chemical analyses that support process design include measurements of pH, nitrogen and phosphorus. Soil type, clay and organic matter content, and particle size distribution analyses as well as total suspended solids analysis is used for water bodies. Microbiological analyses supporting process design include biological oxygen demand (BOD), plate counts, and shake flask and/ or column degradation studies with indigenous microbes or introduced cultures.

Bioremediation is usually carried out near neutral pH, although fungi often require an acidic environment. Most microorganisms are mesophilic, requiring temperatures in the 25–37°C range. Oxygen and nutrient supply are more difficult to optimize than pH, though. Most bacteria capable of degrading organic compounds are heterotrophic and require an organic compound as a source of carbon and energy.

In the selection of a microbial system and bioremediation method, some examination of the degradation pathway is necessary. At a minimum, the final degradation products must be tested for toxicity and other regulatory demands for closure.

7.2.4 *Bioremediation of polluted environments*

After site and microbial characterization, suitable bioremediation techniques can be applied to reduce the amount of toxic substances in the polluted environment. Bioremediation can be applied to an environmental problem in five broad ways — aboveground bioreactors, solid phase treatment, composting, landfarming and *in situ* treatment. These five processes largely cover the variations among bioremediation procedures, though there is considerable diversity in technologies within any one area.

7.2.4.1 *Aboveground bioreactors*

Aboveground bioreactors are used to treat toxic liquids arising from industrial processes, contaminated streams or pumped groundwater. These bioreactors are also used to treat vapors (e.g., solvents vented from contaminated subsurface environments, factory air) or solids in a slurry phase (e.g., excavated soils, sludge, or sediments and plant materials). Usually, detoxifying these substances would involve a variety of methods which include suspended microorganisms and/or adsorbed biofilms, native microbial populations indigenous to the material being treated, pure microbial cultures isolated from appropriate environments or genetically engineered microorganisms designed specifically for the problem.

Several factors determine success:

- Microorganisms involved in bioremediation may or may not need oxygen and other electron acceptors (nitrate, sulphate, carbon dioxide, etc.) to operate.

- Supplying the microorganisms involved with nutrient feeds like nitrogen and phosphorus-rich substrates may not be required.
- The ratio of solid to water in the reaction mixture must be controlled for optimum reaction.
- The biodegradation rates for specific pollutants or mixture of pollutants must be taken into consideration as well as the pH, temperature and redox potential of the mixture.

7.2.4.2 *Solid phase treatment*

Soils are often treated by solid phase technologies. This usually means placing excavated soils within some type of containment system, e.g., a pit lined with leachate collection and/or volatile compound entrapment equipment before percolating water and nutrients through the pile. Oxygen may or may not be supplied, depending on the bioremedial process being encouraged. Also, inocula may or may not be added, depending on whether an indigenous microbial population can be stimulated to remove the target pollutants. To date, solid phase treatments are particularly useful for petroleum-contaminated soils. Fungal mycelia carried on materials such as wood chips have been incorporated into contaminated soils to promote biodegradation of xenobiotic contaminants, a process receiving considerable interest among bioremediation scientists (Lamar, 1990).

7.2.4.3 *Composting*

Composting is a variation of solid phase treatment that involves adding large amounts of readily degradable organic matter to a contaminated material, followed by incubations, usually aerobic, lasting several weeks or months. Adjustments of carbon:nitrogen ratios in composting systems require particular attention in order to achieve optimal results. Also, the compost piles need to be frequently turned to ensure aeration, making composting a labor-intensive treatment technology. Although this technology is a well-known means to convert waste organic matter (e.g., leaves, agricultural wastes, manures) to useful products like fertilizers, it has only recently been applied to the bioremediation of hazardous compounds.

Composting is usually carried out at temperatures of 20–30°C or 50–60°C and typically contains aerobic, microaerophilic and anaerobic microorganisms. These mixtures of microorganisms promote simultaneous growth of fungi, actinomycetes and eubacteria. As such, when these organisms work together to biodegrade harmful substances in the compost, the combined biodegradative processes in the compost system can be very complex. For example, some xenobiotic compounds are polumerized into the organic compartments of composted soils (Williams *et al.*, 1992). Xenobiotics are chemicals found in organisms but not expected to be produced or present in them; or they are chemicals found in much higher concentrations than usual. To date, composting has been used industrially for the treatment of petroleum-contaminated soils.

7.2.4.4 *Landfarming*

In landfarming, contaminated soils, sludges or sediments are spread on fields and cultivated in much the same manner as a farmer might plow and fertilize agricultural land. This method of bioremediation has been used most commonly as an inexpensive and effective process for the treatment of petroleum-contaminated materials. Though simple in design, landfarming must be performed carefully to avoid creating a possibly more serious waste contamination problem.

As an environmental precaution, landfarming should only be used for readily biodegradable chemicals. Also, proper precautionary measures are needed to prevent toxic chemicals from leaking into groundwater. Most regulatory agencies require that groundwater be deep below a landfarming site, or that there be some type of confining layer made out of substances like natural clays or reinforced liner between the cultivated material and subsurface water.

The moisture content as well as nitrogen and phosphorus fertilization in a landfarm site must be monitored closely in order to ensure safe and efficient bioremediation. Figure 7.1 shows a diagrammatic representation of the technique of landfarming.

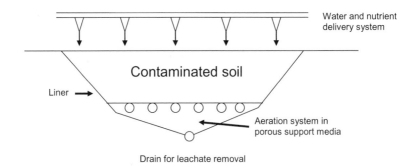

Figure 7.1.   Landfarming of contaminated soil.
Source: Adapted from Admassu and Korus (1996).

7.2.4.5 *In situ bioremediation*

In situ bioremediation is currently receiving a lot of research attention. This technique has been very expensive when it comes to treating vast amounts of contaminated vadose-zone soils, or when it involves prolonged treatment for large aquifers. As such, research aims to reduce such costs and potentially solve problems that are not approachable by off-the-shelf technologies.

Most *in situ* processes involve the stimulation of indigenous microbial populations so that they become metabolically active and degrade the contaminants of concern. An example of *in situ* bioremediation involved the treatment of aquifers contaminated by petroleum hydrocarbons in the mid-1970s (Raymond, 1974). Free products floating off the aquifer surface were first removed by pumping. Nutrients (primarily nitrogen and phosphorus) were then injected and electron acceptors (oxygen and nitrate) were supplied either by sparging wells with air or through the addition of solution of hydrogen peroxide or nitrate salts.

A process known as "bioventing" has become increasingly attractive for promoting *in situ* biodegradation of readily biodegradable pollutants like petroleum hydrocarbons. Bioventing was pioneered by Robert Hincher of Battelle Memorial Institute of Columbus, Ohio. This process involves the forced movement of oxygen through the vadose zone of contaminated sites (Hinchee, 1994). When oxygen is provided as a terminal electron acceptor, indigenous microorganisms multiply at the expense of the carbon present in the contaminating material. The goal is to provide sufficient oxygen to allow degradation of the pollutants to proceed to completion, without vaporizing contaminants to the surface. Air may be forced through the vadose zone either by injection through sparging wells or by vacuum extraction through appropriately located infiltration and withdrawal wells.

In soils that are impermeable (e.g., clay-rich soils), bioventing may not be possible since air cannot be moved through these soils at sufficient rates to supply microbial populations the electron acceptors required to power the processes required for them to bioremediate the soils. Sometimes, such soils can be "opened" by fracturing with pressurized air or water, improving permeability for air transport.

In theory, bioventing should work for both volatile and non-volatile contaminants and petroleum or non-petroleum compounds, as long as the contaminants are inherently biodegradable and an indigenous degrader population of microbes exists in the zone of contamination. Bioventing is expected to be one of the most popular bioremediation techniques in the future. Figure 7.2 shows a diagram of the process of bioventing.

7.2.5 *Phytoextraction of metals — Bioremediation using plants*

Excessive toxic metal levels in soils pose significant hazards to human and animal health. Anthropogenic sources of heavy metal deposition have increased as a result of the Industrial Revolution. Agriculture, mining, smelting, electroplating and other industrial activities have resulted in the deposition of toxic metals such as As, Cs, Cr, Cu, Ni, Pb and Zn in soil. Although trace metals are an important part of the soil ecosystem, the accumulation of these metals may be harmful to people, animals, plants and other organisms in direct or indirect contact with the contaminated soil and water.

Soil clean-up criteria are important considerations in determining if phytoremediation techniques would be successful. To date, three

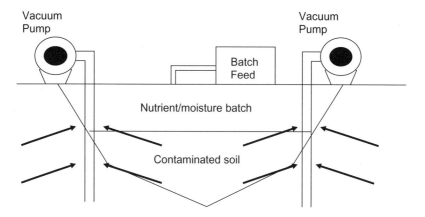

Figure 7.2.   Schematic showing bioventing — Oxygen in the air is used as an electron carrier for microorganisms which are involved in bioremediation.

Source: Adapted from Crawford (1996).

Note: Black arrows indicate the direction of air flow.

main factors influence or determine the ability of phytoextraction to effectively remediate a contaminated site: (1) selection of a site conducive to phytoextraction, (2) metal solubility and availability for uptake, and (3) the ability of the plant to accumulate metals in the harvestable plant tissue to ensure sustainable phytoremediation.

The success of using plants to extract metals from contaminated soils requires a better understanding of the mechanisms of metal uptake, translocation and accumulation by plants. The efficiency of metal phytoextraction is a function of a number of factors. The major factors are plant species, metal availability to plant roots, metal uptake by roots, metal translocation from roots to shoots, and plant tolerance to toxic metals.

Plant species vary significantly in their ability to accumulate metals from contaminated soils. There are a small number of plant species endemic to metalliferous soils that can tolerate and accumulate high levels of toxic metals. These plants, termed metal hyperaccumulators, can accumulate more than 0.1% of Pb, Co, Cr, or more than 1% of Mn, Ni, Zn in plant shoots when growing in their natural habitats (Baker and Brooks, 1989).

The phytoextraction process utilizes the roots of the plants to absorb, translocate and concentrate toxic metals from the soil to the aboveground harvestable plant tissues. The concentration process results in a reduction of contaminated mass and also a transfer of the metal from an aluminosilicate-based mix (soil) to a carbon-based matrix (plants).

The carbon in the plant material can be oxidized to carbon dioxide, further decreasing (and concentrating) the mass of material to be treated, disposed of or recycled. The phytoextraction process is dependent on the metal being translocated to harvestable plant parts after being accumulated in the roots. The harvestable parts are generally regarded as aboveground plant biomass, although roots of some crops may be harvestable.

Usually, soil amendments are required for plants to successfully uptake heavy metals. Plants grown on heavy metal-contaminated soils generally do not accumulate high levels of the targeted metals in the plant tissue, with the exception of certain metal hyperaccumulators such as Zn or Ni hyperaccumulators.

Two major limitations to the phytoextraction of heavy metals are the low metal bioavailability in the soil and the poor metal translocation from roots to shoots. A key to the success of metal phytoremediation is thus to increase and maintain metal concentrations in the soil solution. Chelates and other chemical compounds have been used to increase the solubility of metals in plant growth media, and could significantly increase metal accumulation in plants.

7.3 How is Value Created and Captured?

The development of bioremediation technology requires a combination of basic laboratory research to identify and characterize promising biological processes, pilot-scale development and testing of new bioremediation technologies, their acceptance by regulators and the public, and ultimately, field preparation of these processes to confirm that they are effective, safe and predictable (Crawford, 1996). Value creation is done by assuming intellectual property of the processes and the biological organisms needed for such processes. Novel organisms may well be the target of R&D, especially through new genetic engineering techniques.

7.4 Current Market Size

According to Porta *et al.* (1994), Western European nations spend a total of about $6.5 billion annually on bioremediation, with the greatest expenditures by Germany ($3–$6 billion per year). Total bioremediation estimates for Western Europe could range as high as more than $250 billion.

An estimated current market size of plant bioremediation according to Glass (2000) is shown in Table 7.1.

The USA market for remediation of metals from groundwater may be as high as $2 billion per year. Much of this results from common industrial sources, but much of the metal-contaminated groundwater arises from acid mine drainage and acid rock drainage. In the USA, it has been estimated that $1 million is spent per day to clean up 19,300 km of rivers and 73,000 ha of lakes. The total cost of phytoremediating acid mine drainage is estimated to be about $70 million.

Table 7.1.   Cost estimates of phytoremediation in US$.

Cost	Soils
$1–$10/m³	($2,500–$15,000/ha; S. Cunningham, DuPont)
$15–$20/ton	(E. Drake, Exxon)
$25–$50/ton	(Phytotech)
$29–$48/m³	($60,000–$100,000/acre at depth of 50 cm; Salt *et al.*)
$80/yd³	(R. Levine, DOE)
$100–$150/m³	($200,000–$300,000/acre, R. Chaney, USDA)
	Water
$0.64 per 1,000 gal treated	(V. medina, EPA)
$2,000–$6,000 per 1,000 gal treated	(Phytotech)

Source: Glass (2000).

7.5 Who and Where are the Players in the Bioremediation Business?

Despite the promise and growth of the bioremediation industry, there were less than 20 technical bioremediation companies in the United States in 1994 (Howard and Fox, 1994). The US bioremediation industry was fuelled by the identification of contaminated "Superfund" sites. Three-quarters of Europe's bioremediation companies are equipment suppliers.

There is a great need for bioremediation in Asia, especially for fouled waterways. So far, the biggest player in the bioremediation industry in Asia is Japan. Japan is actively pursuing R&D in bioremediation, focusing on air quality through removal of sulphur from emissions, and on removal of CO_2 from air and incorporating the carbon into polymers or other potentially useful products (Atlas, 1995).

Bioremediation companies can be divided into two categories: companies are either dedicated, having entered the industry to exploit specific biotechnologies; or they are established companies which have long been present in the market and in recent years, have incorporated new biotechnological developments into their traditional activities.

Dedicated companies are typically spin-outs from universities or large companies. They usually specialize in certain products and services like microbial inoculants, nutrient supplies or bioreactor design. Technologies developed by dedicated companies are licensed out to other users. Should these companies face any difficulties, it is likely to be financial constraints. They also usually need a large company for distribution of products.

Established diversified companies, on the other hand, are vertically integrated and engineering-driven rather than bioscience-driven. These type of companies usually contract out licenses in innovative technologies and are characterized by strong distribution, marketing and regulatory functions.

Some examples of dedicated and established bioremediation companies are listed in Table 7.2.

Table 7.2. Some selected examples of established and dedicated companies in the bioremediation sector worldwide.

USA	Europe	Other Countries
Established diversified companies	*Established diversified companies*	*Established diversified companies*
1 Batelle	1 Shell Research (UK, Netherlands)	1 Grace Dearbourn (Canada)
2 Du Point Environmental	2 AMEC (UK)	2 Broken Hill (Australia)
3 Fluor Daniel	3 Solvay (Belgium)	3 Mitsubishi Petrochem (Japan)
4 Groundwater Technology Inc.	4 Elf Aquitaine (France)	4 Obayashi Corp. (Japan)
Dedicated companies	*Dedicated companies*	*Dedicated companies*
1 Bio-recovery Systems Inc.	1 Viridian Bioprocessing (UK)	1 CRA (Australia)
2 Detox Industries	2 Ebiox (Switzerland)	2 Griffin Remediation (Canada)
3 Oil Spill Eater International	3 Biodetox (Germany)	3 Biocentras (Lithuania)

Source: Shohet (1998).

7.6 SWOT Analysis

7.6.1 *Strengths*

Bioremediation techniques enable companies and governments alike to save much on pollution control costs. Levin and Gealt (1993) estimated the costs of biotreatment of biodegradable contaminants in soils to range between $53 and $130 per cubic m, as compared with costs as high as $327–$1,046 per cubic m for incineration and $196–$327 per cubic m for landfilling.

Phytoremediation (i.e., bioremediation using plants) is proposed to be a cost-effective alternative for the treatment of contaminated soil. The most widely utilized alternative to phytoremediation is excavation and disposal of hazardous soil. A direct comparison of the costs associated with landfill-excavation and phytoremediation reveals the outstanding economic advantage of phytoremediation. While the cost estimate of remediation of a site contaminated with lead using the conventional excavation-landfill approach is approximately US$150–$350 per ton, the cost of phytoremediating the same site is estimated to be US$20–$80 per ton (Ensley, 2000).

Using bioremediation to treat contaminated soils is advantageous due to its low capital intensity, low energy usage and minimal site disruption. The complete degradation of some toxic substances in the soil to harmless products is also possible.

Bioremediation of solid waste allows selective concentration and removal. Furthermore, the operating and investment costs in bioremediating solid waste are only moderate. Solid waste which has undergone bioremediation also has the potential to be recycled, adding value to the material.

A further benefit of bioremediation is its application to polluted water bodies. Biosorption of toxic chemicals in water bodies can take place at low concentrations. Also, heavy metals in the waters can be easily recycled.

7.6.2 *Weaknesses*

In situ bioremediation may be expensive at this stage with regards to the treatment of large amounts of toxic waste. In the bioremediation of aquifers contaminated by petroleum hydrocarbons (see Section 7.2.4.5), problems encountered during *in situ* stimulation of microbial populations include the plugging of wells and subsurface formations by the tremendous amounts of biomass that may be generated through microbial growth on hydrocarbons. Also, there were difficulties in supplying sufficient oxygen to the subsurface, and the inability to move nutrients and electron acceptors to all regions of heterogeneous subsurface environments. It is impossible at this stage to remove all free products, so reservoirs of slowly released contamination may be present for many years at a site in some situations.

Despite the many pros of bioremediation, cons regarding this technology still exist as it is nowhere near being fully developed.

Bioremediation may not be suitable for use on contaminated soil if the soil contains complex mixtures of chemicals. Also, the pollution clean-up performance of microorganisms may not be constant and rate of clean-up is dependent on external factors such as pH and ground temperature.

Bioremediation of solid waste also poses a problem to certain microorganisms which give unnaturally low reaction rates during treatment. Some wastes are also resistant to microbial degradation.

In terms of phytoremediation, there is a need to recover and recycle metals from the plant biomass once they have been accumulated in various parts of the plant. However, the need to harvest the biomass, and in some cases to dispose of it as hazardous waste, creates an added cost that can be a potential drawback to the technology.

Phytoremediation can also be a much slower way of reducing the amount of pollutants in the environment compared to other conventional methods like landfilling and excavation. Plants are also seasonally dependent and require specific ranges of temperature, sunlight, salinity and other conditions to function optimally. Other disadvantages are the slow growth of natural hyperaccumulators, the limitation of phytoremediation to the upper soil layers and the potentially limited applicability of phytoremediation to mixed wastes.

7.6.3 Opportunities

In the rapidly modernizing world of the 21st century, the global community faces an increasing demand for power from fossil fuel sources. Unfortunately, this would lead to an increase in the amount of "dirty" coal deposits in the environment.

Asia has seen some of the fastest increases in demand for fossil-fuel generated power. The Indonesian national electric utility plans to more than double its 10-gigawatt generating capacity by the early 21st century. Since 1980, Indonesia has aimed to reduce its dependence on oil, moving instead to coal, hydro and geothermal reserves for power generation. In 1995, the country's power-generating capacity comprised 20% diesel, 20% hydro, 25% gas turbine, about 35% steam turbine and a small percentage of geothermal energy.

By 2019, these percentages are expected to be 50% or greater of coal, 40% oil and gas and 6% nuclear.

Coal deposits around the world have been deemed environmentally hazardous because of their high sulphur content. As power plants seek lower-cost approaches to meet the 1990 Clean Air Act Amendment's sulphur emission control requirements, the bioremediation of sulphur from coal deposits has become increasingly relevant in the USA.

In 1993, a patent was secured on a microorganism that could break down dibenzothiothene (DBT) in coal. When untreated, DBT combines with hydrocarbons in the fuel-producing process to form sulphur dioxide when fired. However, with bioremediation, about 90% elimination of DBT was achievable. Therefore, bioremediation effectively enabled industries to eliminate the need to deal with polluting emissions. Also, the United Nations Environmental Program (UNEP) has called on governments to support "ecologically appropriate technologies" to protect the environment.

7.6.4 *Threats*

Bioremediation must compete economically and functionally with alternate remediation technologies, which are often incineration and chemical treatments. Bioremediation usually competes well on a cost basis, especially with petroleum products and many solvents. A drawback, however, is the large amount of preliminary information necessary to support process design. When information on waste characteristics, microbial physiology and the complex options for process design and operation are lacking, bioremediation can be more difficult to apply than alternate technologies.

7.7 "Freedom to Operate" Issues

There are many factors which influence the market entry and diffusion of products in the bioremediation sector. However, in general, there is scant economic analysis of this specialized area, and it is necessary to draw on the wider literature concerning environmental technologies and biotechnology, while making references to bioremediation where appropriate (Shohet, 1998).

When considering whether to implement phytoremediation techniques, several regulation and evaluation steps need to be put in place. According to the USA's Environment Protection Agency (EPA), the evaluation criteria which determines if phytoremediation is the choice of pollution clean-up consists of:

(1) Overall protection of human health and the environment;
(2) Compliance with applicable or relevant and appropriate requirements;
(3) Long-term effectiveness and permanence;
(4) Reduction of contaminant toxicity, mobility or volume through treatment;
(5) Short-term effectiveness;
(6) Implementability;
(7) Cost;
(8) State acceptance; and
(9) Community acceptance.

Many of these criteria are equally applicable in other world regions.

7.8 Growth Potential

To date, only a minute fraction (approximately less than 1%) of naturally occurring bacteria have been cultured on media. As such, there is great potential for the development of new techniques to identify, maintain and utilize the earth's massive numbers of microbial species. Researchers are currently searching soils, hot vents and springs to find potentially useful or unidentified microbial species.

The potential for the bioremediation industry to expand is enormous. Furthermore, governmental and intergovernmental agencies are likely to support this ecologically friendly research. The US National Science Foundation, along with the US EPA, published a request for proposals for projects aimed at stimulating "green" process chemistry and materials manufacturing in order to minimize or prevent the generation of wastes.

One of the first steps in determining the size of the market is the promulgation of legislation recognizing the problem and establishing a mechanism to report, classify and remediate it. Although this has been done in America and Western Europe, areas such as the developing regions of Asia have been slower to do this. Nonetheless, the international market for bioremediation is growing at a rapid pace and is expected to continue to expand in the foreseeable future.

In America, recent reports predict that cleaning up of underground storage tank sites will yield about US$375 million per year at the start of the 21st century (Howard and Fox, 1994). Hazardous site clean-up is projected to increase from US$100 million in 1995 to nearly US$200 million by the start of the 21st century in the United States alone (Kreeger, 1995).

OECD members (Australia, Austria, Belgium, Canada, Denmark, Finland, France, Germany, Greece, Iceland, Ireland, Italy, Japan, Luxembourg, Mexico, the Netherlands, New Zealand, Norway, Portugal, Spain, Sweden, Switzerland, Turkey, the UK and the US) are projected to spend $300 billion on bioremediation, for which as much as $160 billion would go to solid waste treatment by the early 21st century.

Growth potential of phytoremediation of metals from soil and groundwater has been predicted to be great. According to Glass (2000), the estimates of the total market sizes were about $0.8–$1.0 billion per year for soil, and $1.6–$2.0 billion per year for water.

Phytoremediation is a very promising technology for the remediation of metals from the soil as there are currently very few viable alternatives and those that are used tend to be very expensive. Some examples of alternatives include soil washing ($75–$200 per ton), incineration ($200–$1,500 per ton) and landfilling ($100–$150 per ton), compared to $25–$100 per ton for phytoremediation.

Phytoremediation is also attractive for metal remediation for other reasons besides cost. It can be used at sites where excavation is not practical or possible. The ability to conduct sustainable remediation through collecting and properly disposing of plant parts used in phytoremediation offers opportunities for expanded use.

Phytoremediation of metals from soils has been successfully demonstrated in the field, and is being aggressively promoted. According to Glass (2000), the estimated market in 1997 was low (US$1–$2 million per year), but the potential for growth is great because of the advantages of phytoremediation and because revenue per site is likely to be substantial (i.e., a few successful jobs can lead to a substantial increase in the overall market size). The estimated market growth from 1997 was about $15–$25 million by 2000, and later, up to $10–$100 million in the next 10 years.

Phytoremediation of metals in groundwater has been estimated by Glass (2000) to be about US$1–$3 million in the next 10 years.

Bioremediation is indeed a promising environmental clean-up technology with many benefits. This low-energy technology generates few secondary wastes with potentially lower operating costs of more than 20% when compared to conventional chemical and physical methods of removing pollutants from the environment. In a future of soaring energy costs, the comparative advantage of bioremediation is likely to become stronger.

References

Admassu, W. and Korus, R.A. (1996). Engineering of bioremediation processes: Needs and limitations. In *Bioremediation: Principles and Applications* (Eds. R.L. Crawford and D.L. Crawford). Cambridge University Press.

Atlas, R. (1995). Bioremediation. *Chemical and Engineering News,* 73: 32–42.

Baker, A.J.M. and Brooks, R.R. (1989). Terrestrial higher plants which hyperaccumulate metallic elements — A review of their distribution, ecology and phytochemistry. *Biorecovery,* 1: 81–126.

Crawford, R.L. (1996). Introduction. In *Bioremediation: Principles and Applications* (Eds. R.L. Crawford and D.L. Crawford). Cambridge University Press.

Ensley, B.D. (2000). Rationale for use of phytoremediation. In *Phytoremediation of Toxic Metals: Using Plants to Clean Up the Environment* (Eds. I. Raskin and B.D. Ensley). John Wiley & Sons, Inc.

Glass, D.J. (2000). Rationale for use of phytoremediation. In *Phytoremediation of Toxic Metals: Using Plants to Clean Up the Environment* (Eds. I. Raskin and B.D. Ensley). John Wiley & Sons, Inc.

Hinchee, R. (ed.) (1994). *Air Sparging for Site Remediation.* Boca Raton, FL: Lewis Publishers.

Howard, J. and Fox, E. (1994). Review of current research projects and innovations in bioremediation. *Genetic Engineering News,* 1 October.

Kreeger, K.Y. (1995). Growing bioremediation industry presents a potential boom in jobs for life scientists. *The Scientist,* 9(2): 1, 8–9.

Lamar, R.T. (1990). *In situ* depletion of pentachlorophenol degradation by *Flavobacterium* sp. strain ATCC 39723. Ph.D. Dissertation, University of Idaho.

Levin, M.A. and Gealt, M.A. (1993). *Biotreatment of Industrial and Hazardous Waste.* New York: McGraw-Hill.

Porta, A., Young, J.K. and Molton, P.M. (1994). *In situ* bioremediation in Europe. In *Applied Biotechnology for Site Remediation* (Eds. R.E. Hinchee, D.B. Anderson, F.B. Metting, Jr. and G.D. Sayles), pp. 1–20. Boca Raton, FL: Lewis Publishers.

Raymond, R. (1974). *Reclamation of Hydrocarbon Contamination Waters.* US patent 3 846 290.

Shohet, S. (1998). Bioremediation: An economic perspective. In *Environmental Biomonitoring: The Biotechnology Ecotoxicology Interface* (Eds. J.M. Lynch and A. Wiseman). Cambridge University Press.

Williams, R.T., Ziegenfuss, P.S. and Sisk, W.E. (1992). Composting of explosives and propellant-contaminated soils under thermophilic and mesophilic conditions. *Journal of Industrial Microbiology,* 9: 137–144.

Chapter 8

Biodetection — Diagnosing Plant Diseases and Detecting Genetically Modified Food

Plant diseases cause major crop losses, estimated to average 10%–20% of potential production each year before crop harvest. Early detection of the disease agents (bacteria, fungi and/or viruses), coupled with correct diagnosis, can help to reduce these potential losses with appropriate action.

Several countries, notably those in the European Union, have required that food containing ingredients made from biotech crops be labeled so that consumers can have informed choice. Detection of the genetically modified (GM) ingredients is now a multi-million-dollar business. GM food is produced from biotech crops (Chapter 9). The global area of biotech crops has grown to more than 114 million hectares in 2007, from the first commercial plantings in 1996. Worldwide, 674 products have been approved by 53 countries for public use. These products in turn generate secondary items used in food preparation; for example, GM corn kernels have several hundred secondary processed items ranging from molasses to ethanol.

The development of diagnostic kits for plant diseases and detection kits for genetically modified food (GMO) has been considered a subset of the field of molecular biology. Molecular biology is the study of biology at a molecular level. This specialized area of study straddles the gap between biology and chemistry, especially genetics and biochemistry. A large bulk of molecular biology concerns itself with the understanding of interactions between the various systems of a cell (e.g., the interrelationship of DNA, RNA and protein synthesis and the study of how these interactions are regulated). Applied molecular biology is a term which is used to describe molecular biology used for industrial purposes.

8.1 Diagnostic Kits for Plant Pathogens

Diagnosing plant diseases is of high importance, as accurate identification and early detection of pathogens is essential to disease management in many crops. Many plant pathogens are difficult to identify using visible morphological criteria, which can be time-consuming and challenging.

Furthermore, identifying infected plants by morphological criteria requires extensive knowledge in taxonomy. Molecular detection techniques can generate accurate results rapidly enough to be useful for disease management decisions.

The proper control of plant diseases has been very essential in the production of crops for commercial purposes. In Asia, crop losses caused by diseases have been estimated to run in millions of tons of the major grains annually.

The era of modern diagnostic technology in plant disease management began in 1976, with the first application of the Enzyme-Linked ImmunoSorbent Assay (ELISA) technique to detect plant viruses.

This was soon followed by the highly specific monoclonal antibodies (MAbs) to detect most classes of plant pathogenic microorganisms. Combining the speed and sensitivity of ELISA with the specificity of MAbs, the rapid and accurate diagnosis of plant diseases and detection of pathogens in a variety of substrates was made possible.

During the mid-1980s, it became possible to detect plant pathogens in a very short time (i.e., 10 minutes). The molecular kits which enabled such quick detection could usually perform molecular diagnosis in a few simple steps. They could also be used by people who did not have prior specialized training in molecular diagnosis techniques.

A decade later, development of more advanced technology resulted in assays that could be completed ten times faster. These assays were targeted at the detection of plant pathogenic fungi, including species of *Phytophthora*, *Pythium*, *Rhizoctonia* and *Septoria*, as a diagnostic method and for decision making. Information provided by the kits was used to select the appropriate fungicide and also to indicate the appropriate time of application.

The use of such kits contributed to reducing the environmental impact of fungicides and is an important component of modern-day precision agriculture. However, the cost of developing such tests has been relatively high, making them available for only a relatively small number of applications in the developed countries, whereas most of the potential beneficiaries are in the developing countries with the most plant disease problems in their agricultures.

Diagnostics technology for plant pathogens uses chemicals, antibodies or enzymes to detect certain DNA/RNA chain sequences in bacteria, fungi and other plant pathogens. Practical use of nucleic acid-based detection technologies in plant pathology was limited until the introduction of the polymerase chain reaction (PCR) assay in the late 1980s.

8.1.1 *The science and technology behind biodetection of plant pathogens*

The first and most important step in managing a plant disease is to correctly identify it. Although some diseases can be diagnosed quickly by visual examination, others require laboratory testing for diagnosis. To facilitate the detection and identification of plant pathogens, a variety of diagnostic kits have been created (Flynn, 1993). The more common ones are described in the sections below.

8.1.1.1 *ELISA diagnostic kits*

The ELISA (Enzyme-Linked ImmunoSorbent Assay) kits use proteins called antibodies to detect plant pathogens. The assay is based on the ability of the antibody to recognize and bind to a specific antigen.

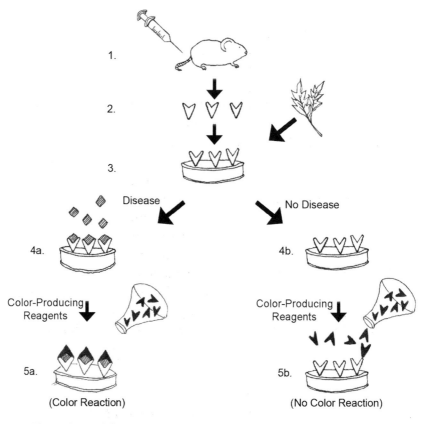

Figure 8.1.   Schematic to show the workings of an ELISA detection kit.
Source: Flynn (1993).

The antigen is often associated with a plant pathogen. A diagrammatic process of how the ELISA detection kit works is illustrated in Figure 8.1.

The antibodies used in the ELISA diagnostic kits are highly purified proteins produced by injecting a warm-blooded animal (e.g., a rat) with an antigen associated with a particular plant disease (**1**). The animal reacts to the antigen and produces the related antibodies required to combat the antigen (**2**). The antibodies produced recognize and react only with the proteins associated with the pathogen which causes the plant disease.

These antibodies are bound to a plastic plate or a similar detector unit in the ELISA test kit. The individual running the test prepares the plant sample to be tested by grinding it finely. The ground sample is then placed in a bottle filled with extraction liquid to extract substances in the sample to be analyzed.

The mixture of the extraction liquid and the sample are then poured into the wells in the plastic plate containing the bound antibodies (3). If the disease-causing pathogen is present in the sample, the specific antibodies in the plastic plate will bind to the proteins associated with the pathogen and adhere to the unit (4a).

A second antibody which also reacts with the proteins associated with the pathogen is added to the mixture. This antibody should be able to react with color-producing chemicals called reagents (5a).

Color changes on the unit's surface indicate a positive (disease present) reaction. If no pathogen-associated proteins are present (4b), the detector antibodies cannot bind to the color-carrying reagents and are washed away (5b).

ELISA kits are used mainly in the laboratory, although field kits have been developed. ELISA kits can detect the pathogens in diseases such as rice blast, bacterial canker of tomato, soybean root rot and bacteria blight of geranium.

8.1.1.2 *Direct tissue blotting*

Direct tissue blotting uses specific antibodies as a detection tool. Different plant tissues from the host plant are selected and pressed on special paper (Figure 8.2). Once the antibodies are added to the tissue sample, those tissue samples which contain the plant pathogen would bind to the antibody. Upon addition of color-producing reagents, the antibody-pathogen complex would show a distinctive color change. With this technique, the location of a disease-causing pathogen within the host plant can be determined, allowing earlier detection and a better understanding of how a disease progresses through a plant.

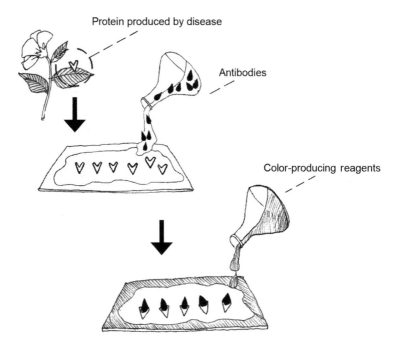

Plant tissue is pressed on a special paper. Diseased tissue binds antibodies, producing a color change when other chemicals are added.

Figure 8.2.   Procedure for direct tissue blotting.

Source: Flynn (1993).

8.1.1.3 *Nucleic acid probes and hybridization testing*

Another set of tools that can be used in plant disease diagnostics is nucleic acid probes. These probes are fragments of nucleic acid arranged in a sequence complementary to that of the deoxyribonucleic acid (DNA) or ribonucleic acid (RNA) of the disease-causing pathogen. Because the sequences complement each other, the probes can be used to identify specific diseases.

Hybridization testing is a method used to detect certain types of plant viruses. Usually, antibodies can be used to detect viruses because each virus has a unique protein coat that an antibody will stick to. However, the viroid group of pathogens has no protein, but a circular piece of RNA. To detect viroids, a hybridization test to detect the RNA is utilized. RNA "hybridizes" when two single strands come together like a zipper to form a double strand. To detect viroid RNA, a labeled piece of RNA called a probe is used to form a "hybrid" with the RNA from the sample.

RNA from plant samples are first extracted and attached to a membrane. The RNA probe is labeled with a chemical called "DIG" and applied to the RNA sample on the membrane. If a viroid is present, the probe hybridizes with it. If not, the probe is lost when the membrane is washed. The membrane is treated with a process which gives off light if DIG is present. Usually, film is exposed to the membrane to detect the light emitted. A spot on the film means that the viroid is present. Companies like Agdia Inc. (www.agdia.com) have used this approach in some of their products.

Chrysanthemum chlorotic mottle disease is caused by the chrysanthemum chlorotic mottle viroid (CChMVd). Just like any viroid, CChMVd consists of a small, closed circular RNA (398 to 399 nucleotides), and lacks the ability to code for proteins. Despite its simplicity, CChMVd is capable of replicating and causing disease in a suitable plant host.

Chrysanthemum chlorotic mottle disease has been reported in chrysanthemums in the USA, Denmark, France and India. Infected plants may have leaves showing mild to acute mottling, which may eventually develop into complete chlorosis on the leaves. Dwarfing of leaves and flowers and stunting of the whole plant may also be observed.

Nucleic acid hybridization is an important method in detecting CChMVd. The Agdia™ hybridization test involves the extraction and enrichment of RNA from infected plants and the use of a probe that is specific to CChMVd RNA. When samples are prepared as recommended, the test is highly specific and highly sensitive (Dimock *et al.*, 1971; Navarro and Flores, 1997).

8.1.1.4 *Squash blot method*

The technology involved in the nucleic acid probe squash blot method is similar to direct tissue blotting (see Figure 8.3). Tissue

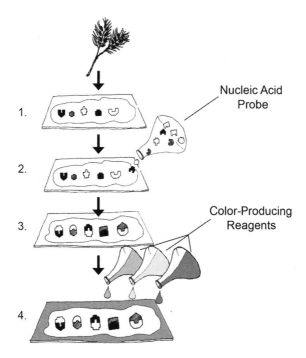

Figure 8.3.   Procedure for nucleic acid probe squash blot method.
Source: Flynn (1993).

from a plant that is suspected to be diseased is "squashed" onto a special piece of paper, called a membrane (**1**). This membrane is then treated with a probe (**2**) that can bind or hybridize with nucleic acid of the plant pathogen suspected to be in the plant tissue.

Hybridization or binding will occur when like sequences are present (**3**). After adding several more substances to the membrane, a color reaction (**4**) indicates that the probe and pathogen nucleic acid sequences have hybridized and the disease is present. No color reaction means the test for the disease is negative.

8.1.1.5 *Polymerase chain reaction (PCR)*

PCR has great potential for raising the sensitivity of various assays that use nucleic acid probes. PCR is used to produce enormous numbers of copies of a specified nucleic acid sequence. This technique could thus allow the detection of very small amounts of a pathogen in a sample by amplifying the pathogen sequences to a detectable level (Flynn, 1993). PCR tests are mainly used for detecting groups of plant viruses rather than for a specific type of virus. For example, different PCR kits are able to detect different groups of plant viruses like the *carlavirus* group, the *carmovirus* group and the *llavirus* group.

8.1.2 SWOT analysis

8.1.2.1 Strengths

Diagnostic kits are very versatile, some of which may be used by people without much laboratory training or background. The use of these kits to detect disease-causing organisms in plants is especially useful in crop disease management, enabling growers around the world to save millions of dollars annually by reducing disease-related crop losses.

Usually, diagnostic kits have a very long shelf life and can be stored without refrigeration or special storage. These kits also enable early detection of plant pathogens so that appropriate measures can be taken. Some of the kits in the market are able to detect a range of plant pathogens at one testing, saving growers time and money in the detection of plant diseases.

Other diagnostic kits are, however, highly specific, and are of use in laboratory analysis for the study of plant-pathogen interactions. Highly specific diagnostic kits are also used after general detection kits in the field to determine the exact pathogen infecting the plant and the subsequent steps which are required for the effective elimination of the pathogen.

A variety of modern biotechnology methods have been employed in the diagnosis of plant pathogens. Some of these methods include the polymerase chain reaction (PCR) and the formation of antibody-pathogen complexes. Using PCR primers for the detection of plant virus groups has many advantages: for one, the test allows for the detection of members and their strains within a virus group in a single test. As such, the test is easily carried out and saves on a lot of time, expertise and effort. The PCR test also allows for the detection of plant viruses for which commercial antisera is not available, and is able to detect very trace amounts of viruses, which typically go undetected by other methods. PCR is used commonly to confirm the test results of other tests and for the detection of uncharacterized viruses and demonstration that they belong to a specific group.

ELISA technology is routinely used in home pregnancy tests, blood tests for AIDS and hepatitis, and sampling for pesticide residues. Some ELISA test kits can give very reliable results in a matter of minutes to a few hours. Besides diagnosing the cause of poor plant health, on-site test kits are useful for regular monitoring for viruses in symptom-free plants of susceptible crops. In particular, regular testing is carried out for "mother plant stocks" and areas where cuttings or other new plants are received or shipped out for propagation.

Routine testing can be especially useful when plants are young; most crops are more severely affected by pathogens if plants are infected during early growth (Kabashima *et al.*, 2002). Some tissue culture companies (see Chapter 3 of this book) use ELISA to produce pathogen-tested disease-free seed material.

On the whole, the direct tissue blotting and the squash bolt method are general tests in the diagnosis of plant pathogens. However, an advantage is that the tests are easy to use and can be used on-site. Cost is saved as samples need not be sent to a laboratory for analysis. Also, the test can pinpoint exactly which part of the plant the pathogen is affecting, making it very useful in research studying plant-pathogen interactions.

The nucleic acid hybridization method is advantageous as it is highly specific, involving DNA strands which "detect" specific DNA strands in a pathogen. As such, although this test may be more expensive, it is highly accurate owing to the more sophisticated materials and method used.

8.1.2.2 *Weaknesses*

A major weakness in applying the technology is that most farmers and growers in Asia are small-scale and have found these kits relatively expensive as regular tools. Identifying plant diseases in the field may not always be straightforward. In the case where simple observation is unable to determine if the plant is infected with a given type of plant pathogen, laboratory tests are required to test for the presence plant pathogens.

Some diagnostic kits may take days or even weeks to complete and are, in some cases, relatively insensitive. Delays are frustrating when a quick diagnosis is needed so that appropriate disease control measures may be taken to prevent plant injury, especially when high-value cash crops, turf grass or ornamentals are at stake. Certain types of diagnostic kits also require skilled laboratory personnel to operate.

With the ELISA method, results obtained may not be conclusive. Negative results in a specific ELISA test do not rule out the possibility that another pathogen is causing disease. Negative results can also be obtained if the wrong tissue is sampled and tested.

Usually, when testing for viruses, the youngest symptomatic leaves are sampled. Accurate diagnosis of certain problems may require other tests, including the sampling of water on the media.

Other methods like the squash blot and the direct tissue blotting method are not very convenient for commercial use as the tester must be able to roughly locate the region of the pathogen in the plant before testing the tissue of the suspected part. Therefore, this method may be time-consuming and requires a degree of knowledge on how to spot diseased plant parts (taxonomy). This test is thus used in research laboratories for the investigation of plant-pathogen interactions rather than in the industry where speed and accuracy matter most for commercial crop disease management.

8.1.2.3 *Opportunities*

Monoclonal antibodies, ELISA and DNA-based technologies such as the polymerase chain reaction have been the basis of molecular detection in modern plant pathology. Genomics and biosystematics research are fast growing databases that can be used to design molecular assays for simultaneous detection of a large number of pathogens and beneficial organisms.

The medical research field has been progressing rapidly in the 21st century and would create platforms which would increase multiplexing capability, and facilitate high throughput and portability, which will provide new opportunities for plant pathology. As new molecular testing devices gain wide acceptance in medical diagnostics, tools for monitoring of pathogens and beneficial organisms should become more commonly used in plant pathology (Lévesque, 2001).

The development of new tools for functional genomics and for medical diagnostics is probably one of the most heavily researched areas around the world. There is likely to be many opportunities in which platforms developed through medical research can be subsequently adapted and used for plant diseases.

As researchers discover that proteins are involved in pathogenesis and as detection abilities of portable detection devices reach a few hundred molecules, DNA and amplification techniques to detect plant pathogens may be replaced by electronic sensors that will monitor the environment for the presence of pathogens in the same way that we use electronic sensors to measure temperature (Lévesque, 2001).

The greatest opportunity for the Asian region is still its cost advantage to produce diagnostic kits *en masse*. As capacity in molecular biology improves in countries such as China, India and Singapore, it is likely that the geographic advantage to market will also play a role in influencing investments in this sector. Asia has the world's largest number of small farmers and is also the region with the most need to reduce crop losses due to diseases.

8.1.2.4 *Threats*

As useful and effective as PCR plant pathogen diagnostic kits may be, the widespread application of PCR-based technologies in plant health management remains at this time constrained by cost, including prohibitive royalty obligations, and relatively complicated assay technology.

Also, due to the relative sophistication and high cost of molecular diagnostic kits today, molecular approaches are still not being used routinely in epidemiology, plant breeding or disease management. While the physical environment is monitored using very sophisticated instruments, relatively crude techniques are still being used to monitor plants and plant diseases.

8.1.3 *"Freedom to operate" issues*

Companies providing diagnostic services are likely to need certification by the International Organization for Standardization (ISO), which would probably entail that all suppliers of reagents and kits in the field of molecular detection be required to follow the same stringent quality assurance certification.

8.1.4 *Product range*

There are countless varieties of diagnostic kits in the market today which test for a wide range of plant pathogens. Only a select illustrative number of diagnostic kits are mentioned here:

- **DAS ELISA test system for Alfalfa Mosaic Viruses by Agdia Inc. (International)** — Alfalfa Mosaic Virus (AMV) is a RNA virus with bacilliform particles of different lengths. AMV is transmitted by aphids in a non-persistent manner, is easily transmitted by sap inoculation and is seed transmitted in some hosts. It is common in most countries, and infects many herbaceous and some woody hosts. Symptoms can include mosaic, mottle, necrosis and stunting. Infections can also be symptomless. The test uses rabbit anti-AMV for capture and enzyme conjugated to monoclonal antibody: clone AL72B6 for detection following a typical DAS ELISA protocol. The test is very sensitive and appears to detect all known strains of AMV.
- **Compound direct ELISA test system for Blueberry Shock Virus by Agdia Inc. (International)** — The test utilizes a polyclonal antibody to capture the virus and monoclonal antibody for the detection of the virus. The virus is sap transmittable.
- **PCR test system for Carlavirus group by Agdia Inc. (International)** — This offers a sensitive diagnostic method to

detect members of the Carlavirus group. The PCR primers are based on conserved genome regions and can detect unidentified viruses and isolate members of the Carlavirus group. This test can be used as an aid for identification of viral etiology of unknown plant diseases, test for known viruses when other tests are not available and can be used to confirm results from other test methods.

- **DAS ELISA test system for Kalanchoe Latent Virus by Agdia Inc. (International)** — Kalanchoe Latent Virus (KLV) is a sometimes-latent virus, often referred to as Kalanchoe Virus, found frequently in Kalanchoes. Two strains of the virus, KaV-1 and KaV-2, have been described. Since KLV often does not show visible symptoms, infection is difficult to determine without a diagnostic laboratory technique. Some methods, such as leaf dip microscopy, have shown to be difficult due to the thick, slimy sap of Kalanchoes. On the other hand, ELISA has proven to be a sensitive and reliable technique for detection of this elusive virus. The virus is captured and detected by a polyclonal antibody.
- **IDENTIKIT™ and IDENTIKIT-Q™ by Neogen Europe** — This product is a 96-well immunoassay test kit that comes complete with all the required reagents. The IDENTIKIT™ format is for the qualitative or semi-quantitative detection of the chosen pathogen. IDENTIKIT-Q™ is a fully quantitative version of the kit and is available for the determination of selected fungal pathogens (Neogen Europe Ltd.).
- **EXPRESS™ by Neogen Europe** — This kit can test for bacterial pathogens in the plants in under a minute. Bacteria tested for include *Calvibacter michiganensis* subsp. *Sepidonicus*, *Erwinia amylovora* and *Xanthomonas campestris pv perlargonii*.

8.1.5 *Value creation in the biodetection industry*

Much of the information on mass production of diagnostic kits remains proprietary. The costs of reagents are relatively low when compared to the R&D costs and the costs of the medium to carry the reagents. Value is created when scientific discoveries on very specific relationships at the molecular level between molecules can be translated into simple kits for use by a variety of people.

ELISA kits in a laboratory format and reagents are commercially available from several firms worldwide. The markets for these kits include public laboratories operated by universities or government organizations; private, for-profit testing laboratories and corporations; private, non-profit organizations (e.g., crop improvement associations); and individual researchers. ELISA and other related antibody-based technologies such as immunofluorescence and dot immunobinding, developed commercially or in the public domain, are widely used in seed and plant certification programs, as well as in laboratories and clinics for routine diagnosis.

The value proposition lies in the size of the potential problem caused by the disease (or diseases) and the value of the crop. Thus, diagnostic kits are more common for the high value ornamentals and higher priced vegetative seed material than for the extensively grown food staples such as rice or wheat.

8.1.6 *Players in the business*

Table 8.1 provides an overview of the key players in the biodetection industry who are involved in the detection of plant diseases.

8.2 Biodetection of Genetically Modified Organisms (GMOs) in Food

Plant products have been the main target for genetic modification in the food industry, which has been estimated to make up 6.5% of the world's commerce. The term "transgenic plants" usually refers to a genetically modified plant which has one or more foreign genes from diverse source(s) introduced through DNA recombinant technology (Chapter 9). Transgenic plants are commonly grouped under the umbrella of "Genetically Modified Organisms" (GMO) as they are considered to be plants modified through the use of biotechnology.

Over 50 countries import millions of tons each year of GM produce for conversion into processed products in the food chain.

Table 8.1.   Players in the biodetection business — A representative sample.

Company	Remarks
NeoGen Europe Ltd. (Europe)	NeoGen Europe Ltd. is a dedicated diagnostics company, providing products and services to discerning customers in over 90 countries worldwide. A wide range of diagnostic reagents and kits with applications for disease detection in temperate and tropical crops are available via NeoGen Europe's Plant Disease Diagnostics Catalogue. These include many unique monoclonal antibodies, novel liquid substrates as well as buffers and reaction controls all packaged in sizes convenient for large- and small-scale testing. NeoGen Europe also has extensive experience of PCR-based tests for fungal pathogens with a quantitative PCR-ELISA soon to be available
Agdia Inc. (United States, International)	Agdia's objective is to help growers produce healthy and thus, profitable crops. The company's focus has been on assisting crop producers in their operations by identifying the presence of plant pathogens before they become serious problems in a crop. Tests and services the company offers encompass not only pathogen detection, but also diagnostics for insect identification, and plant quality factors, all of which allow researchers, diagnosticians, propagators and producers alike to make more informed management decisions
Strategic Diagnostics Inc. (United States, International)	The Group's principal activities are to develop, conduct research, manufacture and market immunoassay-based test kits for inexpensive detection of a variety of substances in water quality, industrial testing and agricultural markets. The Group's test kits include chemicals used to treat drinking water, proprietary chemicals used in industries, environmental contaminants, pesticides, genetically engineered traits and diseases in crops. The Group provides developing and marketing test kits and strip tests, fully integrated monoclonal antibody development and manufacturing services to pharmaceutical and medical diagnostic companies through its subsidiary. The Group sells products market through a network of over 50 distributors in Canada, Mexico, Latin America, Europe and Asia. Test kits and strip tests accounted for 57% of 2002 revenues, and monoclonal antibody development services 43%

All of these have been approved by government regulatory agencies and are subject to monitoring during the import and export process.

In 2006, soybean made up the bulk of all the transgenic crops planted worldwide (59 million hectares, or 57% of total area), followed by corn (25 million hectares) and cotton (13 million hectares). The increase in planted area of transgenic crops has been accompanied by increased publicity.

In some countries, consumers have not been very forthcoming in their acceptance of food products from genetically modified plants due to concerns about their safety. Governments have reacted with action to give consumers more choice, but this action requires that GM ingredients be detected, often at low levels, in processed food (Auer, 2003). The number and importance of rapid and cost-effective GMO testing processes has grown significantly as a result of this.

GMO detection kits are used to certify if the percentage of GMO in the product is within acceptable thresholds. Irrespective of the lack of scientific reasons, consumers generally prefer that food be tested for GMO in order for them to have choices (Figure 8.4).

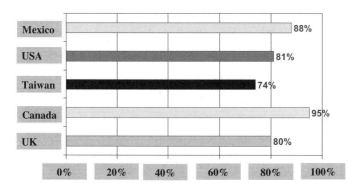

Figure 8.4.   Estimates of the number of customers who prefer GM food to be labeled.

Sources: Mexico (www.globalexchange.org), March 2001; USA, MSNBC, January 2000; Taiwan, *Cropchoice News*, October 2000; Canada, *Ottawa Citizen*, April 2000; UK (www.justfood.com), September 2001.

Due to the high percentage of people who want GM food to be identified and marked, the market potential is thus very promising in relation to detection kits for GMO products. The GMO testing market has been variously estimated at US$1,910 million for 2,122.2 million metric tons of genetically modified food in 2000, and is expected to grow as world governments consider if genetically modified food could be the answer to the sustainable food resources in the coming years.

8.2.1 *The science and technology behind detecting genetically modified organisms through biodetection*

For the testing of genetically modified ingredients in a food product, a detection kit should be able to fulfill the following criteria: detect all the GMOs present in the market and provide quantitative information on the GMOs; be maximally reliable and reproducible; and be able to work on a wide range of foods and agricultural products. Currently, there are two types of detection methods — the detection of new genes in a foodstuff or agricultural product, and the detection of new proteins produced by a genetically modified product. Figure 8.5 illustrates the two approaches of GMO detection.

8.2.1.1 *DNA-based detection of new genes*

There are several techniques for the detection of new genes in a GMO. DNA-based detection of new genes has been considered the most "foolproof" as all GMOs contain foreign DNA sequences. However, the southern blot and PCR analyses have been the most widely used. Microarray-based technology for detecting gene expression is currently under development. The tests rely on the complementarity of two strands of DNA double helix that hybridize in a sequence-specific manner (Ahmed, 2002). The DNA that has been introduced into a GM crop or food product contains a promoter sequence, a structural gene sequence and a stop sequence.

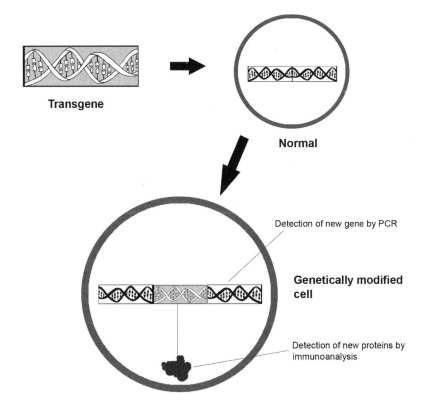

Figure 8.5. Diagrammatic representation of the steps required in the identification of GMOs in food.

8.2.1.2 *Southern blot technique*

In the southern blot technique, sample DNA is affixed onto a nitro-cellulose or nylon membrane and is probed with double-stranded nucleic acid probes that are specific to the GMO tested. These probes detect hybridization radiographically, florimetrically or by chemiluminescence.

In many laboratories today, the conventional phosphorus-labeled probes have been replaced by non-radioactive fluorescein-labeled DNA, digoxigenin- or biotin-labeled DNA probes (Ross *et al.*, 1999), with sensitivity equal to ^{32}P probes. These probes are as sensitive as radioactive probes, so radioactivity is not employed. Although the new probes reduce the detection time for GMO to less than an hour (^{32}P probes require a day), because only one probe is used for each test and no amplification of the GMO gene is carried out, the southern blot method is considered less sensitive than the PCR method, which employs the DNA of two primers.

8.2.1.3 *Qualitative PCR technique*

PCR allows the amplification of specific DNA segments which occur in minute quantities in a mixture of other DNA sequences. In a typical PCR test, the forward sense strand primer ($5' \rightarrow 3'$) and the antisense strand primer ($3' \rightarrow 5'$) are used. Through a series of thermal steps, the primers hybridize opposite sides of the sequence of interest and amplify that sequence many times over. The millions of pieces can then be separated by size using separation methods like High Performance Liquid Chromatography (HPLC) and capillary electrophoresis (CE).

DNA extraction and purification has been a crucial rate limiting step in PCR analysis of GMO. Currently, DNA is extracted and purified using the STAB method (food sample is incubated in the presence of a detergent) (Tinker *et al.*, 1993) or the Wizard method (DNA-binding silica resins are employed) (Meyer *et al.*, 1994). Both methods are able to isolate DNA while managing to avoid DNA degradation, and are cost-effective.

Most currently available GMOs contain the cauliflower mosaic virus (CaMV) 35S promoter, the nopalin synthase (NOS) terminator or the kanamycin-resistance marker gene (nptII). These elements also occur naturally in some plants and soil microorganisms, which, when detected by PCR, can yield false positive results. In this case, product-specific PCR methods have been developed for a range of different GM foods. These methods utilize a set of primer pairs that spans the boundary of two adjacent genetic elements (e.g., promoters, target genes and terminators), or that are specific for detection of the altered target gene sequence. Detection limits are in the range of 20pg–10ng of target DNA and 0.0001%–1% of the mass fraction of GMOs (Yates, 1999).

Recently, GeneScan Europe has introduced a test kit for the detection of GMOs in food products, which allows a multiplex PCR for the specific detection of DNA sequences from plant species and GM traits (GeneScan Europe, 2001).

8.2.1.4 *Quantitative competitive PCR*

Quantitation is a crucial aspect of analysis of GMOs in food as maximum limits of GMO in foods are the basis for labeling in the EU. PCR was shown to be quantitative if an internal DNA standard was co-amplified with target DNA (McPherson and Møller, 2000).

In quantitative competitive PCR (QC)-PCR, the presence of PCR inhibitors will be noticed immediately because the amplification of both internal standard and target DNA would be simultaneously affected (Hübner *et al.*, 1999). Generally, QC-PCR is carried out in four steps: first, standard and target DNA are co-amplified in the same reaction tube; the products are then separated by an appropriate method, such as agarose gel electrophoresis and staining the gel by ethidium bromide. The gel is then analyzed densitometrically, and the relative amounts of the target and standard DNA is estimated by regression analysis. In the QC-PCR, the competition between the amplification of internal standard DNA and target DNA generally leads to loss of detection sensitivity. Nevertheless, the Swiss example allows as little as 0.1% GMO DNA to be detected (Studer *et al.*, 1999), which is within the threshold limits specified by the European Novel Food Regulations (Anonymous, 1997).

8.2.1.5 *Quantitative real-time PCR*

To avoid some of the problems of QC-PCR, a real-time Q-PCR was introduced. In theory, production of PCR products should proceed without end; however, in practice, it reaches a halt between 30 and 40 cycles because of limiting reagents in the reaction.

In the conventional QC-PCR, products of the reaction are measured at a single point in the reaction profile. Real-time Q-PCR allows the determination of the precise initial DNA (then GMO) content in the sample, as the concentration of DNA in real-time PCR reaction is proportional to the PCR cycle number during the exponential phase of PCR. In order to determine the initial DNA amount, the number of cycles it takes for a sample to reach the same point in its exponential growth curve should be determined. Real-time PCR allows this determination easily. Real-time PCR also allows for detection of low copy DNA number.

Several commercially available real-time PCR thermal cyclers automate the analytical procedure and allow cycle-by-cycle monitoring of reaction kinetics, permitting calculation of the target sequence concentration. Among the several formats used to estimate the amount of PCR product, the most common are the ds-DNA-binding dye SYBR Green I, hybridization probes or fluorescence resonance energy transfer (FRET_ probes, hydrolysis probes (TaqMan® technology)), and molecular beacons. These systems also permit the thermal differentiation between specific and non-specific PCR products (non-specific products tend to melt at a lower temperature than longer specific products).

8.2.1.6 *Exhaustive limiting dilution PCR method*

The basis of this method is optimization of the PCR so that amplification of an endogenous control gene will take place in an all-or-nothing fashion, derived from the terminal plateau phase of the PCR; and the premise that one or more targets in the reaction mixture (e.g., GMO) will give a positive result.

Accurate quantitation is achieved by performing multiple replicates at serial dilutions of the material(s) to be assayed. At the limit of dilution, where some end points are positive while some are negative, the number of targets present can be calculated using Poisson statistics from the proportion of negative end points (Sykes *et al.*, 1999).

8.2.1.7 *Protein-based testing methods*

Immunoassay technologies with antibodies are ideal for qualitative and quantitative detection of many types of proteins in complex matrices when the target analyte is known (Stave, 1999). Depending on the amounts needed and the specificity of the detection system (i.e., antibodies to whole protein or specific peptide sequences), the particular application, time allotted for testing, and cost, both monoclonal (highly specific) and polyclonal (often more sensitive) antibodies can be used (Ahmed, 1999).

On the basis of typical concentrations of transgenic material in plant tissue (> 10μg per tissue), the detection limits of protein immunoassays can predict the presence of modified proteins in the range of 1% GMOs (Stave, 1999).

The two more common methods of protein-based testing methods are the western blot and enzyme-linked immunosorbant assay (ELISA). However, protein-based techniques are preferred less to DNA-based detection techniques for GMOs as some GM foods will not express enough protein to be detected.

8.2.1.8 *Western blot*

This test is a highly specific way to determine whether the sample contains the GM protein above or below a preset threshold level and is particularly useful for the analysis of insoluble protein. However, the western blot method is considered more applicable to research applications than commercial testing.

The test samples are solubilized with detergents and reducing agents and are separated by sodium dodecyl sulfate (SDS)-polyacrylamide gel electrophoresis. These components are then transferred to a solid support like a nitrocellulose membrane. The binding immunoglobulin sites on the membrane are blocked with non-fat milk before probing with antibodies (either a high-titer polyclonal anti-serum or a mixture of monoclonal antibodies raised against the denatured antigenic epitopes).

Finally, the bounded antibody is stained with Ponceau, silver nitrate or Coomassie, or a secondary immunological reagent (i.e., protein A coupled to horseradish-peroxidase (HRP) or alkaline phosphatase). The detection limits of the western blot vary between 0.25% for seeds and 1% for toasted meal (Yates, 1999).

8.2.1.9 *ELISA*

There are currently two formats for the ELISA test: the microwell plate (or strip) format, and the coated tube format. The former, with removable strips of 8–12 wells, is quantitative, highly sensitive, economical, provides high throughput and is ideal for quantitative high volume laboratory analysis for undenatured proteins. The typical run time for a plate assay is 90 minutes, and an optical plate reader determines concentration levels in the samples. Detection limits for CP4 EPSPS soybean protein was 0.25% for seeds and 1.4% for toasted meal (Yates, 1999).

The latter format is suited for field testing, with typical run times ranging from 15–30 minutes. Tubes can be read either visually or by an optical tube reader. Results are, however, qualitative. Because there is no quantitative internal standard within the assay, no extra information can be obtained regarding the level of GMOs in food (Ahmed, 2002).

8.2.1.10 *Lateral flow strip*

This test is a variation of ELISA that uses nitrocellulose strips rather than microtiter wells (see Figure 8.6a). Immobilized double antibodies, specific for the expressed protein, are coupled to a color reactant and incorporated into a nitrocellulose strip, which, when placed in a plastic eppendorf vial containing an extract from plant tissue harboring a transgenic protein, leads to an antibody sandwich with some of the antibody that is coupled to the color reagent.

This colored sandwich flows to the other end of the strip through a porous membrane that contains two captured zones, one specific for the transgenic protein sandwich and the other for untreated antibodies coupled to the color reagent. The presence of only one (control) line on the membrane indicates a positive result (Figure 8.6b).

The lateral flow format gives results in 5–10 minutes, making it economical and suitable as an initial screening method early in the food chain. These strips have been developed commercially to detect endotoxins expressed by the bacterium *Bacillus thuringiensis* that

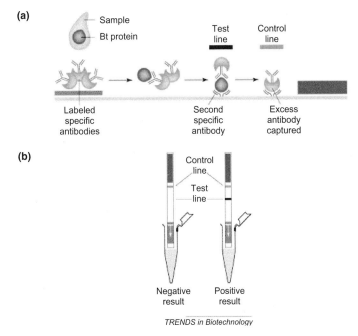

Figure 8.6. Lateral flow strip assay format (Courtesy of D. Layton). (a) Side view illustrating principles of the immunological test, and relative location of control and test lines on a nitrocellulose strip. (b) Vertical view of test strips dipped in an eppendorf containing genetically modified material, and showing both negative and positive test results.

Note: Abbreviation: Bt = *Bacillus thuringiensis* (Ahmed, 2002).

protects against insects, as in CryI(Ab) in corn plants, seeds and grain, in addition to CP4 EPSPS protein in soybean, canola, cotton and sugar beet. Commercially available lateral flow strips are currently limited to few biotechnology-derived protein-producing GM products.

The ELISA is the method of choice to screen for a particular GMO in raw material, semi-processed foods and processed ingredients, provided the expressed protein is not degraded and can be detected. However, because ELISA has lower detection power than PCR methods, it is less sensitive for testing finished food products with many ingredients, especially if the threshold for detection is low

Table 8.2.   Summary of methods that specifically detect rDNA products produced by GM foods.

Parameter	Protein-based			DNA-based			
	Western blot	ELISA	Lateral flow strip	Southern blot	Qualitative PCR	QC-PCR and limiting dilution	Real-time PCR
Ease of use	Difficult	Moderate	Simple	Difficult	Difficult	Difficult	Difficult
Special equipment	Yes	Yes	No	Yes	Yes	Yes	Yes
Sensitivity	High	High	High	Moderate	Very high	High	High
Duration	2 days	30–90 minutes	10 minutes	6 hours	1.5 days	2 days	1 day
Cost/sample (US$)	150	5	2	150	250	350	450
Quantitative	No	Yes	No	No	No	Yes	Yes
Suitable for field test	No	Yes	Yes	No	No	No	No
Employed mainly in	Academic labs	Test facility	Field testing	Academic labs	Test facility	Test facility	Test facility

Note: Abbreviations: rDNA = Recombinant Deoxyribonucleic Acid; PCR = Polymerase Chain Reaction; ELISA = Enzyme-Linked Immunosorbent Assay.
Source: Ahmed (1999).

(Table 8.2). Although protein-based tests are practical and effective, some GM products do not express a detectable level of protein.

8.2.1.11 *Reference materials for GMO testing*

Appropriate reference materials are important in GMO testing to validate the analytical procedures (Ahmed, 2002). Reference materials should be raw materials or base ingredients rather than finished food products (i.e., grains, altered DNA or expressed proteins). Reference materials should also be independent of the analytical methods used. Each GMO requires specific reference materials.

In contrast to protein detection methods, in which a single standard can be settled on easily, DNA-based methods are better served through combinations of several positive controls. The availability of reference materials is currently limited owing to concerns over intellectual property rights (Serageldin, 1999).

8.2.2 SWOT analysis

8.2.2.1 *Strengths*

Of the two main methods developed for the detection of GMOs, PCR-based methods are the most popular due to their high accuracy. A transgenic element in a food sample can be easily and unambiguously detected by PCR if information on the modified sequences is available (European Union, 2004).

The PCR test is described by many as a high-throughput method suitable for automation (i.e., routine analysis in a commercial biotechnology firm). The test is also able to detect and quantify very minute amounts of GMOs in a food product, making it very useful for GMO labeling.

Immunoassay techniques are technically simpler to use compared to PCR techniques. Transgenic plants or foodstuffs would have genetically modified cells which produce a certain type of protein coded by the new DNA in the cell.

8.2.2.2 *Weaknesses*

Another problem with PCR and other DNA-based techniques is that they do not allow differentiation between GMOs and the natural occurrence of transgenic elements, such as the 35S-promoter of cauliflower mosaic virus (CaMV) or the NOS-terminator of *Agrobacterium tumefaciens*. This may result in false-positive detection of GMOs. Thus, it is critical to develop new approaches involving PCR for specific results.

The detection of GMOs based on foreign proteins produced by the GM cell is not as sensitive as DNA-based detection methods. The test may not be able to detect the presence of GM content in food or crops if the amount of protein produced by the GM cell is below detection limits. Reliability of such protein-based detection methods may be questionable. Furthermore, few protein-based detection methods are quantitative.

8.2.2.3 *Opportunities*

Methods are being developed for increasing the sensitivity of detection of PCR products in GMO food and crops. Fluorescence is the favored signaling technology and several techniques rely on energy transfer between a fluorophore and a proximal quencher molecule (Whitcombe *et al.*, 1999).

Recently, an alternative southern blot technology has been attempted with near infrared (NIR) fluorescent dyes (emitting at ~700 nm and 800 nm), coupled to a carbodiimide-reactive group and attached directly to DNA in a 5-minute reaction. The signals for both dyes are detected simultaneously (limit in the low zeptomolar range) by two detectors of an infrared imager, something not yet possible with conventional radioactive or chemiluminescent detection techniques.

Lateral flow strips that can detect multiple proteins are being developed. Also, improvements in immunoassays are expected to occur via advances in antibody technology and improved instruments (Meyer *et al.*, 1994). Advances are being made in combining antibody methods with instrumentation techniques. Considerable advances in relative observation of antibody binding to target molecules using biosensors have been reported.

In the near future, other technologies like biosensors and microarrays would be used in the detection of GMOs. Biosensors and microarrays are two emerging fields with very high potential. Both are rapid, sensitive, specific and yield results in real-time. However, each has its own problems with biosensors proving difficult to commercialize due to inherent instability issues, while microarrays yield a vast amount of data which are complex for analysis.

8.2.2.4 *Threats*

Threats to the operation and sale of detection kits for GMOs come mainly in terms of governmental regulations against the labeling of GM food. The issue of whether to consume GM food, whether GM food is harmful to the environment and/or detrimental to human health and the subsequent labeling of GM food so that consumers can make informed choices are all part of the debate on GM food.

8.2.3 *"Freedom to operate" (FTO) issues*

There does not appear to be any FTO issue concerning the use of biodetectors for plant diseases. On the contrary, detection of GMO ingredients will rest largely on decisions regarding whether foodstuff is required to be correctly labeled for presence (or absence) of GM ingredients. If more countries require mandatory labeling, then the market for GMO detection kits will increase.

The labeling of genetically modified foodstuff has become a controversial issue since the late 1990s. The United States, Canada, Argentina and Egypt have taken the first step in filing a formal dispute with the World Trade Organization against the EU moratorium on GMOs, asserting that the moratorium would become a trade barrier and that it did not adhere to the Sanitary and Phytosanitary Agreement of the WTO.

In response to these disagreements, the Labeling Committee of the Codex Alimentarius has been meeting since 1994 to work out international standards for the labeling of GM foods.

Countries against the labeling of GM food have alleged that the procedure would lead to a waste of capital, delay advances in other aspects of biotechnology and might cause unnecessary alarm to customers. Also, there is the potential for discrimination against producers or GM-friendly countries. The term "GM-free" is also ambiguous and may cause problems in different countries and companies.

The following sections outline the situation in selected countries, in particular on how each country arrived at its current policy, and why the policies differ among them.

8.2.3.1 *United States*

The USA focuses more on the safety of the final product rather than the manufacturing process. In 1992, the Department of Health issued a statement which stated that GM food did not need to be labeled if the nutritional function of the GM food was the same or more beneficial to human health as the food in its non-GM form.

In 1997, there was a major outcry when GM foods were included in the United States Department of Agriculture's (USDA) draft of regulations about the standard of organic food in the nation. In March 2000, the draft was revised and the section on GM foods was removed.

The report "Guidance for Industry" was issued by the Food and Drug Administration (FDA) in January 2001. The report reiterated that only GM foods which differed from their natural counterparts in terms of nutritional content and function were required to have a label. The report also stated that companies needed to inform the FDA four months in advance before they could put a GM food on the market.

During these four months, a "scientific description of the product" should be posted on the internet for review by specialists and the general public alike. Firms can then opt to label their product as one which contains GM content (Ahmed, 2002).

Companies which choose to label their food as containing GMOs must follow certain FDA guidelines: labels cannot contain the words "genetically modified" as consumer studies show this phrase incorrectly leads buyers to believe the food has different characteristics than the natural form. The terms "genetically engineered" or "made through biotechnology" were suggested by the FDA to replace the "genetically modified" term.

At government levels, the USA has been against the EU moratorium on GM crops, introduced in 1999, mainly from the standpoint that scientific evidence shows the safety of the products. This shows that very different views can arise from the same scientific information.

8.2.3.2 *European Union*

The most controversy over the labeling of GM food has taken place in Europe. There have been more protests against GM food in Europe than in USA where the technology is more widely accepted. The European Union (EU) sets minimum standards for countries in the EU, but individual countries may place stricter policies if they see fit.

Since April 1998, the EU has had a *de facto* moratorium on the approval of any new GM foods for use within the EU. The Novel Foods Regulation in 1997 made labeling of GM foods mandatory. With this regulation, any GM food on the market had to pass two requirements: it had to be shown that it was not harmful to human health, and that it had a label which stated that GM content in the food was at a detectable level. The Novel Foods Regulation did have downfalls, however. It did not set a minimum percentage for a detectable level of GM content, and it "left several exemptions to labeling".

In January 2000, the Commission of the Council modified the Regulation and stated that GM foods must be labeled as "genetically modified" if at least 1% of GM material was detectable. The moratorium on new approvals was still in place as of February 2001, and Austria, Denmark, France, Greece, Italy and Luxembourg have stated that they would not favor the lifting of the ban on new GM products until more stringent laws are passed.

In December 2002, the EU drafted a law to extend labeling policy to foods containing soy or maize oil. However, to avoid a trade war with the US, the ban on GM food approvals was lifted on 2 July 2003, but strict labeling policies are still in place and new biotech crops stringently screened before being allowed into the market.

The majority of Europeans do not want GM food, yet almost all want the option of choosing to eat it. As recently as January 2004, the EU had "taken one more step towards removing a five-year unofficial ban on new biotech crops and products". A proposal to import GM sweetcorn was executively backed, but EU ministers did not authorize use of the corn, which is produced by a Swiss company. This corn would not be allowed for planting, but just for eating from a can.

More GM approval applications are expected, but diplomats will not acknowledge a complete lifting of the GM ban until seed GMOs are approved for planting in the EU. Although Norway and Sweden are not EU members, these two countries require all food containing GMOs to be labeled (Ahmed, 2002).

8.2.3.3 *Canada*

As of September 2001, Canada only required labeling for GM foods that had potential "health or safety issues". Currently, a voluntary labeling policy is being considered. The Canadian Food Inspection Agency supports the passing of a uniform standard for labeling GM foods on an international level.

8.2.3.4 *Australia and New Zealand*

In December 2001, the Australia New Zealand Food Authority (ANZFA) passed regulations that required GM foods to be labeled if the "novel DNA and/or novel protein" was present in the finished product. As in the EU policy, labeling is only required if the GM content or any ingredient is 1% or more. If an ingredient is considered

GM, it must be labeled as such on the list of ingredients, and the phrase "genetically modified" must be next to the name of the product on the front of the label.

Highly refined foods, food using "GM processing aids" and food served in restaurants are exempt from the standards. Australia has a nationwide food standard system, but some states within the nation want to have more liberty in labeling policies in their own area.

8.2.3.5 *Japan*

On 1 April 2001, a new policy was passed requiring the labeling for 28 products, including various soy and corn products as well as unprocessed potatoes and tomatoes. If the GM content is less than 5%, the products do not have to be labeled as GM, but companies may volunteer the information on the label if they wish. For products which are voluntarily labeled, they must carry one of the following phrases: "genetically modified", "inseparable" or "no GMOs present". Amendments to the Food Sanitation Law make it illegal to "sell or import GM foods that have not been approved or inspected".

8.2.3.6 *China*

Up until 2001, China was considered liberal with its policies toward biotechnology and GM food. However, in 2001, China regulated several GM crops including corn, cotton and soybeans. China did not want to have their crops banned from import to other nations, and did this to avoid trading disputes.

In May 2001, a 56-article regulation on biotechnology was passed in an attempt to strengthen control over agricultural aspects, but the report was "vaguely worded" and concluded that there would be "safety certification for all GM food and all GM foods will have to be labeled".

8.2.3.7 *Why all the different policies?*

The four main reasons a country (or an individual) would oppose GM foods are: concerns about human health, ethical objection, concerns about the environment and "worries about trading with other countries".

Countries place different emphasis on each of these factors, and this causes different labeling policies to arise. Out of these different objections, the objection against "messing" with nature and environmental concerns are among the most swaying factors in making a political decision on GM food.

In European politics, environmental groups have actively opposed GM food. GM safety is a concern in countries like Australia, New Zealand, China and Japan, although the scientific communities in these countries are almost without exception supportive of the safety of GM crops and food. In these countries, labeling is required to give consumers a choice in whether they want to buy GM foods or not. Countries of the EU are also concerned about GM food safety, especially in the light of recent government safety standards (the BSE crisis, the HIV/AIDS-tainted blood scandal in France, and the dioxin scandal in Belgium).

China is mainly concerned with losing trading partners, especially in Europe. Canada and the US feel the "potential threats from genetic modification [are] minor compared to the potential rewards". The US has a lax policy compared to the rest of the world when it comes to labeling GM foods, but historically the US has had stricter food safety standards. European fears may be unfounded, but GM producers in the US will nonetheless have to deal with EU policies.

8.2.4 *Product range and players in the business*

Table 8.3 provides a representative sample list of the biodetection kits for GMOs currently in the market. Apart from companies directly involved in the manufacture of GM detection kits, there are also those doing consulting work to advise on techniques.

8.2.5 *Value creation*

Value creation occurs mainly from translating the knowledge on molecular biology into tools which allow for the quick, simple and

Table 8.3.   Biodetection kits for GMOs.

Company	Kit name	Primary matrices
Applied Biosystems	TaqMan^R GMO Maize 355 Detection Kit	Processed foods and ingredients, including flour, meal, seeds, grain, plant tissues and oils
Applied Biosystems	TaqMan^R GMO Soy 355 Detection Kit	Processed foods and ingredients, including flour, meal, seeds, grain, plant tissues and oils
BioteCon Diagnostics GmbH	Bt-176 Maize	Corn
BioteCon Diagnostics GmbH	Round-up Ready Soya	Soya bean products
EnviroLogix	QualiPlate Kit for Roundup Ready Corn, Event 603 and Cotton	Roundup Ready corn, Roundup Ready cotton, soybean and soy flour
EnviroLogix	QuickStix Kit for Roundup Ready Bulk Grain. *This product received the recognition: USDA GIPSA Certificate 2002–2003 (soy), USDA GIPSA Certificate 2002–2007 (corn)	Roundup Ready corn, soybeans, canola
EnviroLogix	QuickStix Kit for Roundup Ready Leaf & Seed	Roundup Ready corn, soybean, cotton, canola
Hong Kong DNA Chips Limited	GMO Watcher 1.0 (DNA extraction & quantitative GMO detection kit for unprocessed food)	Genetically modified ingredients, unprocessed foods

(*Continued*)

Table 8.3.   (*Continued*)

Company	Kit name	Primary matrices
Hong Kong DNA Chips Limited	GMO Watcher 2.0 (DNA extraction & quantitative GMO detection kit for unprocessed food)	Genetically modified ingredients, unprocessed foods
Investigen, Inc.	CommodityCheck PCR-Based GMO Detection Kit	Soy, corn, potato, canola in raw, processed, intermediate food products
Perkin Elmer	HyPure	Seed
Promega Corporation	Wizard Magnetic DNA Purification System for Food	Corn, soybeans, cornmeal, corn starch, soy flour, cornflakes, soy milk
Qualicon	BAX for Screening Qualitative GMO	Food
Qualicon	BAX for GMO Quantification	Soy products
Scil Diagnostics/ GeneScan	GMO*Ident* Kit LibertyLink™ T25 Corn	Plant tissues, seeds, meals, flours, grits, processed and unprocessed foods/feeds, food additives and unrefined oils
Scil Diagnostics/ GeneScan	GMO*Ident* Kit Maximizer™ Bt176 Corn	Plant tissues, seeds, meals, flours, grits, processed and unprocessed foods/feeds, food additives and unrefined oils
Scil Diagnostics/ GeneScan	GMO*Ident* Kit Roundup Ready™ Soya	Plant tissues, seeds, meals, flours, grits, processed and unprocessed foods/feeds, food additives and unrefined oils
Scil Diagnostics/ GeneScan	GMO*Ident* Kit StarLink™ Corn	Plant tissues, seeds, meals, flours, grits, processed and unprocessed foods/feeds, food additives and unrefined oils

(*Continued*)

Table 8.3. (*Continued*)

Company	Kit name	Primary matrices
Scil Diagnostics/ GeneScan	GMO*Ident* Kit YieldGard™ Mon810 Corn	Plant tissues, seeds, meals, flours, grits, processed and unprocessed foods/feeds, food additives and unrefined oils
Strategic Diagnostics	GMO Check Food Ingredient Testing	Soybean flour
Strategic Diagnostics	Trait Check Crop and Grain Testing	Soybean bulk, soybean flour, corn
Tepnel BioSystems, Ltd.	BioKits DNA Extraction Kit (GM Foods)	Raw, processed, or intermediate food products
Tepnel BioSystems, Ltd.	BioKits GMO Identification Test Kit	Food

Source: AOAC Research Institute. Genetically modified organisms. http://www.aoac.org/testkits/kits-gmo.html.

accurate detection of the molecules linked to GM ingredients. The biological ingredients for such tools inherently have no value if the demand for detection is not existent. The value created is therefore proportional to the overall size of the GM crop and food market, and the laws or rules set by importing countries.

Public information on the costs associated with producing any detection kit is scant as the sector is predominantly private and much of the information is proprietary. It is known, however, that the biological material costs are low relative to the costs of the carriers of the biodetectors.

8.3 Current Market Size and Growth Potential for Biodetection

The annual food safety testing market in the USA is estimated to be about US$53.4 million. Pathogen-specific food testing, which is a subset of food safety testing, was valued at US$20 million in 2001.

Plant diseases have and continue to cause significant losses in potential production throughout Asia. The outlook for agriculture, with increased demand, reduced land and water availability for crop growing, and the need to input more fertilizer, all suggest that disease problems will increase from the drive to grow more food per land unit. Early detection of diseases and their correct diagnosis are key to successful management of these diseases and the losses they cause.

The area under biotech crops is predicted by ISAAA to grow to > 150 million hectares by 2010. This estimate does not take into account the continued liberalization of regulations in the EU and China about planting such crops, and the increased secondary processing of GM products from biotech crops in fast-growing economies. As more countries implement international agreements such as Codex Alimentarius and the Cartagena Protocol on Biosafety, it can be anticipated that the demand for GM detection kits and services will further increase.

References

Ahmed, F.E. (1999). Safety standards for food contaminants. In *Environmental Contaminants in Food* (Ed. C.F. Moffat and K.J. Whittle), pp. 500–570. Sheffield Academic Press.

Ahmed, F.E. (2002). Detection of genetically modified organisms in foods. *Trends in Biotechnology*, 20(5): 215–223.

Anonymous (1997). Council regulation (EC) No. 285/97, concerning novel foods and novel food ingredients. *Official J. Eur. Communities: Legislation*, 43: 1–5.

Auer, C.A. (2003). Tracking genes from seed to supermarket: Techniques and trends. *Trends in Plant Science*, 8(12): 591–597.

Dimock, A.W., Geissinger, C.M. and Horst, R.K. (1971). Chlorotic mottle: A newly recognized disease of chrysanthemum. *Phytopathology*, 61: 415.

European Union (2004). Development of methods to identify foods produced by means of genetic engineering. http://europs.ed.int/comm/research/quality-of-life/gmo/04-food/04-03-project.html.

Flynn, P.H. (1993). Biotechnology Information Series (Bio-5), North Central Extension Publication, Iowas State University — University Extension August, 1993. http://www.nal.usda.gov/bic/Education_res/iastate.info/bio5.html.

GeneScan Europe (2001). GMO chip: Test kit for the detection of GMOs in food products. Cat. No. 5321300105, Bremen, Germany.

Hübner, P., Studer, E. and Luthy, J. (1999). Quantitative competitive PCR for the detection of genetically modified organisms in food. *Food Control*, 10: 353–358.

Kabashima, J.N., Mcdonald, J.D., Dreistadt, S.H. and Ullman, D.E. (2002). *Easy On-Site Test Kits for Fungi and Viruses in Nurseries and Greenhouses*. University of California, Division of Agriculture and Natural Resources.

Lévesque, C.A. (2001). Molecular methods for detection of plant pathogens — What is the future? *Can. J. Plant Pathol.*, 24: 333–336.

McPherson, M.J. and Møller, S.G. (2000). *PCR*. Springer-Verlag.

Meyer, R., Candrian, U. and Luthy, J. (1994). Detection of pork in heated meat products by polymerase chain reaction. *J. AOAC Int.*, 77: 617–622.

Navarro, B. and Flores, R. (1997). Chrysanthemum chlorotic mottle viroid: Unusual structural properties of a subgroup of self-cleaving viroids with hammerhead ribozymes. *Biochemistry*, 94: 11262–11267.

Ross, R., Ross, X.-L., Rueger, B., Laengin, T. and Reske-Kunz, A.B. (1999). Nonradioactive detection of differentially expressed genes using complex RNA or DNA hybridization probes. *Biotechniques*, 26: 150–155.

Serageldin, I. (1999). Biotechnology and food security. *Science*, 285: 387–389.

Stave, J.W. (1999). Detection of new or modified proteins in novel foods derived from GMO-future needs. *Food Control*, 10: 367–374.

Studer, E., Rhyner, C., Luthy, J. and Hubner, P. (1999). Quantitative competitive PCR for the detection of genetically modified soybean and maize. *European Food Research and Technology*, 207(3): 207–213.

Sykes, P.J. *et al.* (1999). Quantitation of targets for PCR by use of limiting dilution. In *The PCR Technique: Quantitative PCR* (Ed. J.W. Larrick), pp. 81–93. Eaton Publishing Co.

Tinker, N.A., Fortin, M.G. and Mather, D.E. (1993). Random amplified polymeric DNA and pedigree relationship in spring barley. *Theor. Appl. Genet.*, 85: 976–984.

Whitcombe, D., Theaker, J., Guy, S.P., Brown, T. and Little, S. (1999). Detection of PCR products using self-probing amplicons and fluorescence. *Natural Biotechnology*, 17(8): 804–807.

Yates, K. (ed.) (1999). *Detection Methods for Novel Foods Derived from Genetically Modified Organisms*. ILSI Europe.

Chapter 9

Biotechnology Crops
(Genetically Modified Plants)

9.1 Introduction

One of the most rapidly adopted new agricultural technologies in the modern era is biotechnology crops (also known as genetically modified plants). There has been an exponential, double digit percent per annum growth in the global area of biotech crops since the first plantings on a commercial scale in 1996, culminating in over 114 million hectares in 2007.

In 2007, with petroleum prices reaching their highest levels ever, renewed interest has been shown in the potential to use biotech crops for "biofuel" by genetically modifying plants for increased efficiency to produce potential fuel chemicals such as ethanol. All this has created excitement over the "New Agriculture", in which plants are treated as "biofactories", grown and managed to help humankind meet its needs through a more sustainable use of natural resources and in a manner which minimizes negative long-term effects on the environment.

Genetic engineering is a set of techniques, based on discoveries in molecular biology and related disciplines, that has enabled the spectacular growth of a new industry in genetically modified plants or crops, often called "GMOs" (Genetically Modified Organisms) or more recently, "Biotech crops". Biotech crops are those with traits which are derived either using recombinant DNA technology, such as genetically engineered cultivars, or through marker-aided selection.

Ten years have passed since biotech crops were first commercialized, and many countries now have well-developed R&D capacity to conduct cutting-edge plant biotechnology research (although most technological innovations still come from the industrialized countries). The social acceptance situation has also changed in line with the increasing levels of awareness and publicity surrounding GMOs. Over a decade of consuming food derived from GMOs in over 50 countries worldwide, including the European Union, has confirmed their safety.

The first commercial planting of any biotech (genetically modified) crop occurred in China in the form of tobacco; yet, of the 114 million hectares that made up the global area of biotech crops in 2007, only less than 10% were in Asia. After the initial excitement in China and India subsided, the annual regional growth rate in biotech crop area in Asia has been less than anticipated relative to other regions of the world. Concerns have been and continue to be raised about the effect of planting biotech crops on the export trade with other regions, in particular with the European Union. As a result, decisions on the commercialization/release process of key biotech crops in Asia, such as rice and oil palm, have been delayed.

On the other hand, several governments in the region have been visible in articulating their support for crop biotechnology as a new engine for economic growth, especially India, Vietnam, the Philippines and Malaysia. Contradictions between policy and practice are obvious in the cautious approach adopted by many countries, some of which in turn have been influenced by ongoing international discussions over biosafety (the Cartagena Protocol on Biosafety), food safety and labeling (Codex Alimentarius Commission), trade (WTO TRIPS), and global initiatives focused on building biosafety regulatory frameworks (UNEP-GEF) — all of which will be discussed in this chapter.

Four significant changes have occurred since the first biotech crops were commercially planted in 1996: regulatory approval frameworks, the R&D capacity of developing countries, the social acceptance environment, and the technology itself. Countries which have commercialized biotech crops in Asia have developed regulatory frameworks to review and approve such crops for planting and for their subsequent use as food, feed or fiber. Although only four Asian countries *grow* a significant area of biotech crops, many more *import* biotech crop products for processing into food items. As of November 2007, about 670 biotech crop products had been approved worldwide by 53 countries for food, feed and processing.

In Asia, countries which have formal regulations to approve the importation of biotech products are Japan, Australia, Korea, Philippines, China, Taiwan, Thailand, India, Indonesia, Malaysia and Singapore. Many more countries import biotech food products but do not have the formal regulations.

The public sector investment in agribiotech R&D in Asia outweighs the private sector investment, and is estimated to be over US$6 billion per year. This situation augurs well for the future, as a deep and diverse pipeline of biotech crops with various traits has been developed in countries like India, China and the Philippines. In contrast, R&D investments by multinational companies in the EU and North America dwarf that of governments.

9.2 The Science and Technology Behind the Business

The primary aim of modern biotechnology is to make a living cell perform a specific useful task in a predictable and controllable way. The task could be to ferment soya beans to make soya sauce, or to breed a plant that yields better fruit or resists insect attacks.

Whether a living cell will perform these tasks is determined by its genetic make-up, i.e., by the instructions contained in the collection of chemical messages found within its genes. These genes are passed on from one generation to the next so that offspring inherit a range of individual traits from their parents.

In 1953, scientists discovered that deoxyribonucleic acid (DNA) is found in all living things, and that a gene is a segment of DNA that has a specific sequence, or code, of chemicals. This code determines various characteristics or traits such as eye or hair color. In 1973, scientists identified a way to isolate genes and by the 1980s, they had developed the tools necessary to transfer genes (and therefore traits) from one organism to another.

With the discovery of enzymes that could be used to cut or remove a gene segment from a chain of DNA at a specific site along the strand, scientists were able to introduce new instructions that would cause cells to produce needed chemicals, carry out useful processes or give an organism desirable characteristics. This technique is called "recombinant DNA" (rDNA) technology. The end result is modern biotechnology — the science of transferring specific genetic instructions from one cell to another.

9.2.1 *A history of scientific progress*

At the beginning of the previous century, scientists carefully selected plants with beneficial traits and began breeding them together to create new varieties and hybrids — new plants with some of the qualities of each of the parents. Scientists today understand many more biological processes and this has allowed the development of new techniques to alter or copy some of these natural processes. Techniques of modern biotechnology allow scientists to create crops and foods that are equivalent to or even improved over those made using traditional methods. The new methods are faster, cheaper and more reliable.

Traditional plant breeding techniques using the controlled pollination of plants had limitations. Firstly, sexual crosses could only occur within the same or related species. This limits the genetic sources that breeders can depend upon to enhance desirable characteristics of plants. Secondly, when two whole plants are crossed, each having some 100,000 genes or so, all the genes from both plants are pooled and the offspring may express both desirable and undesirable traits of the parent plants. Because of this, breeders must spend many years to slowly breed out the tens of thousands of genes they do not want. Traditional plant breeding takes time, sometimes as long as 10 to 12 years, to produce a variety with the desired properties.

Biotechnology is a collection of knowledge, techniques and tools showing a gradient in sophistication of the applications (Figure 9.1). Generally, cost and complexity of biotechnology applications have increased along with technological improvements. However, it is the former two that have caused understandable concern that only

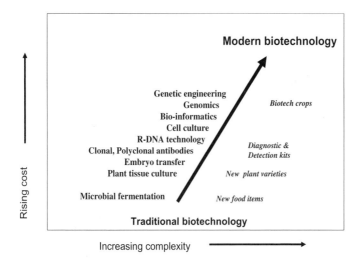

Figure 9.1.   The biotechnology gradient and its applications.

Source: Adapted from Doyle, J.J. and Persley, G.J. (1996). *Enabling the Safe Use of Biotechnology: Principles and Practice*, ESDS & Monograph Series No. 10. Washington, DC: World Bank.

well-resourced institutions can afford to use biotechnology in their R&D process, even though the evidence suggests that many large developing nations have now invested heavily in building capacity for modern biotechnology.

Tissue culture is an essential part of the process to develop a genetically modified ("biotech") plant, and in its own right, has created much value for entrepreneurs (see Chapter 3 in this book). Tissue culture is now well-established on a commercial scale as a means to mass produce plants of the same genetic make-up and expressing the same desired traits. Figure 9.2 shows, schematically, the role that tissue culture plays in this process. Recombinant DNA technology is the epitome of the new biotechnology and has, associated with it, many specialized areas of knowledge such as genomics, proteomics and bioinformatics.

A brief chronology of modern biotechnology is presented in the Annex of Chapter 1 in this book. Modern biotechnology began in the 1970s when bacteria were genetically engineered to produce human

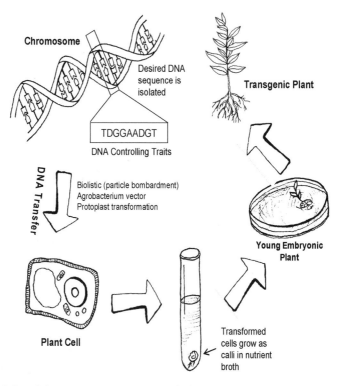

Figure 9.2.   Schematic representation of the process to develop a genetically modified plant expressing the desired gene and trait.

insulin. Scientists immediately recognized the industrial possibilities of this discovery.

The 1980s saw great advances in biotechnology when genetically modified organisms (GMOs) were released into the environment, genetically modified (GM) crop and foods were created, and DNA fingerprinting was discovered. The 1980s saw further intensification of biotechnology applications, but also the emergence of organized resistance, accompanied by increased public awareness of the issues surrounding GMOs. The era of intellectual property protection and intellectual property rights on life forms was created. In 1980, Cohen and Boyer were awarded a US patent to make human insulin from GM bacteria. Also in 1980, a landmark decision by the

US Supreme Court granted a patent for a GM bacterium that could break down oil. In 1983, Stephen Lindow from Berkeley in the USA was given approval to release the first GM bacteria into the environment for the first agricultural application of the modern biotechnology. These bacteria gave protection to potato leaves at low temperatures by making the leaves less frost-sensitive. But the release of the GM bacteria was delayed until 1987 due to legal battles with anti-biotechnology activists and the demand for risk assessments to be done.

There is much parallel development of the science and technology between agricultural, pharmaceutical and industrial uses of biotechnology. However, there are sharp contrasts in public acceptance of this technology between the different applications. The use of GMOs to produce medicinal products has found wide acceptance due to the relative increase in availability of the products and also the decline in costs, while for agriculture and food, there is continuing controversy even after more than a decade of safe use and of over 10 million farmers plating over 100 million hectares in 2006.

9.3 Product Range of Biotech Crops

9.3.1 *Products in the marketplace*

Biotech products include disease diagnostic kits and seeds of plant varieties developed using rDNA genetic modification techniques. Data compiled by the International Service for the Acquisition of Agri-Biotech Applications (ISAAA — www.isaaa.org) from the AGBIOS database and other sources show that as of November 2007, there were 674 products approved by 53 governments to be in the marketplace for FFP (Food, Feed, Processing) as follows: 81 products approved in the USA, 60 approved in Canada, 32 products approved in the EU, 97 approved in Japan, 46 in Australia, 50 in Korea, 40 in Philippines, 50 in Mexico, 35 in New Zealand, 16 in Russia, 27 in China and 140 in 19 other countries. This shows that the use of biotech crop products is prevalent over all regions of the world.

The biotech seeds that have been approved may generally be classified by the crop and trait expressed, for example, corn — insect resistance, to confer protection against one or more harmful pests.

9.3.2 Insect-resistant plants

Devastation of crops by insect pests is a major problem for farmers, causing estimated losses annually of more than 10% of potential production. To fight crop pests, farmers usually spray insecticides. These sprays have limitations as they may degrade in sunlight or be washed away by rain. Also, some insecticides are highly toxic and if safety precautions are not taken, may affect human health. By introducing a specific gene into the genetic make-up of a plant, the plants are able to continuously produce proteins to protect against harmful insects. This built-in protection offers farmers an alternative to the use of chemical pesticides. When the usage of chemical pesticides is decreased, beneficial insects survive and, in turn, help control harmful insect pests.

9.3.3 Herbicide-tolerant plants

Weeds compete with crops for water, nutrients, sunlight and space. They also harbor insect and disease pests, lower crop quality and deposit weed seeds in crop harvests.

Farmers fight weeds by tilling, the use of herbicides or by using a combination of these two methods. Tilling exposes valuable topsoil to wind and water erosion and increases the chances of serious long-term environmental consequences. Environmentally conscious farmers try to reduce tilling and limit their use of chemical herbicides. By introducing into a plant a gene that confers tolerance to a specific herbicide, a farmer can apply this herbicide in judicious amounts to control weeds without destroying the crop, and at a time of his choosing. This technology allows the grower to apply herbicide only when the presence of weeds requires it, a practice that fits within the concept of integrated pest management. It may also shift weed control practices to herbicides with more favorable environmental profiles and reduce the use of tilling.

9.3.4 *Disease-resistant plants*

Plant diseases, including fungal and viral diseases, can adversely impact both the yield and quality of crop harvests. Worldwide, losses of up to 30% of potential yield are common. To minimize these, farmers often plant more than they expect to harvest. This increases the costs of planting, fuel, water and fertilizer. In addition, farmers use chemical insecticides to destroy pests such as aphids that carry viral disease. Researchers have developed crops protected from certain types of plant viruses. By introducing a small part of the DNA from a virus into the genetic make-up of a plant, scientists have developed crops that have in-built immunity to specific viral diseases. This allows reduced dependence on chemical inputs and improves both productivity and crop quality. An example is the Papaya Ringspot Virus, which has stopped farmers growing papayas in many parts of tropical Southeast Asia. Papaya Ringspot Virus-resistant papaya is commercially grown in the state of Hawaii, USA, and scientists are currently cooperating to have the same technology benefit farmers in Southeast Asia as well.

9.3.5 *Improved food and crop quality*

Genetic modification makes possible beneficial changes to crops. Examples include:

* Consistently high-yielding oil palms;
* Potatoes and tomatoes with a higher content of solids, making the plants more suitable for food processing;
* Tomatoes, squash and potatoes with higher levels of nutrients such as vitamins A, C and E;
* Corn, potatoes and soya beans containing higher levels of essential amino acids;
* Oilseeds with lower levels of saturated fat; and
* Slow-ripening tomatoes, peppers and tropical fruits with better keeping qualities and better flavor.

Crop improvements like these can help ensure food security. Increasing the nutritional content of staple foods further helps certain populations get more nutrients without having to change their diets significantly.

9.4 Value of Biotech Crops

9.4.1 *Value creation and market size*

Value creation in biotech crops is done through several mechanisms, namely:

- Ownership of intellectual property in the gene or genetic modification processes, and the resulting seed;
- Increased efficiency in exploiting the potential of the seed through improved traits; and
- Value accrued from a cleaner environment and improved health.

The developers of biotech seeds accrue value from their patents through licensing the use of the proprietary technology in their own seeds to third-party seed companies. These licensing fees can be quite substantial and may account for as much as a third of the cost of the seed to the farmer. Biotech seeds are commonly more costly than conventional, non-biotech seeds, yet the strong evidence is that farmers are willing to purchase these improved seeds due to their higher potential for value.

The growth in demand for biotech seeds, as monitored by ISAAA and reflected in the area planted to biotech seeds, has globally been in the double digit percentages per year since 1996. Farmers find value in biotech seeds as the traits reduce input costs (cost of insecticides, cost of labor for applying insecticides, cost of fuel to drive spraying equipment), increase yield and provide more flexible timing of spray operations (as with herbicide application). The global value of biotech seeds was estimated at about US$6.9 billion for 2007, representing 16% of the $42.2 billion global crop protection market in 2007 and 20% of the $34 billion global commercial seed market (James, 2007).

The market value of the global biotech crop market is based on the sale price of biotech seed plus any technology fees that apply. The

Table 9.1. The global value of the biotech crop market, 1996–2007.

Year	Value (US$ million)
1996	115
1997	842
1998	1,973
1999	2,703
2000	2,734
2001	3,235
2002	3,656
2003	4,152
2004	4,663
2005	5,248
2006	6,151
2007	6,872
Total	42,344

Source: James (2007).

accumulated global value for the twelfth-year period in 1996 to 2007, since biotech crops were first commercialized in 1996, is $42 billion (Table 9.1). These figures do not take into account any potential release of seed produced by the public sector through government sources. The data show that there is as yet a large untapped growth potential for biotech seeds for the current range of traits and crops. Analysts often have to be reminded that so far, the significant value creation has only been with five crops!

Total transgenic crop sales grew more than 52-fold in their first decade, from US$115 million in 1996 to $6.9 billion in 2007. The market is projected to increase to about $20 billion in 2010 on a planted area of 150 million hectares, as more crops and more traits are introduced (James, 2007).

One way to provide a global perspective of the status of biotech crops is to characterize the global adoption rates as a percentage of the respective global areas of the four principal crops — soybean, cotton, canola and maize — in which biotech technology is utilized (Table 9.2).

The global adoption rates for all four biotech crops — soybeans, maize, cotton and canola — all increased significantly between 2003

Table 9.2.　Biotech crop area as % of global area of principal crops, 2007 (million hectares).

Crop	Global Area	Biotech Crop Area	Biotech Area as % of Global Area
Soybean	91	58.2	64
Cotton	35	15.1	43
Canola	27	5.4	20
Maize	148	35.5	24
Total	301	114.2	37.9

Source: James (2007).

and 2007. The data indicate that in 2007, 64% of the 91 million hectares of soybean planted globally were biotech. Of the 35 million hectares of cotton, 43% or 15.1 million hectares were planted to biotech cotton in 2007. The area planted to biotech canola, expressed on a percentage basis, increased from 16% in 2003 to 20% or 5.4 million hectares of the 27 million hectares of canola planted globally in 2007. Similarly, of the 148 million hectares of maize planted in 2007, 24% was planted to biotech maize, up significantly from 11% in 2003.

The ISAAA statistics focus on the major biotech crops. While their areas are small, other biotech crops are known to be grown, such as alfalfa, flowers and some vegetables. The area under these will not grow to the same magnitude as the big four, but their market value will nevertheless be high.

Although 23 countries were reported to grow biotech crops in 2007, a larger number were known to have such crops in various stages of development leading up to commercial plantings. Indeed, Cohen (2005) has suggested that the public sector will be an important source of biotech crop products for poor farmers, as there are currently known to be more than 99 crop variety-trait modifications undergoing different stages of testing by public institutions in Asia. Furthermore, it is also known and acknowledged by some countries that biotech crops are being grown, with or without government regulatory approval, within their boundaries due to zealous farmers bringing in seeds from other countries.

9.4.2 *Key players in the business*

The biotech seed market is dominated by a handful of private sector companies, some of which have exhibited a classical "first entry" advantage by virtue of their pioneering R&D and product development efforts. This is strongly reflected in their market share of the biotech seed market, their ownership of proprietary technology, and their share of the number of regulatory approvals worldwide for growing and importing biotech seeds. ISAAA data (James, 2007) show that > 85% of the products approved by 53 countries as of November 2007 were owned by less than ten separate companies (Table 9.3).

However, it is also significant that while all these companies have their origins in the industrialized, Western hemisphere, significant public investment is now evident in Asia by concerned governments. No reliable data is available on government investments in agricultural biotechnology, but it is known to total > US$5 billion per year in recent years in Asia. Countries with significant public sector investments in agricultural biotechnology are the People's Republic of China, India, Korea, Australia, Singapore, Thailand, Malaysia, Vietnam, Pakistan and the Philippines.

Table 9.3. Key players in the agricultural biotechnology business: Ownership of biotech crop products approved by regulatory systems, 2006.

Monsanto Company	49%
Bayer CropScience	10%
Aventis Crop Science	7%
Syngenta Seeds	6%
Dow AgroSciences LLC	5%
Pioneer (DuPont)	3%
Dekalb Genetics Corporation	3%
Pioneer Hi-Bred International Inc.	1%
Hoechst/AgrEvo	1%
Seminis Vegetable Seeds (Upjohn/Asgrow)	1%
Total	86%

9.4.3 *Costs for establishing and operating a biobusiness based on biotech crops*

There are few reports in the literature on costs to commercialize a biotech crop product since almost all products in the market today have been developed by private companies which commonly view this kind of information as confidential. Commercialization costs may be divided into several categories:

- R&D costs, which are variable and depend on the purchasing power parity of currencies in the particular country;
- Product development costs, which cover the laboratory evaluations, large-scale field tests, ecological studies on potential risks, and which again depend on the costs associated with the respective country; and
- Regulatory approvals for food and feed safety, including the submission of complete dossiers of information required by regulatory agencies and the conduct of public hearings.

Experience with commercialization in several Asian countries shows that the costs range from US$700,000 to US$4.2 million per crop-event (Cohen, 2005). In the Philippines, the total cost of taking an insect-protected corn variety from R&D to market was estimated at about US$2.6 million over a five-year period; two-thirds of the costs were involved in getting regulatory approval (Manalo and Ramon, 2007).

9.5 The Commercialization Process of Biotech Crops

There is much ongoing research in Asia using recombinant DNA technology to produce genetically engineered plants with improved traits (Asian Development Bank, 2001; Cohen, 2005; Teng, 2006; Asia Productivity Organization, 2007). Unfortunately, most will not lead to commercialized products or products available to farmers on a large scale, largely because the work has been "technology-pushed" rather than "demand-driven". In commercial product development, it is important to first conduct the market analysis of demand before any initial "proof of concept" research is done.

9.5.1 *Stages in developing a biotech crop product — "Stage gating"*

The steps needed to commercialize a crop biotech product are many, starting from "product concept" to "market product", and the required time ranges from 10–13 years. The individual steps may vary by country, depending mainly on the regulatory regime in place for biosafety and food/feed safety. These steps may be illustrated by means of the "stage gate" procedure that directly or indirectly is used by private companies to plan and "drive" the commercialization of a biotech crop (Figure 9.3).

Each step is represented by a stage, and to get from one stage to the succeeding one requires that all requirements are met before the

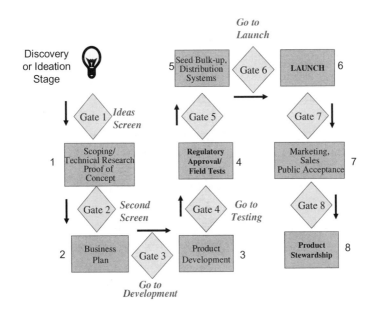

Figure 9.3.   Schematic illustrating the "stage gating" of a biotech crop commercialization process — Main stages.

gate is cleared. Although the schematic shows a linear process, in practice there are concurrent stages going on and multiple responsibilities to ensure concurrent fulfillment of requirements.

Commonly, a **Discovery Group** identifies a valuable protein which helps to confer a useful trait, such as insect resistance. The B.t. protein is an example. At this stage too, many questions are asked about the history of the protein, especially its safe use in its conventional form. When the history of safety is satisfied, a next step commonly is then for molecular biologists to develop artificial constructs of the gene which makes the protein. These steps may take up to a year. So far, there is little biosafety consideration. The insertion of the artificial gene construct into target plant cells is next done through the process commonly called "transformation" (see Figure 9.2).

The target cells are from plant varieties with desirable commercial traits as well as being useful parents in a breeding program. The successful fraction of transformations is very low, hence in the same laboratories, facilities are developed for automation. Successfully transformed cells containing the desired gene are then grown to whole plants using tissue culture techniques. All the above is done under biosafety regulatory purview, usually by means of an Institutional Biosafety Committee made up of representatives from research, government and society. Next comes testing the plantlets or whole plants to determine if the desired trait is expressed in strong enough levels to justify a useful product. For example, a plant purported to contain the B.t. gene may be tested by exposing it to insect larvae from the pest which it was developed to resist. This screening process again is often done *en masse* under biosafety supervision in greenhouses, and may take 1–3 years.

The "**Proof of Concept**" stage is completed when the transgene in a new variety successfully expresses itself by producing proteins in high enough quantity to have the desired effect. Most likely, at the time the "proof of concept" stage is proceeding, another team would be developing the business plan, which includes both market analysis, and also "table-top exercises" on any potential regulatory, intellectual property protection, safety or public acceptance issues.

If the particular crop variety containing the desired improved trait clears the first two stages (Figure 9.3), it then goes into the **product development** stage, when enough seed is multiplied for the many tests required by regulatory authorities, commonly starting with a single location, and progressively, to multiple locations and crop seasons. All this is done to comply with the **regulatory approval** system of the country concerned, which in turn is governed by the existing biosafety regulations of that county. Commonly, countries also require public notification and hearings, for the technology proponents to dialogue with communities. At the same time that this is going on, companies or public institutions proposing commercialization or release of the biotech crops in question are also conducting or accumulating evidence on the food/feed safety of the biotech crop. After 2–3 years of field evaluations and food/feed safety testing, the government body empowered to make a decision to approve or disapprove the product must weigh all the evidence and render its decision.

Assuming the biotech crop product passes all the gates and is approved for wide area planting by farmers, the company or government institution (if it is a biotech crop developed by the public sector) then undergoes **seed multiplication** in preparation for sale or release to farmers.

In Asia, only the Philippines, China and India have much experience with the full cycle of commercialization. An important question that must be asked is whether governments will expect public institutions to be subject to the same long and expensive process of testing a biotech crop before it is approved. In North America, the experience shows that regulatory agencies are willing, on a scientific basis, to allow data sharing between products so that the process can become less cumbersome.

On top of regulatory requirements, producers of GM crops further have to assure the safe use of their products through **product stewardship**. What product stewardship implies is providing the subsequent after-sales support to ensure that the product is properly used. This includes resistance management schemes, especially for the insect-protected products (B.t. corn, B.t. cotton), and detection techniques, among others. Much has been researched on the scientific basis for insect resistance management *vis-à-vis* B.t. crops (Gould, 1998).

In North America, resistance management strategies for B.t. crops rely on deployment of non-B.t. crops within specified geographic areas, a strategy commonly called refugia management (Gould, 1998). Resistance management for diseases using conventional resistances has been practiced in developed and developing countries for decades, and it is only now that the lessons learnt are being applied to the management of transgenic resistance for disease control. The public sector may not be as strong as the private sector in product stewardship. Thus, international organizations like the Food and Agriculture Organization (FAO), United Nations, can play an important role here, especially in developing and strengthening public sector capacity in product stewardship.

9.5.2 *Regulating the safety of biotech crops*

Before any biotech crop can be released for commercial planting or public use, it has to be approved through a regulatory process set up and operated by the government of a country using internationally recognized principles, techniques and technology. This is commonly done for biosafety (environmental safety) and food/feed safety. Regulatory approvals for food and feed safety include the submission of complete dossiers of information required by regulatory agencies, and the conduct of public hearings (Thomas and Fuchs, 2002). The status of biosafety approvals in Asia is shown in Table 9.4.

9.5.2.1 *Safety assessment systems and processes*

The commercialization of any biotechnology product in agriculture produced using genetic engineering (rDNA technology) requires that there be policies and procedures to ensure that these products are environmentally safe. Such policies and procedures have come to be known collectively as "biosafety". Biosafety is now

Table 9.4. Status of regulatory approval and regulatory systems for biosafety in selected Asian countries.

Country	Status of Contained Experiments	Status of Confined Field Trials	Status of Open Field Trials, Precommercialization	Status of Biosafety Regulatory Systems
China	+	+	+	+
India	+	+	+	+
Australia	+	+	+	+
Philippines	+	+	+	+
Thailand	+	+	(+)	+
Vietnam	+	(+)	−	+
Korea	+	+	−	+
Japan	+	+	+	+
Malaysia	+	(+)	−	+
Singapore	+	−	−	+
Cambodia	−	−	−	−
Indonesia	+	+	(+)	+

Source: Teng (2006).
Notes: "+" indicates current, existing strength and/or activity. "−" indicates no known activity. "(+)" indicates either (a) activity using international norms; (b) activity done, but rescinded; or (c) activity done before implementation of country-specific regulations.

the subject of an international protocol, called the Cartagena Protocol on Biosafety (CPB) under the Convention for Biological Diversity. The CPB has been ratified by 147 countries as of 25 April 2008, and provides the international legal basis for the movement of biotech products such as GM seeds used for food, feed or processing. Trade in GM products is worth several US$ billion per year.

The CPB requires that countries have clear and transparent national policies and procedures to deal with research and development involving modern biotechnology. It also requires that risk assessments be conducted before laboratory and field experiments are done using GM seeds. It further requires that frameworks exist to conduct biosafety evaluations prior to the commercial release of any

GM product for food or feed. Key issues revolve around biosafety, such as liability and redress, risk assessment/management technique, economic considerations, public awareness, handling and packaging of GM products, and notification and labeling requirements. A science-based approach is endorsed under the CPB.

Biosafety is assessed using a process called "risk assessment" (Hancock, 2003) and takes into consideration properties of the biotech plant, the ecosystem in which it is to be grown, and societal concerns as well as economic benefits.

A robust and responsive regulatory framework is essential to ensure that the benefits of modern biotechnology can be realized while still assuring food, feed and environmental safety. A regulatory system should be clear and unambiguous in terms of its scope and objectives, with clear differentiation in regulations and guidelines regarding distinct activities associated with the development and commercialization of GM events. For example, regulations and implementing guidelines for experimental, confined trials of GM plants should be distinct from those used to address food safety or the approval of GM plants for cultivation. There should be no doubt as to what is subject to regulation and to the division of responsibilities between government ministries (if there are any). Additionally, the interrelationship with other existing regulatory systems must be clear, and intersecting areas of responsibility rationalized. For example, the regulation of transboundary movement of living modified organisms (LMOs) should be integrated with existing regulatory systems that address phytosanitary concerns.

One of the most important means of developing and maintaining confidence in a regulatory system is to ensure that it is transparent. Within the context of government regulatory systems, transparency refers to the extent to which governments provide information on why and how certain products are regulated, how risk assessments are performed and decisions made, and as well, the conclusions and decisions that have been reached. Transparency can also involve the perceived independence and objectivity of the regulatory decision makers.

9.5.2.2 *Risk assessment and risk management*

Central to all biotechnology regulatory systems is a framework that leads to decision making. Science-based safety or risk assessment is central to this, but may not be the only factor that informs the decision to approve or not approve a GM food.

Risk assessment is a scientific process used to identify hazards, the likelihood of their occurrence, and their impacts on human and animal health and on the environment. It also leads to the identification of possible risk mitigation measures. The risk assessment of a GM food should be evidence-based, scientifically defensible and typically requires a diverse collection of expertise and a significant knowledge base.

At the scientific and technical levels, very similar questions are asked when evaluating the potential human health risks of GM products. In evaluating novel foods, a comparative approach is taken that focuses on the defined differences between the novel food and its traditional counterpart, and the effect these differences have on composition, nutritional quality, toxicology and potential allergenicity. There is a high degree of consistency in the scientific opinion in different countries about the safety of novel foods which have been put forward for commercialization to date.

Those charged with undertaking a risk assessment must ensure that information requirements are scientifically justifiable. In the context of a GM food safety assessment, this means that the information and data required by the risk assessor must be safety-related; risk assessors should be able to identify the biological significance of statistically significant differences where these exist and the context must be safety-related.

The risk assessor is often also required to be a risk manager and risk communicator; however, the roles of risk management, assessment and communication within a regulatory system are distinct and should remain separated so as not to compromise the integrity of the scientific process. Risk assessment should not be driven by a risk communication agenda; requirements and procedures should be determined by real, and not perceived, risks.

In the context of novel food safety assessment, risk management encompasses the decision to approve or not approve a GM food for human consumption. Typically, this is the step where balance is sought between safety and "non-safety" considerations such as socioeconomic, cultural and political concerns that may be associated with GM food products. Additionally, although it rarely happens in practice, potential benefits associated with a GM food may also be applied to informing the decision. Transparency is critical at this point in the regulatory process as the extent to which safety and other concerns are taken into account, and how this is accomplished, should be a matter of public record.

9.6 "Freedom to Operate" Issues

Successful commercialization of biotech crop requires not just sound technology that is relevant to farmers' needs, but also a supporting environment. This supporting environment includes science-based regulatory frameworks, and also a public which understands and supports mainstream government programs and science. Public awareness of biotechnology is therefore an essential ingredient in the overall preparedness of a country to commercialize biotech products. "Freedom to Operate" (FTO) is therefore a composite of the following:

- Effective technology with clear intellectual property (IP) for release;
- IP protection systems;
- Conducive government policies at the national level that are in congruence with international norms;
- Technology distribution systems;
- Transparent, science-based regulatory systems for biosafety and food/feed safety; and
- Public consumer acceptance.

Two FTO components which particularly receive scrutiny are discussed in the following sections.

9.6.1 *Intellectual property protection*

Innovation and creativity thrive best where there is strong protection of intellectual property. Innovative individuals, organizations and enterprises work best in an environment that enables them to protect their competitive advantage and be rewarded for their investment in new products, services and technology development. Typically, this involves obtaining and enforcing (where appropriate and necessary) intellectual property rights including patents, trademarks, copyrights and trade secrets. Asia-Pacific economies that seek to benefit from the life sciences and biotechnology would do well to recognize, respect and safeguard intellectual property rights as a way to protect value that has been created.

In 1930, the US Congress passed an amendment to the Patents Act that allowed some monetary reward to the breeders of fruit trees and ornamental plants. While still excluding open-pollinated varieties, the United States amended its patent law in 1953 to cover "newly found plants in a cultivated state" (Juma, 1989). It was only in 1980 that the US Supreme court tailored patents to cover genetically modified plants "with markedly different characteristics from any found in nature" (Heitz, 1999).

A well-developed intellectual property management strategy enables an economy, institution or enterprise to use cutting-edge technologies, to control the use of such technologies by competitors, to maximize its competitive advantage and revenues, and to obtain rights to use technologies that do not belong to it.

From the FTO perspective, intellectual property protection epitomizes social and ethical concerns about biotechnology. Multinational companies are increasing their ownership of biological material, which will be protected by patents, relative to the public sector. A small number of public institutions have taken out IP protection on their genetic resources as well. Supporters of patenting point out that if the private sector is to mobilize and invest large sums of money in biotechnology R&D for agriculture, it must protect and recoup what it has put in. This is especially so when the returns to investment in agriculture do not compare as favorably as with pharmaceuticals. On the other side of the argument is fear that patenting will lead to monopolization of knowledge, restricted access to germplasm, controls over the research process, selectivity in research focus and increasing marginalization of the majority of the world's population (Serageldin, 1999).

The new developments in biotechnology and information technology have forced a reexamination of the traditional roles of the public sector relative to the private sector. This has affected crops which traditionally have been only of interest to the public sector, such as rice; opportunities for the private sector started with the introduction of hybrid rice but is now extending possibly into biotech rice. When the US Supreme Court upheld a patent in 1980 for a genetically engineered bacterium, it probably triggered what is now called by some as a new "gold rush" to own genes.

An illustration of the proprietary nature of future rice varieties is given for B.t. rice with resistance to stemborers — an insect-resistant rice variety could have as many as seven patents associated with it. This new situation has caused much discussion within international fora with regards to its impact on plant breeders' rights (PBR) and farmers' rights protected by conventions such as the International Union for the Protection of New Varieties of Plants (UPOV). Most Asian countries as yet do not have patent protection for biological material, although plant varietal protection laws exist. The direct effect of intellectual property protection on germplasm exchange is likely to be the requirement for companies or institutions using proprietary material to acknowledge its use in some way.

To cover the commercialization of cultivars produced by normal breeding procedures, various European associations of plant breeders negotiated the International Convention for the Protection of New Varieties of Plants. This convention was first adopted in 1961 and has been revised in 1972, 1978 and 1991 (Serageldin, 1999). The UPOV had 43 member states in mid-1999, with 60 other states having laws or draft laws based on one of the UPOV Conventions (Serageldin, 1999).

In the United States, the Plant Variety Protection Act was introduced in 1970. This legislation sets out that a variety should be distinct, uniform and stable — criteria that are common in UPOV-compatible legislation around the world. The duality of systems to protect intellectual property in plant varieties is ensconced in a provision of the World Trade Organization (WTO) concerning Trade-Related Aspects of Intellectual Property Rights (TRIPS). Members must agree to "provide for the protection of plant varieties either by patents or by an effective *sui generis* system or by any combination thereof". This simply means by an alternative system to patents "of its own kind" (Murray, 2003).

9.6.2 *Public understanding and acceptance of biotech crops*

Public knowledge, attitudes and perception of biotech products are very important factors which determine ultimately whether biotech crops will become an important contribution to the world's food supply. Balancing information and news on biotechnology and GM food has been a real challenge in some parts of the world. How does one separate emotion from science? Most of the big life science companies did not appreciate the many challenges facing them in the early years of the industry. When they started commercializing biotech products, they all believed in the value of the product and were confident of public acceptance. Looking back, this may be viewed as a failure on the part of many companies to anticipate public sentiments about the safety of their food supply.

Many surveys have shown that people want to know how food safety is assured. It is interesting to note that most common food products that are currently eaten have not been subjected to the same rigor of testing that is done now for biotech, genetically modified foods. If so, many of today's common foods would not have been approved. The testing of biotech foods is a science-based process that includes actual and potential information, risk assessment for the presence of allergens or toxins, what genes are transferred, what proteins are produced, among others. The question then is how the current process for assuring food safety can be improved.

Surveys conducted by organizations such as the Asian Food Information Center (AFIC) and several biotech information centers have shown that the public in general has high awareness but low understanding about GMOs; consequently, large segments of the public are uncertain about the technology, and are thus often influenced by sensational media coverage and misinformation conveyed through the internet.

To their credit, government regulators in many countries have approved biotech crop commercialization using sound scientific justification in the face of such controversy. In countries like the Philippines and India — where ardent anti-technology non-governmental organizations operate — the regulatory, scientific and farming communities have shown changes in biotechnology acceptance from negative/neutral to strongly positive.

In the private sector, misstated positions or misconstrued, off-the-cuff remarks can seriously jeopardize a company's freedom to operate, its potential as an investment vehicle, its governance rating and ethical positioning, its bottom line and shareholder value. In the public sector, the consequences can be just as devastating to the credibility of government agencies, impacts on public policy and national R&D budget allocations. These miscommunications can be rapidly disseminated globally by single-issue activists via the internet, with serious and often costly consequences. The current global "war for minds" on biotech crops is a reminder of how high the stakes can become for companies and governments wanting to pursue biotechnology.

Appropriate communication is therefore essential for all stakeholders in the technology arena, whether they are thought leaders, policymakers, managers or researchers. Whilst many stakeholders (e.g., researchers/academic lecturers) have communication skills appropriate to their own specialist areas, communicating effectively in high-concern or high-stress situations presents very different challenges, and a different set of communication skills is essential in such situations. The more fear is separated from the reality of bioscience, the better it is for all parties involved. It is therefore important to demystify the process of biotech crop production and the nature of biotech crop products.

Issues central to public concern fall into three broad categories:

- Environment effects of biotech crops,
- Food safety and effects on human health, and
- Social and economic issues.

It is important that the ethical and social implications of biotechnology be considered by companies and government systems alike. Some general ethical considerations that relate to the application of modern tools of life science and biotechnology include:

- How to weigh the potential benefits against the possible costs?
- Do the processes involve the taking of ethically unjustifiable risks?
- Do the processes themselves constitute an "unnatural" interference with nature, particularly in breaching natural species boundaries and violating the integrity of species?
- From a religious viewpoint, is modern biotechnology to be interpreted as "playing God" or as collaborating in the ongoing work of creation?
- Do these questions suggest any significant ethical differences between modern biotechnology and traditional techniques?
- Are there non-technological alternatives to genetically modified products?
- Who would benefit from the creation of these products and who has access to these products?
- Who would own these products? (Shahi, 2004; Teng, 1999)

Many resources are available to provide information on these issues, especially through the network of biotechnology information centers led by the Global Knowledge Center of ISAAA (www.isaaa.org).

Currently, there are several ways in which government bodies or scientific communities involved in genetic modification of food can clear the doubt surrounding the abovementioned ethical dilemmas. Some of these strategies include specific government- or company-organized sharing and education programs on GM food targeted at a public audience. Other strategies include direct education on GM food at the level of educational institutes and the acceptance of interns by GM food companies.

There is growing need to reexamine biological science education curricula in schools, and to ensure the injection of modern life science and biotechnology into education programs — starting as early as the primary and secondary school levels, but also working to incorporate fundamental knowledge and understanding of the principles of life science and biotechnology in training programs at the vocational as well as tertiary educational levels.

9.7 Growth Potential of Biotech Crops

9.7.1 *Needs and benefits*

Biotech seeds provide benefits for those involved in their value chain, from the technology originators and owners (be they in the private or public sector), to the producer and user of technology, to the consumer. As the demand for more high-quality food, feed and fiber increases due to increases in human population and a higher standard of life, so too will the need be felt for more biotech crops with specific traits.

The current benefits of biotech crops underpin the important role that they will continue to play in ensuring the global supply of food, feed and fiber. Evidence has now accumulated in scientific media to show the following:

- **Improved productivity and income** — Increased yields of 5%–50% from biotech crops, reflected in farm income gains of $5.6 billion in 2005 and $27 billion for the period 1996–2005;
- **Protection of biodiversity** — Doubling crop production on the same area of land, and consequently, helping reduce the deforestation occurring at 13 million hectares loss/year in developing countries;
- **Reducing environmental impact of cropping practices** — Reduce need for external inputs. Such reduction led to the saving of

224,300 million tons per annum of pesticides from 1996 to 2005. Also, about 9 billion kg of carbon dioxide (i.e., about 4 million cars less on the roads) was saved in 2005, contributing greatly to the effort to reduce climate change. Furthermore, sustainability would aid in the conservation of soil and water, creating a sustainable environment for people to live in; and

- **Social benefits** — Contribution to alleviation of poverty for 9.3 million small farmers in 2006 compared with 7.7 million in 2005, and also making food more affordable.

The need to grow more food, feed and fiber with minimal negative impact on the environment has been strongly advocated by Conway (1998) and others, and these benefits support that. The benefits to be derived from biotech crops may be exemplified by the case of insect-protected cotton.

9.7.2 *Benefits of biotech crops — Insect-protected cotton*

China was an early adopter of insect-protected (B.t.) cotton and now has the highest number of hectares in the region. In 2004, insect-protected cotton was grown by seven million farmers in China on 3.7 million hectares (James, 2006). A number of studies have documented the economic, environmental and social benefits from this technology in China (Table 9.5; Huang and Wang, 2002).

The improved economics and reduced use of pesticides seen with the adoption of insect-protected cotton has also yielded social benefits for the individual and society as a whole in China (Huang and Wang, 2002).

India has seen a rapid expansion in the number of acres on which insect-protected cotton is being grown. The product was first introduced in 2002. In 2004, India had the highest percentage annual growth of biotech acres of the eight leading biotech crop countries, with 0.5 million hectares planted, providing a 400% increase over the hectares planted in 2003 (James, 2006). Studies are now being published documenting the impact of the product. For example, the performance of insect-protected cotton under Integrated

Table 9.5.   Impact of insect-protected cotton in China.

Year	Net Revenue (US$ per hectare)		Pesticide Usage (Kg per hectare)	
	Insect-Protected	Conventional	Insect-Protected	Conventional
1999	277	−225	11.8	60.7
2000	367	−183	20.5	48.5
2001	351	−6	32.9	87.5

Source: Adapted from Pray *et al.* (2002).

Table 9.6.   Net returns from different cotton systems.

System	Net Returns (Rs. per hectare)
Insect-protected cotton under IPM	16,231
Conventional under IPM	10,507
Conventional (non-IPM)	9440

Source: Adapted from Bambawale *et al.* (2004).

Pest Management (IPM) regimes was recently assessed in field trials in India (Table 9.6). Insect-protected cotton reduced damage due to bollworms with a reduction in pesticide usage when compared to conventional cotton, and delivered higher net returns (Bambawale *et al.*, 2004).

Significant yield increases, combined with reductions in insecticide sprays, were also found in a previous analysis of insect-protected cotton field trial data in India. Similar benefits have been reported from Australia and the USA.

These benefits serve to emphasize why biotech crops have become the choice of millions of farmers worldwide as they compete in a globalized market in which cost of production and efficiency of production are key considerations to survive.

9.7.3 *The R&D pipeline for GM plants*

Biotechnology holds great promise in the fields of food, feed and fiber production through the "New Agriculture" that has been a recurring theme of this book. Its promise is even greater for energy, medicine and environmental management.

Current agricultural biotechnology products are focused on improving agronomic properties and production systems at the grower level. In the future, traits will be developed to continue improvements in these areas, but also to extend the impact into the food and feed sectors. Future agronomic traits that are being actively pursued include providing stress tolerances as a means of preserving yield under diverse environmental conditions such as cold, heat or salinity. In the future, biotechnology will produce crops with improved feed or food quality or nutritional enhancements. A number of such products are currently in development.

Vitamin and mineral enhancement are two areas of particular importance to the developing world. One well-publicized effort is the initiative to produce rice with increased levels of beta-carotene to address vitamin A deficiency (Ye *et al.*, 2000). Improvement of rice by enhancing levels of minerals is also in development.

Proteins (and their constituent amino acids) are critical components of mammalian diets, so improvement of crop plants to generate food and feed that meet the amino acid dietary requirements of humans and animals is another area of active interest. Lysine and methionine levels are two such essential amino acids whose levels have been increased using biotechnology. Modification of oils is another area of active research in the public and private sector. Plant biotechnology has successfully altered fatty acid compositions of major oilseed crops to produce oils with improved processing characteristics or oils with enhanced nutritional characteristics.

A number of traits of potential relevance to agriculture and the food and feed sector in Asia and Oceania are in development. From a research and development perspective, China and India have been among the most active in the region. In China, for example, 16 different crop plants with biotechnology traits had been approved for commercialization or were in trials in 1999 (Huang and Wang, 2002), and in 2005 China invested about US$500 million in crop biotechnology, making it the second largest global investor in crop biotechnology after the US (James, 2006).

India also has very active research efforts in plant biotechnology in both the public and private sectors. Multiple crops (e.g., chickpea, rice, cotton, mustard and potato) and biotechnology traits (e.g., insect, disease and virus resistance, herbicide tolerance, stress tolerance and fruit ripening) are being pursued. The hope is that the efforts in these countries will provide a number of products of value for these nations and the region. As the ADB (2001) has shown, there is a very large pipeline of products that are undergoing regulatory approval in many Asian countries, summarized as follows:

- Agronomic Traits

  o Biotic stress

    ▪ Insect resistance
    ▪ Disease resistance viral, bacterial, fungal, nematode
    ▪ Weed-herbicide tolerance

  o Abiotic stress

    ▪ Drought, cold, heat, poor soils

  o Yield

    ▪ Nitrogen assimilation, starch biosynthesis, O2 assimilation

- Quality Traits

  o Processing
  o Shelf-life
  o Reproduction: e.g., seedlessness
  o Nutrients (Nutraceuticals)

    ▪ Macro: protein, carbohydrates, fats
    ▪ Micro: vitamins, antioxidants, minerals, isoflavonoids, glucosinolates, phytoestrogens, lignins, condensed tannins
    ▪ Anti-nutrients: phytase, allergen and toxin reduction

  o Taste
  o Architecture

o Fiber

o Ornamentals: color, shelf-life, morphology, fragrance

• Novel Crop Products

o Oils

o Proteins: nutraceuticals, therapeutics, vaccines

o Polymers

• Renewable Resources: biomass conversion, feedstocks, biofuels.

With the recent energy crisis in 2006 caused by high petroleum prices, renewed efforts are underway in several countries to accelerate their R&D programs in improving crop varieties for more efficient biofuel production.

9.7.4 *SWOT analysis*

The following provides a summary of the strengths, weaknesses, opportunities and threats related to the commercialization of biotech crops.

The Strengths	The Weaknesses
— Strong financial support, R&D facilities and incentives	— Lack of expertise in biotechnology commercialization
— High priority in biotechnology R&D in government institution and universities	— The private sector is reluctant to invest in R&D and industries based on biotechnology unless transparent regulatory systems exist
— Governments have identified biotechnology as a core technology to be given priority	— Lack of molecular and genetic information of crops important to the country
— Reservoir of trained personnel in the component technologies for R&D	— Initially, a large sum of money is needed in order to purchase the equipment, land and expertise to start a biotech crop line
— Environmental protection through the use of less crop spray. GM crops are usually more resistant to pests	

(Continued)

(Continued)

The Opportunities	The Threats
— Increased demand for biotechnology products and services — Growing business opportunities for specialized agricultural products to meet increasing demand — Increased demand for biodetection services to identify GM crop for the market — Increased crop yield would result in the expansion of the agricultural market	— Opposition against genetically engineered products leading to delays in commercialization — Non-public acceptance — Worry that the modified genes in GM crops may "infect" organic crops, ruining the businesses of farmers who sell organic produce and reducing customer choice — GM crops may pose a health risk to natural predators if they do not have resistance to the built-in pesticides in the crop

9.8 Future Opportunities

Scientists today are able to improve the appearance of fruits and vegetables, increase the time food can be stored, enhance the nutrient content of plants and foods, and produce crops that are resistant to diseases and pests. In the future, biotechnologists also hope to be able to produce plants that withstand different climatic conditions, such as drought, extreme heat or cold, thereby enabling farmers to cultivate land that is currently poorly used. Biotechnology also offers new opportunities for the protection of our environment. For example, genetically modified bacteria may be used to convert organic wastes to useful products or to clean up oil spills, while research is ongoing to improve the ability of certain plant species to absorb toxic chemicals from soil and water (bioremediation).

In the near future, another set of products which focuses more on nutritional traits may more clearly demonstrate to the general public the benefits of biotechnology. Many of the biotech crop products in the public sector research pipeline will further be able to demonstrate more clearly the benefits to small farmers as they focus on a range of crops collectively known as the "orphan crops"; the private sector so far has only commercialized soybean, corn, cotton and canola. Countries like Malaysia are also working on the concept of plants as factories, in particular, on using the oil palm tree as a manufacturer of hydrocarbons with industrial applications. There is also ongoing work to use crops as carriers of medicine, such as vaccines (Cohen, 2005).

The end of the first decade since the large-scale introduction of agribiotechnology is a relevant time to ask why the adoption of biotech crops in Asia has not been faster. This is especially important because the benefits of biotechnology in this region are so obvious in terms of helping to alleviate the challenges posed by food security, equity, livelihood, farming drudgery and the economics of farming. It is also an opportune time to reexamine the premises on which biotech crop benefits were based, and to explore ways to tap into the largely unexploited potential of this technology to meet Asia's needs for more food, feed, fiber and fuel.

The major bottlenecks to large-scale commercialization of biotech crop products are not technological or scientific, but rather the issues related to public acceptance, trade and adequate frameworks for government oversight.

Developing countries stand to derive the most benefit from this new technology, and any excessive regulation will hinder progress and the sharing of benefits with the small resource-poor farmers in Asia. Asia is unique in its natural biological diversity, which serves as a resource (and therefore justifies protection), but also serves as an important natural buffer to the monocultural cropping systems needed to produce food efficiently in large enough quantities for feeding a growing population. It is hoped that, as experience with biotech crops grows and there is increasing demonstration of its safety, that the misconceptions and misinformation on this technology will decrease. Promising signs are already here, as evidenced by the European Union's recent decisions in favor of selected field trials of biotech crops, and by the continued importation (albeit regulated) of millions of tons of biotech crop products from North and Latin America.

Many countries in developing Asia have espoused national policies to promote biotechnology in agriculture, the most recent being the National Biotechnology Policy of Malaysia (Teng *et al.*, 2007). Most of these have been developed based on the anticipated role that biotechnology has played to create new value and to add value to existing agricultural businesses such as the seed business (Oliver, 2003; Shahi, 2004). Singapore government websites show that Singapore alone has invested over US$3 billion in the past few years to make biotechnology a major engine for economic growth. Its optimism is based on the anticipation that in a new globalized, knowledge-based economy, creating value through biology will likely add or even succeed the value created by the digital information-communication technologies.

Ultimately, it is likely that in Asia, the future of agricultural biotechnology will be decided by its relevance to feeding people and providing the food security essential for national development. Columbia University economist Jeffrey Sachs has noted that most of the world's new technologies are generated and owned by a small group of countries which collectively account for only about a third of the world's population. Asia, in which more than 60% of the world lives, is as yet not a notable contributor to new technologies, but rather, has been a major user and adapter of technology. This will change. Countries which recognize the potential of biotechnology will likely benefit most from it, even in the seemingly mundane business of commercializing biotech seeds.

References

Asia Productivity Organization (2007). *Business Potential of Agricultural Biotechnology Products.* Tokyo: Asian Productivity Organization.

Asian Development Bank (ADB) (2001). *Agricultural Biotechnology, Poverty Reduction, and Food Security.* Manila: ADB.

Bambawale, O.M., Singh, A., Sharma, O.P., Bhosle, B.B., Lavekar, R.C., Dhandapani, A., Kanwar, V., Tanwar, R.K., Rathod, K.S., Patange, N.R. and Pawar, V.M. (2004). Performance of Bt cotton (MECH-162) under Integrated Pest Management in farmers' participatory field trial in Nanded District, Central India. *Current Science*, 86(12): 1628–1633.

Cohen, J. (2005). Poorer nations turn to publicly developed GM crops. *Nature Biotechnology*, 23(1): 27–33.

Conway, G.R. (1998). *The Doubly Green Revolution: Food for All in the 21st Century*, pp. 44–65. Ithaca, NY: Cornell University Press.

Gould, F. (1998). Sustainability of transgenic insecticidal cultivars: Integrating pest genetics and ecology. *Annual Review of Entomology*, 43: 701–726.

Hancock, J.F. (2003). A framework for assessing the risk of transgenic crops. *BioScience*, 53: 512–519.

Heitz, A. (1999). Plant variety protection and cultivar names under the UPOV Convention. In *Taxonomy of Cultivated Plants: Third International Symposium* (Ed. S. Andrews, A.C. Leslie and C. Alexander), pp. 59–65. Royal Botanic Gardens, Kew, UK.

Huang, J. and Wang, Q.F. (2002). Agricultural biotechnology development and policy in China. *AgBioForum*, 5(4): 122–135.

James, C. (2006). Global status of commercialized biotech/GM crops: 2006. ISAAA Brief 35. Ithaca, New York.

James, C. (2007). Global status of commercialized biotech/GM crops: 2007. ISAAA Brief 37. Ithaca, New York.

Juma, C. (1989). Life as an intellectual property. In *The Gene Hunters — Biotechnology and the Scramble for Seeds* (Ed. C. Juma), pp. 149–178. Princeton, New Jersey: Princeton University Press.

Manalo, A.J. and Ramon, G.P. (2007). The cost of product development of Bt corn event MON810 in the Philippines. *AgBioForum*, 10(1): 19–32. http://www. agbioforum.org.

Murray, D.R. (2003). *Seeds of Concern — The Genetic Manipulation of Plants*, pp. 35–37. CABI Publishing.

Oliver, R.W. (2003). *The Biotech Age: The Business of Biotech and How to Profit from It*. McGraw-Hill.

Pray, C., Huang, J., Hu, R. and Rozelle, S. (2002). Five years of Bt cotton in China: The benefits continue. *The Plant Journal*, 31(4): 423–430.

Serageldin, I. (1999). Biotechnology and food security in the 21st century. *Science*, 285: 5426.

Shahi, G.S. (2004). *Biobusiness in Asia*. Pearson Prentice Hall.

Teng, P.S. (1999). Current and future importance of biotechnology to crop protection. Paper presented at the Symposium on International Crop Protection: Achievements and Ambition, The Brighton Conference, 15 November, British Crop Protection Council.

Teng, P.S. (2006). Where does Asia stand in accepting agribiotechnology crops? *Asia Pacific Biotech*, 10(15): 838–845.

Teng, P.S., Arujanan, M. and Dardak, R.A. (2007). Development of Malaysia's biotechnology sector. In *The Malaysian Economy: Development and Challenges*. National University of Singapore.

Thomas, J.A. and Fuchs, R.L. (eds.) (2002). *Biotechnology and Safety Assessment*. San Diego: Academic Press.

Ye, X.D., Al-Babili, S., Kl'ti, A., Zhang, J., Lucca, P., Beyer, P. and Potrykus, I. (2000). Engineering the complete provitamin A (beta-carotene) biosynthetic pathway into (carotenoid-free) rise endosperm. *Science*, 287: 303–305.

Chapter 10
Growing the Opportunities for Bioscience Entrepreneurship in Asia

In Asia, all projections point to an increasing number of people, an increasing demand for food, feed, fuel and fiber, and progressively, a demand for a cleaner environment. By 2025, there will likely be more than five billion people in Asia, with an increasingly affluent but older population, most of whom will live in megacities with over ten million people each. Most of Asia's poor, however, will still live in the countryside.

The area of arable land for agriculture and the availability of potable water are expected to decline. While the threat of dwindling physical resources challenges the goal of increasing agricultural production, it also provides unparalleled opportunities for bioscience entrepreneurship.

Asian economies which aspire to exploit these opportunities will need to reposition themselves by generating and owning the knowledge to use bioscience, and subsequently, form strategic alliances to utilize the knowledge for productive purposes.

For most bioscience enterprises, value capture and value addition can be anticipated mainly from ownership of intellectual property, such as on the bioprocessing activities described in previous chapters. Comparatively less value capture or addition would accrue from the production of the biomaterial itself. The value chain of bioscience enterprises today is different from that of the first "Green Revolution" in the 1960s, and will more closely resemble that of the "Life Science Revolution" in the early 1990s.

Many countries have made projections of the anticipated value of the "bio" sector, which is expected to nurture new industries. For example, the Department of Biotechnology, Ministry of Science and Technology, Government of India estimated that biotechnology in India has the potential of generating revenues to the tune of US$5 billion, with agricultural and industrial biotechnology (biopesticides included) snagging US$500 million worth of market value. BioEnterprise Asia (www.bioenterprise.org) projects that the world market for biobusinesses will likely exceed US$150 billion by 2010 with a growth rate of 15% annually.

Many recent developments have renewed interest in the production of food, feed, fiber, fuel and pharmaceuticals, and consequently, in bioscience entrepreneurship in the Asian region. The 1996 hikes in petroleum prices stimulated rigorous debate on alternatives, with the consequent production of biofuels catalyzing a nascent industry in several countries, and diverting the use of crops such as corn from their primary use for animal feed to biofuel production. More recently, Asia has seen some significant increases in the prices of raw commodities such as corn and palm oil for the same reasons, and while the short-term effects have been disruptive to the food-feed supply chain, the mid- to long-term implication for investments and new industries is one of great potential to create employment and value!

In the 1990s, with rapid developments in biotechnology, Asia saw much interest in "biobusinesses" based mainly on the potential of the new life science industry to spill over into pharmaceuticals and biomedical applications. In reality, many new companies which had entered into this highly competitive field were faced with only limited success, owing to competition from larger multinational companies of the industrialized countries which had strong "first entry" advantage. A few countries, exemplified by Singapore, have been able to grow their own biomedical sectors, but only after large multi-billion-dollar investments. By and large, most Asian countries have not been able to tap into the "biobusiness" potential so ably described in the pioneering book, *BioBusiness in Asia* by Gurinder S. Shahi (2004, Pearson Education South Asia).

The Asian financial crisis of 1996–1997 played a role in dampening investment interest, but also in raising consciousness on the need to address basics before embarking on new ventures. Thailand, through the urging of its Royal Family, embarked on a program of self-sufficiency to address its own food needs; Malaysia refocused its national development plan to move agriculture away from a "sunset industry" status. China's continued economic growth and the corresponding overall uplift in its people's standard of living also contributed to renewed interest to ensure secured supplies of the fundamentals — food, feed, fiber and fuel. The recent spiking of petroleum prices, the general optimism in the Asian region about continued prosperity, the availability of capital through high national average savings rates, are additional factors which have spurred a renaissance in bioscience enterprises for value creation and to meet Asia's growing needs.

10.1 The Demand for Bioproducts and Its Link to Changing Human Demographics

It is estimated that the world's population will double by the year 2033, placing increasing stress on world food production. In Asia, food demand is expected to exceed supply by the year 2010, posing huge supply challenges to its agricultural systems.

Traditional farming equipment and practices are reaching their limits of effectiveness in increasing agricultural productivity. As countries develop, people demand more and better food. These pressures are multiplied by shrinking farmland, rising labor costs and shortage of farm workers.

There are about 800 million hungry people in the developing world today, including 185 million seriously malnourished preschool children. Many of these unfortunates lack adequate food, water and protection from food-related disease. However, the number of starving and malnourished people would have been much larger today if not for the significant progress made to alleviate their sufferings over the past 50 years. Unfortunately, progress has not been achieved everywhere; large numbers of hungry people remain in India and Bangladesh, despite the substantial gains in per capita food production there.

Before the middle of the 19th century, "hunger and premature death" were the norm for most of humanity. At that period of time, 80%–90% or even more of the people in what would become today's wealthy developed countries were farmers. Then came the Industrial Revolution and the application of technology and science to farming. The benefits of science to agriculture have been immense. Food availability increased, notably in Europe, North America and Japan, sparking an increase in life expectancy and population growth in these countries. For example, from 1800 to 1950, life expectancy in England increased from 35 to 68 years of age (Fogel, 2004). However, the benefits of increased food supply were not far-reaching. People residing outside the few aforementioned countries continued to eat simple diets with barely enough to maintain themselves. Even in 1950, life expectancy in countries such as Egypt, India and China was about 40 years; hunger was widespread; stunting and nutritional deficiencies were widespread.

From the middle of the 20th century, the fortunes of many poorer countries began to lift. In the developing world, life expectancy increased from 40 to 64 years as average food consumption increased and real prices of food actually fell, despite the doubling of population — a remarkable achievement (FAO, 2002). Chronic food shortages, manifested in protein-energy malnutrition, fell sharply in Asia largely owing to increased grain yields and farm incomes. These regions went through a process similar to what Europe, North America and Japan had experienced somewhat earlier, where products of the industrial and scientific revolutions were applied to food production.

Without the tremendous gains that have been made in food production and economic development over the past half-century, many more people would be chronically hungry today. Table 10.1 presents some of the basic facts related to current food security in the major

Table 10.1. Indicators of food security and agricultural production.

	% of population under- nourished	Agric. labor force as % total	Agric. land per agric. worker (ha)	Grain yield (kg/ha)	Pesticide applied per ha arable land (kg)	Fertilizer applied per ha arable land (kg)
South Asia	24	59.0	0.7	4,385	0.39	116
Southeast and East Asia	10	62.2	1.2	2,985	1.96	224
Developed economies		7.6	37.6	4,809	1.55	84

Source: The State of Food and Agriculture 2003–2004, Food and Agricultural Organization, Rome, 2004; Compendium of Agriculture — Environmental Indicators (http://www.fao.org/es/ess/os/envi_indi/part_213.asp).

regions of the world. It is saddening to note that about 17% (350 million people) of the population in Asia and the Pacific are hungry. Although China has managed to reduce the percentage of its starving population to about 11%, the total population percentage of hungry people in South Asia still remains at a high 24%.

Increased food production and income are two important factors associated with reduced hunger. Other important associated factors include improved transportation and education of the population, especially with regard to females. Asia has been able to increase grain yield despite a relatively small land area per capita largely because modern agricultural technology has been developed and applied widely over the past 30–40 years. Without the aid of bioscience, Asia would have remained as it was in the 1960s, with similar rates of hunger, low-yielding crops and primitive technology as most of Africa today.

The Green Revolution of the 1970s and its continuation into the 21st century provide ongoing refutation to the idea that farmers are reluctant to adopt new technology. The key determinant of technology adoption is its contribution to farmer well-being, often reflected as greater income, but sometimes as more food, reduction in effort or better working conditions. As farming becomes more technologically advanced, it requires capital investments like wells and buildings that are attached to the land, so farmers must have assured rights to the land to encourage such investments. The institutions that assure land rights, incentive prices and a steady stream of new technology are critical for agricultural development. All these requirements can only be achieved in a stable, non-oppressive political, social and economic context. Hence, well-functioning governments that understand the importance of agriculture and make the necessary investments in agricultural infrastructure and human capital are critical.

Crop yields in the developing world have increased substantially over the past 50 years (see Table 10.2). Significant increases have been observed across most regions with crops like sorghum and potato. Wheat, maize and rice yields today have more than doubled from yields in the 17th century. Although overall crop yields have increased around the world, the increases have been greatest in Asia and Latin America. The gains can be attributed to new modern crop varieties, coupled with fertilizer and irrigation. Generally, the more that countries are willing to implement new biotechnologies to their agriculture, the greater the crop yield.

As mentioned earlier, planting and harvesting new genetic varieties of crops were integral to the increase of nationwide crop yields. From 1960 to 2000, public breeding programs in over 100 countries released over 8,000 new varieties of the major food crops. Since the 1990s, private local and international seed companies have begun creating varieties for developing countries based on "platform" varieties generated by these public sector breeding programs.

The new varieties, the most important component of the Green Revolution, have been widely adopted by farmers, especially in Asia and Latin America, and were central to improving food security of developing countries over the past 40 years. Today, these new varieties are integral to the agricultural processes of Asian and developing countries, with modern varieties of wheat taking up over 85% of all developing country wheat area, and modern varieties of rice taking up over 80% of Asia's rice area.

Table 10.2.   Developing world staple food crop yields, 1961–1965 and 1999–2003 (kg/ha).

	Wheat		Rice		Maize	
	1961–1965	1999–2003	1961–1965	1999–2003	1961–1965	1999–2003
Asia	850	2,750	1,800	3,950	1,250	3,650
L. America	1,500	2,550	1,750	3,550	1,225	2,850
Mid-East NA	950	2,050	3,400	5,750	1,850	5,620
SS Africa	790	1,500	1,250	1,650	850	1,250

	Sorghum		Potato	
	1961–1965	1999–2003	1961–1965	1999–2003
Asia	650	975	8,750	1,450
L. America	1,500	2,850	7,200	15,250
Mid-East NA	1,025	850	11,400	21,950
SS Africa	750	825	6,250	7,550

Source: FAOSTAT.

Food security is fundamental for economic growth and national development. Asia is expected to be the most populous region of the world in the foreseeable future. Therefore, the demands for products of bioscience enterprises are expected to continue playing significant roles.

10.2 Investments in Capacity: Science Parks in Asia

In Asia, the creation of science and technology parks and high technology clusters are key major initiatives for enhancing economic growth. Almost invariably, these parks and clusters are located in close proximity to universities and government laboratories. Universities play an important role in providing skilled personnel, research and access to research-support facilities. Science and technology parks are contributing to the growth of technology-based manufacturing and services in a region where agriculture previously dominated. This section offers a brief scan of some of these parks.

Some of the parks have been created and managed by governments, but most involve public-private partnerships in which park developers get a return on their investment, while governments achieve economic and industry development objectives.

Science and technology parks have their origins in post-war USA. Stanford University's Industrial Park has not only enhanced the high reputation of the University, but also underpinned the high-technology industrial growth in the Silicon Valley. The Silicon Valley phenomenon is something that science and technology parks in Asia seek to emulate. Technology-based clusters — firms with similar business interests located in close geographic proximity with universities — are a key feature of science and technology parks. Science and technology parks help to draw together firms with related interests and provide them with all the features of clusters.

Science and technology parks are playing a major role in the development of knowledge-based industries in Asia. The parks have provided a focus, not only for the major players such as the semiconductor manufacturers, but also for a wide range of supporting industries. The clustering of these industries has created significant competitive advantage — for example, Singapore has become a world leader in disc drives, while Taiwan has become a world leader in memory chips.

Asian countries are now placing a new emphasis on parks which focus on biotechnology and life sciences, with the aim of achieving a strong position in particular areas such as medical devices (Shanghai), agricultural biotechnology (Malaysia, Taiwan), pharmaceuticals (Singapore) and biomedical software (India).

There is generous government support in Asia for science and technology parks as catalysts for technological development. There are many common features of governmental monetary support for science and technology parks. Benefits to bioscience firms include low corporate tax rates, tax incentives, tax holidays, low-interest loans, free or low-cost land, grants, tariff concessions and accelerated approvals. There are even a few cases of personal tax measures designed to help recruit highly skilled foreigners.

The number of science parks in Asia grew rapidly in the 1980s. They were developed in designated areas or zones, usually within close proximity to universities and research institutes. Specialized industries were attracted into the parks as collaboration with the parks ensured that the outcomes of their research and innovation would result in the stimulation of technology transfer between institutions and industry within the parks. Science and technology parks also offer opportunities for synergy between business incubators, technology enterprises and research institutes, particularly to assist with the early development and stimulation of business. For this reason, parks often include business incubators as well.

A feature of most of the science and technology parks in Asia is that they are property-based developments, planned to create and develop high-growth technology businesses that result in high-value jobs. Local authorities, state and provincial governments and national governments encourage the development of science and technology parks through the provision of land and building space at concessional rates and financial incentives such as income tax exemptions.

10.2.1 *Singapore*

Singapore has several science parks of which the Biopolis may be considered comparable in scale to those in other countries. The Biopolis symbolizes Singapore's new direction in encouraging the growth of technology-based sectors. Built at the cost of approximately S$500 million and launched in October 2003, the Biopolis is the center of biomedical research in Singapore and is claimed to be the world's first integrated, purpose-built biomedical research complex. It has the full complement of R&D activities — encompassing basic scientific research, medical research, drug discovery and medical technology research. The Biopolis also boasts both public and private sector research laboratories and is further designed to stimulate interaction and collaboration between industry and public research laboratories.

Biopolis is strategically located close to Singapore's National University and the National University Hospital and the Institute of Molecular and Cell Biology. It is also home to the multi-agency Genetic Modification Advisory Committee, which regulates biotechnology research.

10.2.2 *Malaysia*

Malaysia has both federal- and state-sponsored science parks. The Technology Park Malaysia (TPM), located within the Multimedia Super Corridor, covers 300 hectares at Bukit Jalil in the southern outskirts of Kuala Lumpur. The mission of TPM is to provide first-class infrastructure and services for technological innovation and R&D, facilitating the growth of knowledge-based industries which are able to compete in the global market. TPM's objectives are directed towards:

- facilitating private sector R&D and innovation;
- participating in the commercialization of research results and innovation;
- facilitating smart partnerships between the government and private sector in technology development;

- providing support and services in marketing, management and technical fields to tenant companies;
- creating a conducive environment in order to stimulate a knowledge-based community; and
- participating in wealth creation through technological innovation and creativity development.

TPM's development is divided into three technology-related "Cities" — Engineering City, Biotech City and Communications and Technology City. There is a strong emphasis on maintaining harmony between the buildings and the surrounding tropical environment.

Another noteworthy science and technology park in Malaysia is the Kulim Hi-Tech Park. Covering 1,450 hectares, Kulim Hi-Tech Park is a fully integrated high-technology industrial park in the northern state of Kedah. The Park's masterplan emphasizes quality of life in a self-contained environment that incorporates industries, R&D facilities, and a township with full amenities including a shopping center, a hospital, educational institutions and recreational facilities. The first phase of its industrial zone covering 250 hectares has been fully leased, and tenants have moved into the second phase.

The Selangor Science Park-1 (SSP-1) is supported by the state government and planned by the Selangor State Development Corporation (PKNS). SSP-1 is designed utilizing modular concept to allow technology-based companies to establish facilities that can grow to meet future needs. SSP-1 is located within the Kota Damansara Township, 45 minutes from Kuala Lumpur International Airport, and provides an environment conducive to high-tech manufacturing activities, supported by the nearby MSC and universities. Companies investing in the SSP-1 can access various venture capital funds from the state of Selangor's investment arms. Malaysia also has a number of industry and business parks including the Bayan Lepas Industrial Park on the island of Penang, where Motorola has a major facility. Perak State is developing a state "biovalley" to nurture bioscience enterprises based on modern technology.

A federal "BioValley" project was launched in May 2003 to tap potential benefits from the modern biology. At that time, the National

Biotechnology Directorate identified genomics and proteomics, agriculture, and nutraceutical/pharmaceutical technologies as the three research priorities to be addressed in the Eighth Malaysia Plan. The BioValley project has since evolved into a "BioNexus" program.

Malaysia announced a new National Biotechnology Policy on 28 April 2005. Under the new roadmap for biotechnology, the nation's emphasis has been shifted to agricultural biotechnology, healthcare biotechnology and industrial biotechnology. These areas have been identified based on Malaysia's leading position in plant commodities and the abundance of natural resources which could be sustainably utilized in the healthcare sector. R&D activities and collaborations with industries will take place in existing research facilities in public universities and research institutions throughout the country. The new strategy does not favor the establishment of a biotech cluster as decision was made to put resources into developing and upgrading the existing research facilities.

Furthermore, biotech activities are already taking place at some local universities which are host to a couple of incubators. Industries will naturally thrive around centers that have good connections with research institutes and universities. As such, the upgrading of existing facilities and the encouragement of researchers through provision of supportive research grants and incentives would be the best way to lure investors and companies to set up their biotech entities in these centers of excellence. In order to provide a physical infrastructure to meet the needs of researchers worldwide, Malaysia has developed the BioNexus, as a network of centers of excellence throughout the country, comprising companies and institutions which specialize in specific biotech areas.

Under the National Biotech Policy, three national institutes were set up, namely the National Institute for Agricultural Biotechnology, the National Institute for Pharmaceutical and Nutraceuticals, and the National Institute for Genomics and Proteomics. These institutes are under the purview of the Ministry of Science, Technology and Innovation, with an aim to spearhead research in these areas. As the value proposition of BioNexus is to leverage on existing facilities, the Pharmaceutical and Nutraceutical Institute is being established at the present biovalley site at Dengkil. The Institute of Agro-biotechnology is situated at MARDI, Serdang and the Genomic and Molecular Biology Institute is situated at the present facilities in the National University Malaysia in Bangi.

To streamline biotechnology research, seven Biotechnology Cooperative Centers (BCCs) have been established. The BCCs help to coordinate biotech research in the various research organizations to improve cooperation and reduce duplication. The seven BCCs are:

- Molecular Biology Cooperative Center University Malaya (UM) and Universiti Kebangsaan Malaysia (UKM)
- Plant Biotechnology Cooperative Center Malaysian Agricultural Research and Development Institute (MARDI)
- Animal Biotechnology Cooperative Center Universiti Putra Malaysia (UPM)
- Medical Biotechnology Cooperative Center Universiti Malaysia Sarawak (UNIMAS) and Institute of Medical Research (IMR)
- Environmental/Industrial Biotechnology SIRIM Cooperative Center
- Biopharmacy Cooperative Center Universiti Sains Malaysia (USM), and
- Food Biotechnology Cooperative Center Universiti Putra Malaysia (UPM) and Malaysian Agricultural Research and Development Institute (MARDI).

10.2.3 *Taiwan*

Taiwan is planning to establish a series of Agricultural Biotechnology Parks to concentrate limited resources and provide adequate basic investment conditions to attract both local and international biotech investors. Currently, Taiwan has already established the Agricultural Biotechnology Park in Pingtung, the National Flower Park in Changhua, the Taiwan Orchid Plantation in Tainan, the Medicinal and Spice Herb Biotechnology Park in Chiayi, and the Marine Biotechnology Park in Ilan, combining private capitalization and governmental research and development capacity to create a high value-added industry in agriculture. The Agricultural Biotechnology Park

Establishment and Management Act was announced in April 2004. The law primarily provides full access to factory facilities, and clarifies the amenities and benefits offered to agricultural biotechnology companies.

Among Taiwan's technology parks, the Tainan Park would be one of the most notable. The Tainan Park site was originally chosen because of its proximity to agricultural research institutes such as the National Cheng Kung University, National Sun Yat-Sen University, the World Vegetable Center (a.k.a. Asian Vegetable Research and Development Center), Taiwan Livestock Research Institute and the Tung Kang Marine Laboratory. Tainan is regarded as an agricultural biotechnology center. Its targeted activities are biopesticides, livestock vaccines and aquaculture. The National Science Council has a center for industrial-academic R&D in Tainan, which provides an incubation center. This system includes prototyping facilities, counseling, training, information and legal services, as well as a range of grant, credit and equity financing arrangements.

10.2.4 *India*

Although a relatively recent entry into the "science park race", India has caught up with its large and diverse number of such parks. The Information Technology Park (ITPL) near Bangalore in the state of Karnataka is a joint venture involving Tata Industries Limited, a Singapore Consortium led by Ascendas, and the Karnataka Industrial Areas Development Board. The park provides state-of-the-art infrastructure and professionally managed services to attract global and local investors to Bangalore. The main focuses of the technology park are on biotechnology and bioinformatics.

Another of India's science and technology parks is the Genome Valley, which is spread over 600 square km near Hyderabad in the state of Andhra Pradesh. This Valley is India's first major biotechnology cluster providing infrastructure to more than 100 biotechnology companies. A cluster of biotechnology research, training, collaboration and manufacturing activities is located in Genome Valley. These include several science parks and related facilities such as ICICI

Knowledge Park, Shapoorji Pallonji Biotech Park, centers of excellence in biotechnology (such as India's Center for Cellular and Molecular Biology, ICICI) and some major healthcare organizations. ICICI Knowledge Park is a not-for-profit company set up in partnership with the Andhra Pradesh government and the ICICI Group in 1956. ICICI is a leading financial institution in India, founded by the World Bank, the Indian government and the private sector in 1955 to assist industrial development and investment. The main focuses of this park are biotechnology, pharmaceuticals, new materials and telecommunications.

10.2.5 *China*

China is another Asian country which boasts numerous science parks. Zhangjiang Park was established in 1992 as a national-level park designated for the development of new high technologies. The Shanghai municipal government decided in 1992 to accelerate the park's development by issuing its "focus on Zhangjiang" strategic policy and increased the size of the park with the aim of attracting more R&D companies. The focus of the park was on ICT, biotechnology and pharmaceuticals, with the goal of developing innovation and entrepreneurship. Zhangjiang is the only zone designated by the central government for the development of the pharmaceutical industry.

Caohejing Park is about 11 km southwest of Shanghai. It is a state economic and technological zone as well as a high-technology development zone that received approval from the authorities in 1988. It has a broad focus — semiconductors, optical communications, aerospace and aviation, satellite telecommunications, laser technology, bioengineering, new materials and biomedicine. It is believed that within these industries, there are about 1,000 enterprises, research and service institutes in the park, employing some 45,000 skilled staff.

In 2001, the Shanghai municipal government approved the development of Zizhu Science-Based Industrial Park. The first phase, covering 15 square km, was opened in June 2002. The Shanghai Minhang district government, the Shanghai-based Alliance Investment Company Limited, Shanghai Jiatong University and the Zijiang Group has set up a company to manage the park with a capital base of A$100 million. The Zijiang Group has also injected A$50 million for the development of several colleges and research centers in the park. Zizhu is Shanghai's first science park funded partly by the state and partly by the private sector, unlike most of the other science parks in China which are state-funded, and covers a number of university campuses.

Almost every Asian country that aspires to exploit modern bioscience has declared supportive policies and incentive packages to attract investment. A scan of some notable ones is given here.

10.3 How Ready is Asia to Exploit the Opportunities?

In this book, ten types of bioscience enterprises have been described in eight chapters, namely:

- Hybrid plant and seed varieties
- Tissue culture
- Biofermentation, biofertilizers and biopesticides
- Mushroom culture
- Biofuels
- Bioremediation
- Biodetection, and
- Biotechnology crops (genetically modified plants).

There are obvious differences in the region's readiness to exploit the potential in each; there are also differences among countries in their attitudes towards each of these enterprises and in their readiness to tap the opportunities. Table 10.3 is a simplified diagram to give a "bird's eye" view of the situation.

Asia is particularly strong in the more conventional bioscience enterprises such as production of raw biocommodities like rubber and palm oil. Countries in general are ill-prepared to conduct the sophisticated R&D needed for full exploitation of the developments in modern biosciences such as genomics and its associated biotechnology. The largest potential return to investment in bioscience enterprises

Table 10.3.   Relative readiness of Asian region to exploit bioscience opportunities.

Bioscience enterprise	R&D capacity to generate innovations	Technology adoption & distribution systems	Regulatory frameworks to facilitate commercialization	Investment facilities	Public acceptance
Raw biocommodities	++	+++	+++	+++	+++
High-quality seed material using hybrids	+++	++	+++	++	+++
High-quality seed material using tissue culture	+++	+++	+++	+++	+++
Biofermentation	++	++	++	++	++
Biofertilizers	+++	+	+++	+	+++
Biopesticides	+++	++	+++	+	+++
Biofuels	+	+	++	+	++
Bioremediation	+	+	++	+	++
Biotech seeds	+	+	+	+	+

Notes: "+" indicates strength of current status, activity or capacity (+ = low; ++ = medium; +++ = strong).

is likely to be those developed using modern biotechnology. Biotech seed is one such direct product.

Asia grew approximately 10 million hectares of biotech crops in 2007. Three biotech crops (cotton, corn or maize and canola) are currently planted in significant areas in Asia with government regulatory approval. In China and India, which together account for more than a third of the world's population, over 7 million small farmers are estimated to grow 4.6 million hectares of biotech crops. In China, biotech crops such as tomato and sweet pepper are grown in small areas, while Australia grows biotech carnation. Biotech (B.t.) cotton was first commercially planted in Australia and China in 1996, followed by the approval of B.t. corn in the Philippines in 2000 and of B.t. cotton in India in 2002. Indonesia planted B.t. corn for a brief period in 2000. Official figures aside, it is also known and acknowledged by those concerned that biotech crops are grown in Cambodia and Vietnam using imported seeds.

Within the ASEAN region, the Philippines was the first country to approve a biotech crop for food and feed (i.e., B.t. corn), and has developed a strong public institutional capacity for pioneering agribiotechnology-related R&D. Several biotech crops (rice, papaya, banana, sugar cane, potato and tomato) are in development in the Philippines, and field trials have been conducted with government oversight on rice and corn. Vietnam has also been receptive to the study and implementation of biotechnology related to genetically modified crops. Vietnam has for years been conducting contained experiments on papaya, rice, sugar cane, potato and tomato through the Institute of Biotechnology and the Omon Rice Research Institute. With the impending implementation of a new biosafety regulatory framework, Vietnam seems poised to significantly increase its use of modern biotechnology for crop improvement. Thailand was one of the earliest countries in Asia to initiate agribiotech crop R&D on a large number of species, and to implement a regulatory regime for agribiotechnology. However, it has now appeared to adopt a "wait and see" attitude towards the commercial release of any biotech crop, while maintaining an active research agenda.

In Indonesia, B.t. cotton was momentarily planted in seven regencies in South Sulawesi in 2001; within the public sector, there is ongoing proof-of-concept research on crops like rice, corn, potato and soybean. Malaysia has a very strongly articulated National Biotechnology Policy, in which agriculture is given the highest priority, and institutional capacity for R&D in universities and government agencies is of the highest standard. However, the country at this time has no experience with the commercialization process or with public regulation of agribiotechnology for commercial release, and it has not yet developed a biosafety framework for implementation. Singapore has recently enacted guidelines for the commercialization of agribiotech crops, and it has strengthened its capacity to conduct proof-of-concept research and to develop prototypes for technology licensing and sharing, even though the island-state's economy is not agriculture-dependent. In addition, many other countries which have not been discussed here — such as Bangladesh, Pakistan, Nepal, Japan and Korea — have both upstream (molecular biology, genomics, etc.) and downstream (back-crossing biotech crop parents with local crops) biotech research activities.

10.4   "Freedom to Operate" (FTO) Issues in Acceptance and Adoption of Novel Bioscience Products

FTO issues were discussed in Chapter 9 and comprise the following:

- Effective technology with clear intellectual property (IP) for release;
- IP protection systems;
- Technology distribution systems;
- Transparent, science-based regulatory systems for biosafety and food/feed safety;
- Conducive government policies at the national level that are in congruence with international norms; and
- Consumer acceptance.

Almost without exception, biotech crops have been successfully commercialized and released for farmers' use only by private companies.

The commercial release of biotech seeds in Asian countries has been done by multinational seed companies working either on their own or in partnership with a local company or public institution. The reasons for this are manifold, and include a lack of the following factors among developing countries: resident expertise in agricultural biotechnology and the commercialization process, ownership of the proprietary technology required to develop a viable biotech crop product, knowledge of product stewardship programs, investment capital for the long concept-to-product process, etc. The process of commercializing an agribiotech crop product goes through many stages, each of which is dependent on the success of the preceding stage or is linked to others (Figure 9.3, Chapter 9). Experience has shown that it takes 7–12 years to move from the proof-of-concept stage to the launch stage, while imported technology may require 4–6 years to obtain all the necessary regulatory approvals before a product can be sold or released. The latter is a strong argument for forming partnerships, either private-private or public-private. FTO issues impinge on many of the stages shown in Figure 9.3.

Of the 674 biotech products approved by 53 regulatory agencies worldwide, about 86% are owned by 10 companies, of which about half are directly owned by a single company. This highlights the importance of ensuring FTO in the development of a biotech seed product. Because of the relatively large investment of public funds in Asia to conduct proof-of-concept research, which aims to generate effective technology expressing a desired trait (e.g., improved insect resistance, virus resistance), public institutions need to internalize the capacity to conduct IP audits and manage IP. Until recently, such capacity did not exist in public institutions. However, efforts such as those by the ISAAA to conduct regional training workshops for public sector scientists and science administrators have resulted in pockets of expertise in selected public institutions in Thailand, Philippines, Indonesia and India. Several meetings convened under the Asia-Pacific Economic Cooperation (APEC) umbrella have also helped to focus attention and create awareness of the importance of IP management. Closely linked to IP protection systems are seed variety regulations and protocols; indeed, most biotech seeds rely on hybrid cultivars to capture value. It is difficult to imagine private investment in agribiotechnology without the use of hybrids for technology distribution.

The last two aspects of FTO — government policies and consumer acceptance — receive much media coverage. In the last two years, several governments have visibly promoted agribiotechnology. Most notably, Malaysia announced its National Biotechnology Policy in April 2005, followed by details concerning the restructuring of its operational approaches into three focus areas. The Malaysian Biotechnology Corporation has also been formed, with its prime mandate being to attract investment and develop a new industry. Moreover, Singapore and Vietnam have recently made very supportive policy announcements on plant-based biotechnology. In the context of FTO and commercialization, the crucial element in such policies is whether they translate into regulations or guidelines which would allow the many stages required in product development. For example, most of the Asian countries which have ratified the Cartagena Protocol on Biosafety have yet to internalize their procedures on articles required by the Protocol, such as those concerning liability and redress. The latter is particularly important, as a strict liability regime will stifle or even turn away investors by putting undue financial burdens on researchers.

Consumer acceptance of agribiotechnology, which takes the form of crops growing over large areas and food processed from biotech products, remains a matter requiring much effort in public education and information sharing. Surveys in several Asian countries have shown that, while most consumers rank issues such as pesticides and quality higher than doubts about GMOs in their choice of purchase, a small but significant proportion have negative to neutral perceptions about the safety of foods derived using agribiotechnology. Public acceptance issues fall into three broad categories: food safety, environmental safety and social/bioethical issues. Concerns over the first two categories have decreased as scientific evidence about safety has accumulated, and as experience with the safe use of agribiotechnology has grown among farmers, consumers and regulators. However, social and bioethical issues continue to be debated and revolve around the control over and access to the technology, the morality of the technology, and the religious implications of gene transfer. Many countries now have active biotechnology education and information dissemination activities at many levels, notably among the network of biotechnology information centers coordinated by the ISAAA's Global Knowledge Center on Crop Biotechnology. The network's members have been largely responsible for creating a group of well-informed agribiotech champions among the scientific, government and farming communities in several Asian countries.

10.5 The Important Role of "Innovation and Entrepreneurship" in the Biosciences and in Bioscience Entrepreneurship

In Chapter 1 of this book, I discussed the important role that education plays in fostering the innovation chain leading to successful entrepreneurship. Innovation and Entrepreneurship ("I & E") have become embedded in the policy initiatives of governments such as Singapore through its school education system (www.moe.gov.sg). In education circles throughout Asia, there is much discussion on how to nurture more creativity as a desired outcome of education, with some countries having introduced enquiry-based learning approaches in the science and mathematics curricula. Recognition is made of the role of creative individuals to spark the innovations for creating value that leads to products in the marketplace.

At the National Institute of Education, Singapore, a new approach that explicitly recognizes this has been proposed by this author — the Science Plus (Science$^+$) Paradigm — in which core knowledge and skills as part of a science curriculum is deemed to be core, but value addition is achieved through the "Plus" skills. These plus skills have been divided into three sets, namely "grantsmanship", "teambuilding" and "communication". The author has taught teacher in-service courses on developing I & E skills, in which each of these three sets is detailed with practice and case studies (www.nie.edu.sg). Grantsmanship includes knowledge of the concepts and tools for moving a concept to a project, and an appropriately planned project

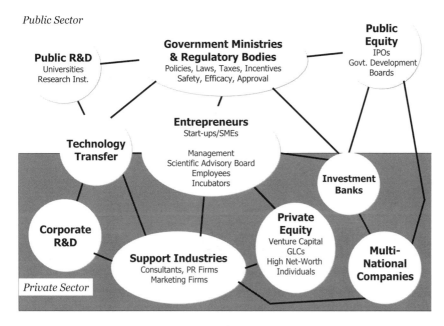

Figure 10.1.   Success enablers for bioscience entrepreneurship.

Source: Modified from M. Arroyo, Hybridigm Consulting, Philippines, 2005 (www.hybridigm-consulting.com).

document in different forms for resource mobilization. Teambuilding includes knowledge to assemble a team of compatible individuals able to leverage off each other's skills to move from a "storming" phase to a "performing" phase.

Apart from education, which builds the capacity to exploit opportunities, other enablers of success are shown in Figure 10.1. Academic institutions (public and private) and company R&D teams will continue to be the main source of technology for bioscience products. This is not to discount the origin of some innovations accruing from farmers and the public, but they have not seen the level of impact as the technologies from organized sources. Science sparks on their own will not give the desired outcomes unless they are connected to other success enablers such as entrepreneurs, regulatory bodies and the investment community. In some countries, bioscience products such as biotech seeds are subject to national and local political influence as well, whether positive (technology champions) or negative (anti-technology activists). Connectivity between parts is key to success, and SMEs have sprouted in number to offer their services in making connections in a proactive manner.

Opportunities to participate in the renaissance of bioscience entrepreneurship can occur in the many components made possible by a community of practice. Some of these are illustrated in Figure 10.2. Most successful bioscience MNCs have exploited opportunities associated with IP generation and product development,

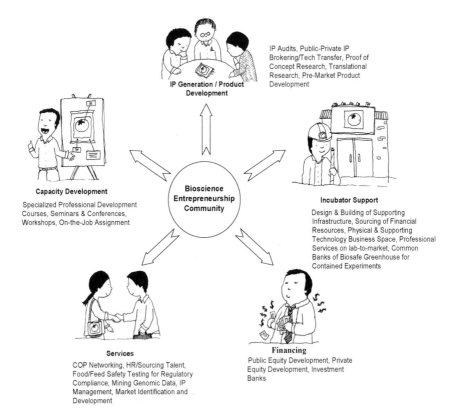

IP Generation / Product Development

IP Audits, Public-Private IP Brokering/Tech Transfer, Proof of Concept Research, Translational Research, Pre-Market Product Development

Capacity Development

Specialized Professional Development Courses, Seminars & Conferences, Workshops, On-the-Job Assignment

Bioscience Entrepreneurship Community

Incubator Support

Design & Building of Supporting Infrastructure, Sourcing of Financial Resources, Physical & Supporting Technology Business Space, Professional Services on lab-to-market, Common Banks of Biosafe Greenhouse for Contained Experiments

Services

COP Networking, HR/Sourcing Talent, Food/Feed Safety Testing for Regulatory Compliance, Mining Genomic Data, IP Management, Market Identification and Development

Financing

Public Equity Development, Private Equity Development, Investment Banks

Figure 10.2.   Opportunities for participation in a bioscience entrepreneurship community of practice.

largely due to their focused R&D teams working in a well-regulated environment which protects investments and allows value capture to occur. However, opportunities exist in many other parts of the entrepreneurship community for new players. In the past five years, the plethora of capacity development activities has mushroomed in the region, to the extent that it is possible to attend several seminars, conferences or workshops each month in different countries. Many institutions offer specialized programs and courses for those wanting either a short primer in bioscience entrepreneurship, or a program leading to a graduate degree. The author's institute had partnered with an SME and international non-profit organization to offer a course on "Commercialization of Agricultural Biotechnology" in 2007, with most participants from APEC economies (www.asiabiobusiness.com). There must be value creation opportunities in these!

Another opportunity which Asia is well-poised to exploit is the area of food/feed safety testing to meet regulatory requirements for novel and biotech foods. The use of specially bred animals or plants for such testing requires specialized equipment, facilities and skilled personnel, all meeting international standards. Cost competition would indicate that this has as much potential for outsourcing as the software industry.

Translational research and pre-market product development are two other areas to have received attention but not shown full exploitation as yet. It is commonly known that public institutions in Asia conduct the most "proof of concept" type of research, many of which will result in nice research papers and credits for their authors but not in any marketable product unless further development is done. Studies by the Asian Development Bank and others show that there are about a hundred near-market possible biotech products in the public sector, some of which require the translational research and pre-market product development to move them the next step towards innovation. To date, only one international non-profit organization appears to have brokered the translation of technology from the private to the public sector, but its experience has not been pursued by others.

10.6 The Future: Accelerating the Renaissance in Bioscience Entrepreneurship in Asia

Asia is characterized by its large number and diversity of people. More than any other region, concerns about food security at the local level (for those depending on the land for their livelihood) and at the national level (in terms of excessive production capacity and trade) are magnified here. Experts claim that Asian countries have to produce more food with less water, less land and a smaller farming population. Agribiotechnology has been acclaimed by the mainstream scientific community as the best (albeit not the only) hope to meet future demands for more and better-quality food, grown with the minimal use of chemicals and environmental disturbance.

Agribiotech crops, or "biofarming", represent the first wave of applications of the "new biology". With renewed interest spurred on by high petroleum prices, greener agriculture and biodiversity conservation, scientists and government planners are now attempting a serious focus on other applications such as "biopharming", "biofuels" and "bioplastics" in response to new needs and as a way to add value to crops functioning as biofactories. Additionally, biofarming has grown beyond just agribiotech crops to include biofertilizers and biopesticides as well. Countries like the Philippines have developed detailed, ambitious multi-year plans to reap the economic benefits from agribiotechnology (Philippines Agriculture and Fisheries Biotech Roadmap for 2006–2016), while Vietnam has embarked on a significant capacity-building program for its physical and human resources.

Support systems to commercialize biotech crops are essential in those countries which choose to pursue the opportunities presented by agribiotechnology. All components of the FTO equation need to be addressed, and support systems need to be developed to nurture or address these components. Without an operational regulatory approval system and IP protection, it is unlikely that developing countries will attract the inflow of technology or investment required to kickstart any local agribiotech industry. In this respect, science and scientists play a vital role to ensure honesty and accuracy in the information base used for decision-making and in the development of such support systems. Scientists and farmers also have important roles to play in creating awareness among urban consumers that the technology is safe and necessary. Public acceptance, which comes from improved understanding, is essential in ensuring that the benefits of agribiotechnology are shared by all.

The Asian continent faces many challenges as it forges ahead in economic and social development. Without food security for all, political stability and economic growth would face additional challenges. The stakes are huge in this populous region. Agribiotechnology offers much hope and, as Nobel laureate Norman Borlaug has stated, is one of many important tools which must be harnessed in order to meet Asia's challenge to feed itself.

The Asian region is uniquely placed to become the global leader in exploiting bioscience entrepreneurship to meet its needs. As physical and human capacity improves, more discoveries will fuel more innovative applications, while the current deep R&D pipeline in many countries will translate into actual products and processes. By 2025, Asia will likely be a leading player in the "Biology Century".

References

FAO (2002). *The State of Food and Agriculture 2001–2002*. Rome: Food and Agricultural Organization.

Fogel, R.W. (2004). *The Escape from Hunger and Premature Death, 1700–2100*. Cambridge, United Kingdom: Cambridge University Press.

Shahi, G.S. (2004). *BioBusiness in Asia*. Pearson Education South Asia.

Index